PRAISE FO. SUPPLY CHA ECOSYSTEMS

'Mark Millar is recognized in Asia as a thought leader in supply chain management. His new book **Global Supply Chain Ecosystems** provides new insight on the multi-dimensional touchpoints across the supply chain, combined with a three-dimensional perspective on the complex ecosystem that dynamically interacts and ultimately defines the optimal movement of product across the globe. He includes discussion on the transformative technologies that can provide competitive advantage, practical case studies and shares his views on how these new methodologies can be creatively leveraged in the evolving developing countries. I strongly recommend this book to both seasoned professionals and college students seeking to embrace this industry from a different vantage point'.
Paul W Bradley, Chairman and CEO, Caprica International

'Mark Millar, one of the best known supply chain experts in Asia and beyond with more than 30 years of global business experience has set a further standard in his latest book **Global Supply Chain Ecosystems**. This book provides valuable insights for business leaders who are managing and developing their global supply chains – with a focus on the upcoming Asian era. Mark describes the different aspects a complex and global supply chain nowadays needs to reflect in order to become strategic as a business enabler and a revenue driver. He also highlights new developments to shape global business, such as the New Silk Road connecting Europe and Asia. Based on solid research and insightful practical case studies, Mark's book offers a perceptive understanding of the roles the business and also the governments can play to create an enabling environment for global supply chains to thrive. **Global Supply Chain Ecosystems** is a must-read for anyone interested

in strengthening their competitive supply chain position in our global economies.'
Rolf Neise, Global Logistics Programme Manager, British American Tobacco

'A generous and erudite exploration of the contemporary global supply chain scene. A genuinely entertaining and informative read by one of the real characters of the supply chain community.'
Kimble Winter, Global CEO, Logistics Executive Group

'A must-read book for freight forwarders and supply chain practitioners – this book delivers an outstanding holistic view of global supply chain ecosystems, including future directions such as the New Silk Road and how Africa could emerge as the next Asia.'
Henrik Christensen, Chairman of African Logistics Club and President of KTZ Express Hong Kong Ltd

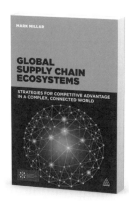

Global Supply Chain Ecosystems

Strategies for competitive advantage in a complex world

Mark Millar

Robert
Thank You
for your great
support at Multimodal 2016.
See you in China!
Mark
12-5-2016
@NEC

KoganPage

LONDON PHILADELPHIA NEW DELHI

> **Publisher's note**
>
> Every possible effort has been made to ensure that the information contained in this book is accurate at the time of going to press, and the publishers and authors cannot accept responsibility for any errors or omissions, however caused. No responsibility for loss or damage occasioned to any person acting, or refraining from action, as a result of the material in this publication can be accepted by the editor, the publisher or any of the authors.

First published in Great Britain and the United States in 2015 by Kogan Page Limited

2nd Floor, 45 Gee Street	1518 Walnut Street, Suite 1100	4737/23 Ansari Road
London EC1V 3RS	Philadelphia PA 19102	Daryaganj
United Kingdom	USA	New Delhi 110002
	India	

© Mark Millar, 2015

ISBN   978 0 7494 7158 3
E-ISBN 978 0 7494 7159 0

British Library Cataloguing-in-Publication Data

A CIP record for this book is available from the British Library.

Library of Congress Cataloging-in-Publication Data

Millar, Mark (Supply Chain Consultant)
   Global supply chain ecosystems : strategies for competitive advantage in a complex, connected world / Mark Millar.
      pages cm
   ISBN 978-0-7494-7158-3 (paperback) — ISBN 978-0-7494-7159-0 (ebk)   1. Business logistics.
I. Title.
   HD38.5.M546 2015
   658.7—dc23

                                                                                    2015015896

Typeset by Amnet
Print production managed by Jellyfish
Printed and bound by CPI Group (UK) Ltd, Croydon, CR0 4YY

CONTENTS

07 The New Silk Road connecting Europe and Asia 131

08 Integrated logistics hubs 149

09 Human capital – the talent pool 169

ABOUT THE AUTHOR

Mark Millar

"One of the region's Supply Chain leaders"

China Supply Chain magazine CHaINA

"One of the most progressive people in world logistics"

Global Institute of Logistics

"One of the Top 50 influential individuals in Asia supply chain & logistics"

Terrapinn, 2015

Mark Millar leverages over 30 years global business experience to provide value for clients with informed and independent perspectives on their supply chain strategies in Asia.

Acknowledged as an engaging and energetic presenter who consistently delivers a knowledgeable, professional and memorable impact, Mark has been engaged by clients as Speaker, Moderator, Conference Chairman or MC at more than 375 corporate events, client functions and industry conferences across 23 countries.

His 'Asia Supply Chain Insights' series of corporate briefings, consultations and seminars deliver practical knowledge and educated insights that help companies navigate the complex landscapes in Asia, improve the efficiency of their supply chain ecosystems, develop new business opportunities and make better informed business decisions.

Mark is a Visiting Lecturer at Hong Kong Polytechnic University and has delivered Guest Lectures at Georgia Tech (Atlanta), RMIT (Ho Chi Minh City) and SP Jain (Singapore and Dubai).

He is a graduate of the Australian Institute of Company Directors (GAICD), Chartered Fellow of the Chartered Institute of Logistics and Transportation (FCILT), Fellow of the Chartered Institute of Marketing (FCIM) and an APICS SCOR-P certified Supply Chain Professional.

Mark achieved an MBA with Distinction from the University of the West of England, is a graduate of the Chartered Institute of Marketing and holds a post-graduate Diploma in Management Studies.

His international track record in the B2B services sector includes 20 years in the Asia Pacific region, where Mark led business development initiatives across ten Asian countries. His distinguished corporate career includes executive positions at Thorn EMI, RR Donnelley, ModusLink, Platinum Logistix, Exel Contract Logistics (now DHL) and UPS Supply Chain Solutions – serving many leading companies across the consumer, retail and high-tech electronics sectors.

He has lived and worked in the UK, the Netherlands, Australia, Singapore, USA, Ireland, mainland China and Hong Kong. Whilst with the Thorn EMI group in the UK, Mark's international sales leadership earned Thorn Secure Science the "Queen's Award for Exports".

Appointments: an active and enthusiastic industry contributor, Mark currently serves as:

- Asia Ambassador, East West Transport Corridor Association, Europe
- Advisory Board Member, Institute for Supply Management, Hong Kong
- Council Member and Chair of Logistics Policy Committee, CILT Hong Kong
- Head of International Relations, Vietnam Supply Chain, Ho Chi Minh City
- Chairman, Logistics Committee, British Chamber of Commerce, Hong Kong
- Industry Advisor, Confederation of International Freight Forwarding Networks

- Chairman, International Relations Committee, Hong Kong Logistics Association
- Advisory Board Member, Logistics & Supply Chain Management Society, Singapore
- International Advisor, Logistics & Supply Chain Management Association, Shenzhen
- APAC Regional Leader and International Advisor, Supply Chain & Logistics Group, Dubai

Accolades: Mark's commitment and expertise has been recognized with several accolades:

- "Top 50 influential individuals in Asia Supply Chain & Logistics" 2015
- "Pro's to Know, Supply Chain Providers" 2014
- "Chartered Fellowship" awarded by Chartered Institute of Logistics & Transport 2010
- "Supply Chain Thought Leader" Pro's to Know 2009
- "One of the most Progressive People in World Logistics" 2008
- "Supply Chain Veteran" Who's Who of Supply Chain in Asia 2008
- "China Supply Chain 20: the Who, What and Why of China Supply Chain" 2007
- "Pro's to Know in Fulfilment and Logistics" 2007
- "Who's Who Top 20 Power Players in Supply Chain Management in China" 2006

PUBLISHER'S ACKNOWLEDGEMENTS

Kogan Page and the author gratefully acknowledge the involvement of Dr Song Hanh Pham, Senior Lecturer at Sheffield Business School, Sheffield Hallam University, and thank her for her valued review of the manuscript for this book. Unless otherwise stated, all individuals quoted in this book were interviewed by the author.

AUTHOR'S ACKNOWLEDGEMENTS

My sincere thanks to:

- Mae – for the wonderful foundations, full of love and support;
- Maureen – for our fantastic journey, full of love and encouragement;
- Many others – colleagues, clients, business partners and friends – too numerous to mention – for their inspiration, guidance and advice over many years, on many topics, in many places;
- Mike – for helping to make it happen;
- Julia and Jenny at Kogan Page;
- You – thank you for buying this book.

Mark Millar

Global supply chain ecosystems

Supply chains are the arteries of today's globalized economy – they enable the international trade flows that empower global commerce. Supply chain management has become an essential topic across all spheres of management and a strategic agenda item in every boardroom. Today's supply chains are evolving to reflect the increased complexity of world trade – a highly competitive, super-connected, fast-changing and increasingly volatile global environment, which is progressively more difficult to predict.

Introduction

Few generations have seen such rapid changes and expansion in technology, trade and globalization as we have experienced in the past few decades. The rise of China and other Far East economies, the internet and e-commerce, volatile fuel prices, automation and environmental issues are just some of the factors that have – and will continue to – influence and transform our business and personal lives.

Companies, business models and management techniques have had to evolve to both reflect and take advantage of these changes which, most critically, have made possible the enormous increase in world trade and global prosperity. Greater use of collaborative partnerships, outsourcing and off-shoring has created elongated networks of organizations that require more sophisticated management and controls than ever before.

Consequently, modern supply chains have become complex, multi-layered, interconnected distribution systems that enable companies and countries to trade more effectively and efficiently. Developed by innovative, competitive and ambitious stakeholders and users, they have been the essential enablers of international cargo flows around the world, bringing economic and social benefits, and leading to a steady improvement in the standard of living for millions.

Confirming how these networks enable business in an increasingly connected world, the *Financial Times'* (*FT*) lexicon describes how 'businesses operate in a broader network of related businesses offering particular products or services – this is known as a business ecosystem'. They further define the business ecosystem as 'a network of interlinked companies, such as suppliers and distributors, who interact with each other, primarily complementing or supplying key components of the value propositions within their products or services'.

From the supply chain perspective, Cranfield School of Management's Dr Martin Christopher adopts an end-to-end perspective of the flows of product and accompanying information from the source of raw materials to delivery to the end customer – and sometimes beyond – to develop a definition of supply chain as: 'The network of organizations that are involved, through upstream and downstream linkages, in the different processes and activities that produce value in the form of products and services in the hands of the ultimate consumer'.

Christopher explains that the notion of networks is particularly important, stressing the key point that modern supply chains are not simply linear chains or processes, 'they are complex networks – the products and information flows travel within and between nodes in a variety of networks that link organizations, industries and economies'.

Supporting the concept that the supply chain can become a source of competitive advantage, the *FT* lexicon explains how, 'Ecosystems also create strong barriers to entry for new competition, as potential entrants not only have to duplicate or better the core product, but they also have to compete against the entire system of independent complementors and suppliers that form the network.'

In this introductory chapter, we build on these principles and explore three critical dimensions of supply chains that have continually evolved during recent years to become the foundations of how and why we have transformed into the world of 'global supply chain ecosystems', namely:

- supply chain is **strategic**;
- supply chain is **complex**;
- supply chain is **global**.

Supply chain management has become strategic

Leading companies are increasingly considering their supply chains as strategic – as a business enabler, as a revenue driver and as a differentiator. In many sectors, companies compete on the basis of their supply chains, as much as on their actual products. For many businesses – particularly those in high-tech and consumer electronics – time to market and effective distribution channels are critical success factors, and therefore supply chain management capabilities become a source of competitive advantage.

The all essential human capital dimension of supply chain management capabilities is covered in Chapter 9, including looking at talent attraction, development and retention strategies as a source of competitive advantage.

Historically there have been many misunderstandings about what exactly is supply chain, with many business managers thinking that it's all about trucks and warehouses – which are in fact components of logistics, which in turn is a part of supply chain management.

What is supply chain?

The Supply Chain Council (SCC) has finely tuned the definition of supply chain as 'the processes that plan and execute the acquisition of materials, transformation of materials into sellable products, delivery and return of products and services, in support of customer orders'.

As defined in the SCC's widely accepted Supply Chain Operation Reference (SCOR) model, at its highest level, supply chain consists of the five key components: plan, source, make, deliver and return.

This broad definition embraces pretty much all the operational aspects of the business, representing substantial critical mass of a company in terms of resources and assets, as well as spend and contribution.

Supply chain is the business

Another perspective is that 'supply chain is the business', advocated by Prakesh Menon, former Supply Chain Director of Myer, Australia's largest department store, and where during 2010–11 he led the supply chain transformation that delivered $25 million to the bottom line. Prakesh is adamant that: 'Supply chain is not just about logistics. Supply chain is the backbone for any retailer and it is about the end-to-end processes. It is about the cash-to-cash cycle. You streamline this and get it humming, you have a world class operation happening in your retail organization and add significant profit to your bottom line. Supply chain is the business.'

The supply chain comprises every single function that enables getting products to customers. World-class organizations no longer perceive the supply chain as merely tactical support for business as usual, but take a holistic position that their supply chain is what drives the business.

Supply chain in the boardroom

A growing trend in recent years is the presence of supply chain managers on the board, with supply chain strategy and performance becoming standing executive agenda items, and the adoption of the role and title of Chief Supply Chain Officer (CSCO).

Research led by Professor Alan Waller (2012) of Solving Efeso, in collaboration with Cranfield, found that in well over half of the companies surveyed, the most senior supply chain person now sits on the board of the business unit and suggests that this trend is accelerating.

This in stark contrast to just 10 years ago, when it was highly un-usual for companies to have supply chain representation at board level and 'supply chain strategy' typically amounted to not much more than the aggregation of individual functional decisions. The research report summarized that 'the supply chain is an intrinsic ele-ment of the enterprise and its ability to adapt quickly to changes in the commercial environment is critical to the financial and market performance of the business.'

A high-profile example of supply chain in the boardroom is Apple. Prior to becoming chief executive, Tim Cook was an acknowledged expert in the quiet but critical world of supply chain management. His level of operational expertise and experience is critical to Apple's continued leadership in global markets with global products amongst global competition, where the supply chain drives competitive advan-tage through time to market, finely tuned global operations, eco-nomically efficient logistics networks and simultaneous worldwide product releases.

Having an increasing presence at-the-table means that supply chain leaders have to learn to speak the language of the boardroom in order to operate effectively and succeed.

Supply chain and the CFO

According to research by the Supply Chain Council, supply chain is responsible for 63 to 90 per cent of a company's total spend, how-ever organizations typically measure and report financial metrics by department or product – not by supply chain.

Even with many companies having supply chain representation in the boardroom, in reality there is still some way to go before the whole board considers supply chain to be the business, in which case there is a risk of sub-optimizing from a strategic planning perspective.

In terms of dialogue with the CFO, in reality the supply chain has significant material impact on multiple aspects of the profit and loss and balance sheet statements. Supply chain managers can therefore readily translate their activities, influence and results into the busi-ness language suitable for the CFO and the boardroom.

From the profit and loss perspective, supply chain will impact the following areas:

TABLE 1.1 Supply chain impact

Profit and loss	Supply chain impact
Revenue	Customer service
Cost of goods	Sourcing and procurement Capacity utilization Operational efficiencies Inventory management Warehousing and transport
Admin expense	Order processing
Interest expense	Inventory financing

Likewise, supply chain activities will impact throughout the balance sheet. Accounts receivable and cash assets will be impacted by order fill rates, invoice accuracy and order lead times; whilst balance sheet inventory will be influenced by supplier relationships, supplier management strategies and inventory policies. The fixed asset categories of property, plant and equipment will directly reflect a combination of the company's warehouse network, insourcing and outsourcing strategies and build-buy-lease decisions. Order quantities will affect current liabilities whilst the financing arrangements for inventory, plant and equipment will influence long-term debt and shareholder equity.

Supply chain and marketing drive the business

There are exciting and evolving synergies between the supply chain and marketing functions, as together they become the primary business drivers for companies in the modern era. Each of them is both a functional discipline and a profession. Taking the broad perspectives of both disciplines, these two functions together embrace all the critical business activities of a company, whilst IT, HR and finance play a supporting role.

With marketing comprising the four Ps of product, price, promotion and place and supply chain encompassing the five operational activities of plan, source, make, deliver and return, then logistics becomes the point of intersection, the linkage between the place (distribution) function of marketing and the deliver function of supply chain.

Hence marketing and supply chain together are becoming the primary engines that drive the business. The Chief Marketing Officer (CMO) and the Chief Supply Chain Officer (CSCO) will therefore become the most critical leadership roles to sit alongside the CEO and CFO in the C-suite of the future.

Supply chain as competitive advantage

In an increasingly competitive world, the supply chain is more and more seen as a key source of competitive advantage and differentiation. Brands strive to build powerful supply chains that will enable them to get their products to market faster, more efficiently and economically than their competition. Businesses are now competing on the basis of their supply chain management capabilities almost as much as their product or their brand.

Any chain is only as strong as its weakest link – and it's the same with supply chains, except that in an ecosystem the linkages are not consecutive and not linear; there are numerous multi-dimensional connections with profound interdependencies.

Nevertheless, the strategy of continuous improvement by consistently and persistently working on strengthening the weakest link(s) still applies, and companies adopting such an approach will leverage their global supply chain ecosystem for competitive advantage in our complex, connected world.

Supply chains have become increasingly complex

In the past, supply chains were vertically integrated within local communities of suppliers and customers, with individual cities or regions specializing in specific sectors – for example automotive in Detroit, steel in Sheffield, shipbuilding on the river Clyde in Glasgow.

In today's connected world of open borders, reduced barriers to trade, cost effective long-distance transportation and low-cost labour markets, supply chains have now become infinitely more complex, compounded by the widespread adoption of outsourcing and off-shoring.

Through globalization, supply chains have developed, evolved and morphed into complex ecosystems, comprising many different organizations, featuring numerous multi-layered interdependencies, spanning the globe, crossing time zones, borders, cultures and languages. All these factors combine to exponentially increase supply chain complexity.

Outsourcing

Defined as 'the act of one company contracting with another company to provide services that might otherwise be performed by in-house employees', outsourcing is generally undertaken in order to benefit from using an external provider – typically through gaining economic advantages and leveraging specialist expertise.

Adopting the Tom Peters' mantra 'Do what you do best and outsource the rest', organizations have taken the approach of focusing on their core competencies – retaining those activities in-house (insourced), whilst seeking external partners to undertake activities that are non-core and that can be undertaken by third party service providers.

Today's supply chain ecosystems inevitably incorporate third party providers offering services on an outsourced basis, ranging from back office services and debt collection through to customer service, warehousing and transportation.

Outsourcing partners typically have specialist expertise and the economies of scale that enable them to deliver the required results better and more cost effectively than could be achieved by the client using their own in-house resources.

These trends have led to industry sub-sectors of firms providing services on an outsourced basis – including call centres, finance, payroll, telecommunications, computing and of course transportation and logistics. In fact, business process outsourcing (BPO) has become a mainstay of employment generation and economic development in certain economies such as the Philippines where over one million people are employed in customer service call centres and in India where a very large software development community provides services for the ICT (information and communication technology) industries.

In addition to leveraging the scale economies that result from servicing multiple clients, these focused outsource service providers also nurture and develop specialist subject matter expertise, domain knowledge, streamlined processes and technology platforms that are above and beyond levels that any single organization could – or would want to, or need to – develop themselves in-house.

Off-shoring

Off-shoring refers to moving business activities out of the company's home country to another location in a different country – usually to take advantage of lower cost environments. Off-shoring has become particularly prevalent for manual oriented production activities, and also to reconfigure the product's country of origin classification, in order to capitalize on preferential trade agreements (PTA) – also known as 'tariff engineering'.

The opening up of emerging economies – enabling access to large scale labour forces that are plentiful and cheap – resulted in numerous low cost country sourcing (LCCS) initiatives, involving the off-shoring of large scale, labour intensive production activities to countries such as Mexico, Hungary, China and Vietnam.

In many cases, these off-shoring initiatives also involved the subcontracting out of the production to third parties – outsourcing – in which case the business activities were both off-shored and outsourced.

Many companies have established their own international subsidiaries in overseas markets and transferred business activities to those lower cost environments, in effect these activities have been off-shored, but are still insourced – ie produced in-house, not outsourced.

In our globalized world, outsourcing is often confused with off-shoring and the terms are sometimes used interchangeably. To be clear, outsourcing refers to the 'who' – the organization performing the services, and off-shoring refers to the 'where' – the location where the services are performed. Outsourcing is still outsourcing irrespective of where the outsourced services are actually performed – whether onshore or offshore.

Elongated, interconnected, multi-layered and interdependent networks

Coupled with the increased accessibility of international markets – and further facilitated by technological developments that enable ships and aircraft to economically undertake ever longer journeys – outsourcing and off-shoring have resulted in increasingly blurred boundaries within-and-across the complex structures that companies deploy in order to efficiently plan, source, make and deliver their products and services.

As such, we have seen supply chains evolve into elongated, inter-connected, multi-layered networks of partners, suppliers, regulators, service providers and customers – with profound interdependencies – which can no longer be described adequately using the linear concept of a 'chain'. The depth and breadth of complexity, connectivity and interdependencies are such that we are now firmly in the sphere of global supply chain ecosystems.

Complex supply chain ecosystems

Within these ecosystems, each configuration is unique to the particular enterprise that owns that supply chain – the principal.

The principal's chosen business partners join together to configure an ecosystem that serves the common purpose of providing an end-to-end channel of distribution – all the way from the suppliers of materials and components, extending through manufacturing processes – whether in-sourced or outsourced – to the distributor and retailer, and ultimately to the consumer.

As a commercial entity, each principal forms their own distinctive supply chain ecosystem, adopting a different composition of similar functional participants, or in several cases, particularly within industry sectors, many of the same actual participants, all contributing in many different supply chain ecosystems for different principals.

And so it goes on, such that today's supply chains encompass complex webs of interdependencies, frequently spanning the globe, designed and deployed to optimize critical attributes – such as speed, agility and resilience – that drive competitive advantage.

Speed is a key differentiator in today's world of high velocity supply chains. Fashion brands are a good example of the 'need for speed' in responding to changes in styles, seasons and trends. Inditex (Zara), H&M and Benetton are companies whose success has been to a large degree based on competitive advantage gained through superior supply chain design and execution involving short production lead times and fast, streamlined distribution channels, that give them the ability to rapidly have the latest styles on sale in stores throughout the world to take immediate advantage of fast-changing demand.

Agility was a key theme of the KPMG 2012 study of supply chain maturity, in which one theme was prevalent across nearly all of their research interviews, that 'supply chain directors need to focus on

FIGURE 1.1 Supply chain ecosystem

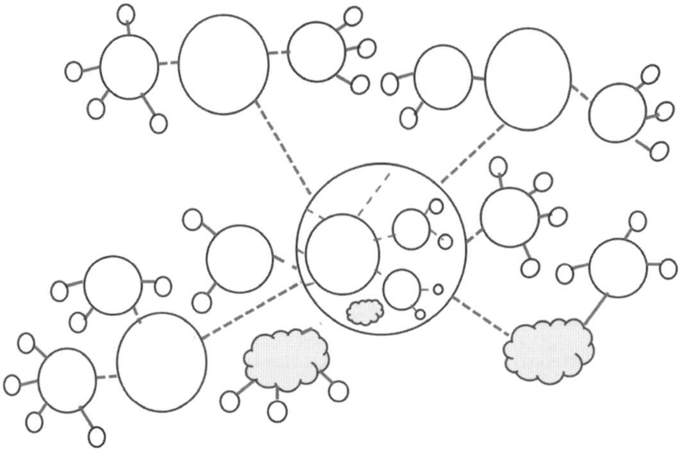

bringing agility to their supply chains, not only to manage current volatility in the markets, but also to put themselves in a competitive position once the long-awaited upturn finally arrives'. KPMG reported that during lean times, the strongest organizations work on strengthening the partnerships that empower their supply chain ecosystems, with 'some focused on driving true collaboration across the supply chain and others adopting new, low-cost technologies and operating models to enhance transparency and facilitate collaboration'.

Today's volatile world means that supply chains are vulnerable to a wide range of risks, which are explored in detail in Chapter 4. Resilience was the focus of the 2004 Cranfield white paper by Martin Christopher and Helen Peck, who used the term 'resilience' as it relates to supply chains as networks, and so adopted a 'dictionary-based definition that is rooted in the science of ecosystems'. Their paper used the definition of resilience as 'the ability of a system to return to its original state or move to a new, more desirable state after being disturbed'. They reinforced the inherent need for flexibility and pointed out that the desired state may well be different to the original state.

As modern supply chains increasingly resemble ecosystems rather than linear chains, the suppliers, manufacturers and service providers that work together to service one client's supply chain could well be fiercely competing against each other to win business to provide services for a different client's supply chain. Indeed, whilst each company has their own supply chain ecosystem – over which they have control – that same company will most likely be a participant in several other supply chain ecosystems, for example for its customers or suppliers.

This combination of complexity and connectedness result in scenarios where a company may find that one single external organization may actually be a supplier, and/or a customer and/or a competitor – depending in whose supply chain ecosystem configuration they are operating! High-tech sector examples would include Apple and Samsung, or Microsoft and IBM. In this context, organizations must therefore develop the capabilities to effectively work with not just multiple different partners in their own ecosystem, but also the same partners playing multiple different roles across other ecosystems.

Two examples from leading global brands illustrate the complexity of today's global supply chain ecosystems:

- Apple's iPhone 6 supply chain involves some 786 suppliers in 31 countries, 60 of which are in the United States and 349 in China.

- Boeing's extended global supply chain procures 783 million parts per year, involving total spend of $28 billion, across 5,400 factories employing 500,000 people.

Global supply chain ecosystems inevitably involve numerous organizations working together for a common purpose, such that by nature of comprising multiple participants, the ecosystems must inherently involve outsourcing – thus requiring collaboration.

Collaboration

Advancing the complexity even further is another of the key factors that empowers competitive advantage through effective global supply chain ecosystems – collaboration. This is something that just about everyone talks about, but is consistently challenging to successfully implement and deploy. It appears that individuals can collaborate quite effectively with each other, but when it comes to organizations, collaboration becomes inherently more difficult to achieve.

Complex globalized supply chains involve numerous suppliers, manufacturers and service providers, such that whatever impacts one link or node, can affect the whole ecosystem. To execute a supply chain efficiently, the participants need to work together and that usually requires open information-sharing between all the partners throughout the ecosystem – something that most participants are reluctant to do.

Companies have a natural resistance to share their business details or reveal information to any outsiders, but economic reality may force supply chain participants to collaborate in order to win business – because the principal customer demands it. Many of the world's Fortune 500 companies – particularly in high-tech electronics, automotive and consumer retail sectors – insist on their chosen business partners embracing a collaborative approach throughout their supply chain ecosystem.

Transport Intelligence (Ti) of the UK, found that a number of logistics service providers have stated that they would consider collaborating with a competitor but only if such collaboration was managed by a neutral third party, with strict confidentiality policies in place.

Whatever type of collaboration, the 'new normal' of complexity and volatility will require more of it – in order for companies to become better positioned to effectively deal with the challenges ahead and to be able to sense and respond to ever changing supply chain dynamics. The need for supply chain visibility is addressed in Chapter 2.

One of the many challenges for today's supply chain professionals is therefore to learn the art and science of practical collaboration, further empowering their global supply chain ecosystems. Typically this involves yet another balancing act – that of leveraging partners for economies of scale and combined competitive advantage, whilst protecting organizational assets, including human capital, tribal knowledge and proprietary customer intelligence.

Collaborative supply chain management therefore – whilst wonderful in theory – can be difficult to achieve in practice – due to the inherent reluctance of organizations to openly share their data and information with other supply chain participants, many of whom are, or are perceived to be, competitors.

As a reminder of this fact, there are two distinct dictionary definitions of 'collaboration': (a) to work with others for mutual benefit; and (b) to willingly assist the enemy!

Back to basics

Amongst all the complexity, let's remind ourselves of the fundamental objectives of supply chain management – to manage the efficient and effective flow of four critical elements throughout the ecosystem: goods, services, funds and information.

And whilst managing these flows of goods, services, funds and information, supply chain managers are continually striving to balance the optimization of three key performance metrics: speed, cost and quality.

All sounds rather straightforward. However, in reality the combination of complexity and volatility make global supply chain management both exciting and challenging, but never boring.

As companies continually try to juggle speed, cost and quality in their supply chains, it becomes apparent that all three elements cannot be optimized simultaneously! One of the three will always have to be compromised to some extent – in order to optimize the other two elements.

For example, if the solution is fast and cheap, then it will most likely have to compromise on quality. Likewise, if the supply chain requires top quality and high speed, then it is unlikely to be the lowest cost solution. In global supply chains, the classic trade off example is the contrast in speed and price between air freight and ocean freight.

Hence the perpetual challenge of supply chain optimization – finding the right balance between speed, cost and quality that is appropriate for the circumstances of any particular supply chain scenario, which of course will vary frequently and on an irregular basis.

Global supply chains for a connected world

The explosion in world trade

Despite the volatility of recent decades – political upheaval, spikes in energy costs, wars and terrorism, environmental issues – the volume of goods moved internationally has grown far beyond what most would have forecast.

World Trade Organization (WTO) figures for gross imports and exports between 1973 and 2013 show just how vast this growth has been. Measured at current dollar prices, the 1973 figure was $1,175 billion; by 2013 the figure had risen to $37,658 billion, a 32-fold increase.

The emergence of China as a world economic power has of course played a major role, with imports and exports rising from a mere $11 billion in 1973 to $4,160 billion in 2013, taking an 11 per cent share of total world trade. During the same 40-year period, the USA has managed a 27-fold increase in trade, from $114 trillion to $3,910 trillion.

Such global developments have considerable social and political implications. In its 2014 annual report, the WTO emphasized the positive link between trade and development. It focused attention particularly on least-developed countries (LDCs), proposing a series of capacity-building initiatives, improving market access for such states and recognizing the potential of e-commerce trading.

The operational impact of globalization is that supply chain ecosystems need to be flexibly configured such that they can effectively serve the full spectrum of developed, developing and emerging markets – across which there are huge variations in consumer tastes, regulatory environments and transport infrastructure. From the geographic dimension, changes to the landscape are driving some key supply chain shifts that have consequences for business leaders and supply chain managers to learn from and respond to, namely:

- carbon footprint considerations;
- shift beyond globalization;
- growth market opportunities.

Carbon footprint considerations

With growing awareness of and concern about environmental issues, the supply chain's carbon footprint – comprising the total greenhouse gas emissions caused by the supply chain – has become a significant strategic consideration.

One inescapable fact about global supply chain ecosystems is that they are significant users of oil – a commodity whose price is extremely difficult to predict. Whether storing goods, transporting them by road, rail, sea or air, the supply chain continuously consumes fuel and consequently generates some level of pollution. Oil prices are notoriously volatile, falling low when supplies are plentiful but rising rapidly when demand is high or political instability affects a major oil producer. In the last decade we have seen prices range from $70 to more than $150 per barrel – and back down to less than $70. New alternative energy sources are challenging the dominance of oil, furthering the volatility in relation to both price and availability of the sticky black gold.

Clean and green supply chains are increasingly in vogue. Environmental issues and legislation add to the complexities involved in assessing how to structure a global supply chain strategy, with progressively more stringent requirements and expectations.

According to MIT, sustainability is now a permanent part of 70 per cent of corporate agendas. Most companies now also consider green supply chain practices as a vital element of competitive advantage, with many businesses confirming that green practices can and do reduce costs – and are therefore contributing to increased profits. According to a Cohn & Wolfe survey (slideshare, 2011), the majority of consumers in all countries say that it is very important or somewhat important, that companies are environmentally-friendly and 35 per cent of respondents say they are willing to pay more for green products.

In reality, thus far there is little evidence of wide-scale consumer willingness to actually pay higher prices for consumer product companies being green. Nevertheless they are demanding it and businesses are implementing it – in many cases adopting modern marketing strategies to adapt it into a differentiator as a source of competitive advantage.

From the supply chain carbon footprint perspective, globalization has significantly increased the total transport miles involved in managing the journey of materials, components, intermediate goods and finished products – all the way from their multiple diverse origins through the complex ecosystem to their final destinations, in turn creating quite a carbon footprint, the perils of which both consumer and business buyers are increasingly aware. More miles means more fuel, more dollars and more emissions. Shortening some of the distances involved in today's elongated global supply chains will reduce total transportation miles, thereby using less fuel and therefore saving money and reducing emissions. Green supply chains are explored in Chapter 3.

Shift beyond globalization

Above and beyond the pressures to reduce transportation miles and improve carbon footprint, the low-cost element of global sourcing has been impacted by inflationary pressures across the emerging and developing markets.

What was once low cost has now become just lower cost – China is no longer as cheap as it once was. In many cases lower cost is no longer low enough to economically justify the additional complexities – and expense – of managing a global supply chain ecosystem.

All low-cost countries are experiencing inflationary pressures. Factory wage inflation in China is running at over 15 per cent per year. Likewise, land and labour costs are increasing across all emerging markets. Transportation costs are subject to fuel price volatility. Ocean freight now takes longer due to the new norm of slow steaming, increasing working capital as a result of finished goods inventory being in transit – on the water – for 20 per cent longer on average.

Companies are consequently rethinking their globalization strategies and exploring options for reconfiguring their supply chain ecosystems – in some cases to move some production closer to the final consumption market – most likely still outsourced – and also to adopt a more regional approach.

In fact, outsourcing and globalization are identified by John Manners-Bell (2015), CEO of Ti, as the two most notable supply chain shifts that have transformed the relationship between manufacturers, retailers and their logistics providers since the 1980s. Now, with the increasing velocity of change in the industry, he predicts an increased focus on supply chain innovations, which will range from those affecting specific sector niches and logistics functions, to those which have the power to transform the entire industry.

Chapter 12 explores several examples of supply chain innovation that are, or soon will be, impacting supply chain ecosystems, specifically focusing on technological developments, inland port developments and game-changing infrastructure initiatives.

Off-shoring to near-shoring to re-shoring

With rising labour rates in China – and elsewhere in Asia – gradually eroding the cost differential with the developed markets, companies in US and Europe are considering moving some of their off-shored production closer to home (near-shoring); or in fact bringing the production all the way home to produce in the domestic market (re-shoring).

Near-shoring in many ways revisits lower cost locations that are in close proximity to the final consumption markets – for example Mexico for North America and countries like Poland and Hungary to serve Western Europe.

Re-shoring initiatives are politically very popular and gain much kudos amongst communities for resurrecting manufacturing and creating jobs. With the wide availability of labour seeking gainful employment, local government incentives and subsidies for job creation, easy and economic access to the efficiencies of automation, if required, and newly available lower-cost energy sources in their domestic markets, many companies in the western developed economies are exploring their options, conscious of the complexities and increasing costs of operating their global supply chain ecosystems.

All these factors are resulting in a trend beyond globalization to more regional supply chains. Whether global, regional or local, today's supply chain ecosystems are dependent on integrated logistics hubs, leading examples of which are explored in Chapter 8.

Trend towards more regional supply chains

Velocity is an additional factor influencing the rethinking of supply chains from global to regional. With product lifecycles continually reducing and speed-to-market a key differentiator, then supply chain velocity becomes another key component of competitive advantage. To increase velocity, companies are exploring how they can shorten their supply chains.

Again responding to increasing labour costs in traditional low cost markets, fluctuations in oil prices, and the trend towards regional free trade agreements (FTA) – explored in detail in Chapter 5 – some companies seek to rebalance their supply chain complexity by adopting a more regional approach.

Hence, for some businesses there will be some – not all – production activities that migrate 'closer-to-home', adopting near-shoring strategies resulting in supply chain ecosystems configured as 'Made in North America for America', or 'Made in Eastern Europe for Europe'.

This will not however be a mass exodus from manufacturing in Asia – largely because of the well-established, finely tuned and highly efficient global supply chain ecosystems that service the Asia-Europe and Asia-America trades, but also because the potential of the domestic consumer markets in the emerging economies is so enormous. Indeed, 'Made in Asia for Asia' will gradually become a leading model for regional supply chain ecosystems that serve the growth markets in the Far East.

For the well-established and very substantial Asia-Europe trade flows, the latest options for ground based bi-directional transportation linkages are explored in Chapter 7 – the New Silk Road.

Growth market opportunities

Over and above the evolving trend towards more regional supply chains is the scramble to capitalize on longer term opportunities in growth markets – those that are rapidly progressing along the emerging-developing-developed continuum, have large critical mass and represent substantial medium- to long-term potential.

Whilst the traditional developed markets in Europe and North America remain in low-to-no growth mode – and the majority of them continue to experience varying degrees of economic, social, political and financial uncertainty – companies will have to focus on some of these new markets to explore new business opportunities.

Reviewing the World Bank's 2013 GDP growth rates for more than 200 countries, the vast majority of 5 per cent-plus growth economies are in either Asia or Africa, whilst the vast majority of the traditional developed markets are hovering below 2 per cent, with the United States a notable exception at 2.2 per cent. 2013 GDP growth for the United Kingdom was 1.73 per cent, Germany and France were at less than one per cent and the euro area as a whole at minus 0.47 per cent.

In contrast, the diverse group of countries growing at above 5 per cent includes Angola, Azerbaijan, Bangladesh, Botswana, Burkina Faso, Cambodia, Cameroon, China, Democratic Republic of the Congo, Djibouti, Gabon, Ghana, India, Indonesia, Kazakhstan, Kenya, Laos, Lesotho, Mauritania, Mozambique, Namibia, Nigeria, Panama, Papua New Guinea, Peru, Philippines, Sierra Leone, Sri Lanka, Togo, Uganda, Vietnam and Zambia.

Consequently, leading-edge companies are focusing on reconfiguring their supply chain ecosystems to take advantage of the opportunities in these rapidly growing economies, which in many cases requires building additional resilience into their supply chains.

Currently, many of these growth markets may be not much more than potential alternatives for off-shoring and outsourcing initiatives. Under-developed economies with abundant sources of labour are increasingly interested to attract foreign investment that helps to build factories, develop infrastructure and create employment, thereby improving economic prosperity for the nation as a whole.

For example, India has only recently begun to show it has the drive to fulfil its potential. The second most populous country on the planet with 1,267 million inhabitants, its GDP is less than a quarter of that of China and less than a third of Japan. Even if it reached the level of half of Japan's GDP, it would add a gross value to the world economy of $1.14 billion – equivalent to another South Korea. Since 2010 its economy has been growing by around 5 per cent per year, albeit starting from a very low base, but even today, despite having a number of world-leading industries, the service sector and agriculture still dominate, and a quarter of the population live in poverty.

Opportunities in Africa are explored in Chapter 11. With its billion-plus population, Africa in the short term offers plentiful low-cost labour resources, but over the medium to long term is likely to represent massive opportunities as a huge consumer market.

The leading modern day example is China. Multinational companies first went to China to take advantage of an abundant supply of low-cost labour and incentives to establish operations in special economic zones. Nowadays they remain in China to sell their products to Chinese consumers in the local market. The development of factories and shops is intertwined. Production and consumption are interconnected and converging. Over time, factory employment has increased economic prosperity across the nation, everyone is better off than they were. The workers have become the shoppers. The latest saying is that the foreign companies 'came to China for the workers, now they stay in China for the shoppers'. With an insatiable appetite for western brands, whether cars, fashion, luxury or entertainment, the massive Chinese consumer market provides huge growth opportunities for all types of trade.

And it's not just China. The global centre of economic gravity is undoubtedly shifting eastwards. Out of all the world's emerging markets, those in Asia will be the fastest growing, such that by 2050 the Asia region as a whole will account for 50 per cent of global GDP growth and by 2030 will be home to 66 per cent of the world's middle class. The opportunities and challenges of the 'Asian Era' are examined in Chapter 6.

Diverse and complex, the Asia region is experiencing unprecedented growth and prosperity, but involves overcoming numerous supply chain challenges in order to embrace the smorgasbord of potential new business opportunities. Multinational brands are following the expansion of Asian consumer markets closely, seeking to build revenue and volume, which means they need to review and reconfigure how their supply chain ecosystems operate to reach and serve these new markets.

The world is connected

The advent of globalization has irreversibly broken down borders between international markets around the globe. The world is undoubtedly connected physically – with all the ensuing consequences for supply chain management.

However, the digital revolution has changed the game! The convergence of internet, Wi-Fi and mobile has resulted in a different version of a connected world.

According to Cisco, 30 years ago there were a total of 3,000 devices connected to the internet. By 2014 that number had become 13.5 billion devices and they predict that by 2020 there will be 50 billion devices connected to the internet.

'Increasingly everything will be connected to everything' says Cisco's Matt Smith, Global Head of Market Development.

Always on, digitally enabled – from anywhere and everywhere – people around the world are connected for business and for pleasure. The digitization of everyday activities, from chat to messaging to social networks to online shopping to mobile commerce, is furthering the complexity of our global supply chains, with profound implications for retail in particular. Digital native consumers equipped with ubiquitous smart hand-held devices and universal wireless internet access are fuelling exponential growth in e-commerce transactions, with profound ramifications for supply chain management. Chapter 10 explores the omni-channel supply chain.

Summary

Once relatively local and comparatively simple, 21st-century supply chains have evolved into worldwide interconnected supply-and-demand networks comprising vastly more complex operations, with profound interdependencies and greater exposure to the volatility in our connected but uncertain world.

The linear concept of a chain is therefore no longer adequate to describe the complex international networks of suppliers, stakeholders, partners, regulators and customers that are involved in ensuring the efficient and effective movement of products, services, information and funds around the world – we are firmly in the era of global supply chain ecosystems.

Supply chain visibility

02

An introduction to supply chain visibility – what, why, where and how

We know that supply chain ecosystems are complex, multi-layered, globally connected, interdependent systems – operating in a volatile and often unpredictable environment. What companies often do not know, is what is happening throughout their supply chain ecosystem – from monitoring and tracking a single but vital shipment, to information on trends, costs, performance metrics and other measurements essential for continuous improvement and development.

Supply chain visibility enables business agility – the ability of companies to build and manage more cost-effective, efficient, responsible and customer-focused supply chains. While it is clear that the vast majority of companies understand and recognize the need for supply chain visibility, it is just a minority that feel they either have – or are close to having – the right systems and technologies in place to provide such visibility.

So just what do we mean by supply chain visibility, what are the benefits, what stands in the way of achieving success? How do we best design, implement and operate visibility within and across our supply chain ecosystem? What IT systems, equipment and technologies are available to best manage and control the visibility of our supply chains? How can we avoid being swamped by too much data or pointless information which rather than aiding visibility may actually hinder our vision of the supply chain ecosystem?

Can we define supply chain visibility?

There is no standard definition of supply chain visibility, and what it implies will vary from industry to industry and from company to company. A simple description that covers the immediate and day-to-day requirements is being able to know which goods are where, at any point in time, against a planned schedule. But this does not address the end-to-end data gathering and visibility needed for a broader understanding of the supply chain ecosystem to help make strategic decisions, or answer the 'What if?' scenario modelling that companies need to consider whilst operating in our volatile environment.

The data that companies need is essential, but often elusive. In order to sense a problem it must be visible – and developing visibility across the ecosystem is a complex process comprising technology, systems and collaborative partnerships – both internal and external. Good visibility provides companies with early-warning systems that alert the relevant stakeholders when events are deviating from plan, enabling adjustments to be implemented promptly, empowering increased performance levels. But if we cannot see what is happening throughout the network, how can we make the right decisions and manage the right balance of levers to pull, knobs to turn, partners to persuade – within, across and throughout our supply chain ecosystem?

Supply chain visibility is about 'connecting the right dots'

Visibility enables agility

Supply chain visibility enables companies to become more agile and responsive. The 2014 'Supply Chain Visibility in Business Networks' Study from Supply Chain Insights LLC found that agility was almost universally recognized as important (95 per cent of respondents), but only one third of respondents considered their businesses to be agile.

An agile business is able to rapidly and cost-efficiently adapt and respond to changes in the business environment, whether from emerging technologies, market trends or changing customer requirements. Agility means the business can readily adjust and modify its strategies and tactics to overcome challenges and take advantage of opportunities.

Collaboration essential to achieve full visibility

Any successful supply chain visibility strategy must adopt a paradigm of openness and collaboration between all partners. As supply chains become more global, they inevitably involve different organizations striving to work in harmony, with multi-party collaboration critical for success.

To successfully achieve visibility needs an open and co-operative approach to information-sharing – on a needs-to-know basis with partners throughout the ecosystem, to enable overall supply chain efficiency, without compromising the proprietary data.

How business leaders view visibility

A number of recent surveys (2011–14) come to similar conclusions – executives responsible for supply chains universally recognize that visibility is one of the biggest, if not the biggest, challenge to their businesses – directly impacting and in many cases impeding their ability to develop the most productive supply chain strategies. They also have a sound understanding of how to improve visibility and the technologies available. However, far fewer believe that they have reached acceptable levels of success, and the majority believe they still have a considerable way to go before they can claim to have full supply chain visibility.

The Economist Intelligence Unit/KPMG International (2014) report for 2013, Competitive advantage: enhancing supply chain networks for efficiency and innovation, reported that 49 per cent of global manufacturing executives admit that their companies currently do not have visibility of their supply chain beyond their Tier 1 suppliers. Moreover, only 9 per cent of the 335 global companies surveyed say they have complete visibility of their supply chains. Amongst USA executives that number is even lower, with only 7 per cent of them claiming complete supplier visibility. For communicating issues about demand changes within the supply chain, 44 per cent of respondents say they still use mail, fax and email – as opposed to using integrated technology platforms. The SCM World survey, *Managing Global Trade* (2013) reported 48 per cent of respondents as saying that lack of visibility in their global supply chains is one of their top five challenges; while only 12 per cent claimed to have fully automated collaborative execution with their global trading partners. Significantly, respondents were acutely conscious of the real economic impact of poor supply chain visibility. Of those listing the issue as one of their top five challenges, some 75 per cent said it was having a material impact on costs. The adverse economic impacts from poor visibility included:

- lack of consistent and timely collaboration with foreign suppliers;
- inability to control costs;
- unpredictable lead times;
- excess safety stock.

Companies do want to build end-to-end visibility throughout their supply chain ecosystems because their operational execution processes are dependent on numerous trading partners across the extended value network. Many claim that they are leveraging technology to build end-to-end supply chain visibility but results show this is not always true. Most companies focus on enterprise automation – which is not sufficient in the context of complex global supply chains. IT investments are primarily focused on enterprise resource planning (ERP) systems and electronic data interchange (EDI) which automate the enterprise, not enable the network.

Companies therefore still have large gaps in their current supply chain visibility capabilities, even though they are seeking to build new and deeper forms of the process through leveraging technology in their business networks. They want to be more agile but are not yet succeeding.

What comes through strongly from these various surveys is that businesses find supply chain visibility to be one of their biggest challenges, but paradoxically not necessarily their top priority. There is limited evidence that organizations have truly effective programs or activities in place to remedy their lack of visibility. Even the successful deployment of technology does not necessarily help the situation – this can frequently result in an explosion of information – so rather than companies having too little information, in fact technology solutions can sometimes result in companies having too much data.

While technology can provide the conduit for increased information visibility, the bigger challenge is often that organizations need the courage to step outside their comfort zones to truly collaborate and openly share information, adopting a more trusting approach among suppliers, customers and even competitors.

Technology – friend or foe?

There is no doubt that enabling visibility across a global supply chain ecosystem requires successful deployment of appropriate IT software, equipment and systems. The sheer complexity of modern supply chains makes it virtually impossible to manage effectively without full visibility provided by a well-designed, fully integrated IT solution. Companies will need to go over and above standard in-house operations, including:

- goods-in;
- manufacturing;
- production-processing;
- accounting;
- order and sales management;
- storage;
- order preparation;
- despatch.

Instead, companies will have to contend with multi-stakeholder external activities and processes such as:

- export and import documentation;
- instructions and reports from partners;
- foreign currency exchange;
- international payments;
- taxes.

However, we cannot overlook the fact that the various participants within the supply chain ecosystem are likely to be using different information technology systems. When seeking to connect and integrate multiple disparate systems, companies will inevitably experience integration challenges that typically consume plenty of time and money to successfully address and overcome.

The harsh reality is that when it comes to technology-enabled visibility, a significant number of businesses are not yet even on the starting blocks. The Aberdeen Group's survey into supply chain visibility (Heaney, 2013) analysed 20 discreet processes in both inbound and outbound operations. Respondents reported that at best half, or usually less than half, of all processes were monitored with visibility software, the rest being handled by phone, fax or email. So there is a long way to go before we see technology-enabled full supply chain visibility as the norm.

To make matters even more challenging, across all sectors of businesses and government, the track record of successfully implementing new IT systems is somewhat patchy, and this applies equally if not more vividly in the context of multi-stakeholder supply chain ecosystems.

The Aberdeen report, 'Enabling Supply Chain Visibility and Collaboration in the Cloud' (Viswanathan, 2010), benchmarked the supply chain application priorities and strategies of 150 organizations. Among the findings, they concluded, 'when undertaking IT projects, multiple roadblocks will be encountered that test even the strongest fortitude. Large doses of commitment and determination are required to successfully drive these projects through to completion.'

The reported success rates for implementing new IT projects presents a daunting picture:

- 21 per cent were judged to be successful;
- 37 per cent ran over budget on either cost or time or both;
- 42 per cent were stopped or aborted.

The report identified some basic ground rules to improve the chances of a successful IT implementation, including:

1 start by being clear about the project's objectives and realistic about the starting point;

2 involve all stakeholders and partners in the initial specification and supplier proposals;

3 set a realistic budget and timescale;

4 appoint a project champion whose sole task is to direct and lead the task;

5 include testing, training and implementation procedures.

On a more positive note, the same Aberdeen Group survey found that the role of cloud-based solutions – such as Software as a Service (SaaS) – in promoting collaboration and enabling visibility are proven to provide businesses with a competitive advantage in areas that require multi-enterprise collaboration. Best-in-class IT system adopters achieved material supply chain benefits, including:

- improving perfect-order rates to 88 per cent;
- achieving cash-to-cash conversion cycles of 22 days;
- managing order-to-delivery cycles of four days;
- whilst being able to on-board new B2B trading partners within 14 days.

Data, information or garbage?

So you have deployed a powerful and expensive software system to help provide the holy grail of full visibility into every corner and byway of your supply chain ecosystem? As with any piece of equipment or process its usefulness, value and survival will depend on the fuel supply – both volume and quality.

'Garbage in, garbage out' (GIGO) may be somewhat of an exaggeration, but incomplete or inaccurate inputs to the system will seriously impact the effectiveness of information and reports, potentially leading to wrong decisions. Even when we have the technology engines seamlessly integrated and synchronized, there will still be challenges in providing clean fuel in the form of high-quality data.

Cloud technology provider GT Nexus advocates three critical steps for ensuring quality supply chain data is feeding into your supply chain software applications:

1 Accuracy – data must be accurate in order to provide a sense of meaningfulness; think of budget reviews where different parties have different numbers.

2 Completeness – missing data can and will distort the information derived and can therefore impact supply chain decisions as badly as incorrect data.

3 Timeliness – data that arrives too late may as well be missing data; in the world of high-velocity supply chains, the need for speed applies equally to bits and bytes as it does to cartons and pallets.

So how can organizations ensure that they keep garbage at bay and not allow it to clog up the flow of genuinely useful data? Everyone involved in the gathering, analysis and use of data should be encouraged to look for errors, gaps and delays so that staff can take remedial action to improve data quality and accuracy.

It's not just garbage that can affect the value and quality of data. Management needs to watch that the sheer volume of data does not overwhelm the system and staff. Better to have limited data that can be acted upon than a flood of information that no one has the time to fully analyse and use. This also applies to regular daily, weekly or monthly reports that may have been set up for a specific purpose which may no longer be relevant but which no one thinks to stop. So it's worth considering regular reviews of reports and analyses to make sure they continue to serve a useful purpose and have not become just part of the system that no one questions.

Big Data

With modern hardware and software technology now able to collect, collate and process billions of pieces of data, users face the challenge of how best to harness the power of Big Data – which can be both a blessing and a curse. Often businesses are dealing with data sets so large and complex they become difficult to process using traditional database management tools or data processing applications. It's possible to be drowning in data yet starved of real, usable, actionable information.

In striving for end-to-end visibility, companies are seeking to deploy a single platform through which the participants can view all the data involved in the supply chain – including through to their suppliers' suppliers – and then to convert the masses of data into meaningful information.

The data management challenges run from the gathering and storage of the data itself, through to the compiling, sharing, transferring and analysis of information.

Big Data grows in size in part because they are increasingly being gathered by ubiquitous information-sensing and data collecting mechanisms, including:

- mobile devices;
- aerial sensory technologies;
- software logs;
- cameras;
- scanners;
- microphones;
- RFID readers;
- wireless networks.

Big Data is difficult to work with using most database management systems, desktop statistics and visualization packages, requiring instead massively parallel software running on tens, hundreds, or even thousands of servers. What is considered Big Data varies depending on the capabilities of the organization managing the set. For some organizations, facing hundreds of gigabytes of data for the first time may trigger a need to reconsider data-management options. For others, it may take tens or hundreds of terabytes before data size becomes a significant consideration.

The real issue is not that you are acquiring large amounts of data – it is what you do with the data that counts. The vision is that organizations will be able to take data from any of multiple sources, extract and harness the relevant data and then analyse it to find answers that deliver usable and practical levels of supply chain visibility, resulting in specific business benefits including:

- Ecosystem-wide visibility to see and monitor the flows of materials, components and finished goods throughout the extended network.

- The ability to determine root causes of failures, issues and defects in near-real time.

- The optimization of transportation routes for many thousands of delivery vehicles whilst they are on the road.

- The ability to analyse millions of SKUs to determine prices that maximize profit and optimize inventory.

- The ability to generate retail coupons at the point of sale based on the customer's current and past purchases.

- The ability to transmit tailored location-based offers to mobile devices while customers are in the relevant vicinity.

What do we mean by IT systems in supply chains?

None of the plans, guides, recommendations and projects addressed so far would be possible without the tools of the trade. Hundreds of suppliers and designers worldwide now offer thousands of solutions and an infinite number of bespoke packages, so it helps to be familiar with the main technologies and IT categories on the market.

Supply chain management software for execution and optimization

The American Production and Inventory Control Society (APICS) dictionary describes supply chain management (SCM) as the 'design, planning, execution, control, and monitoring of supply chain activities with the objective of creating net value, building a competitive infrastructure, leveraging worldwide logistics, synchronizing supply with demand and measuring performance globally' (APICS, 2013).

And so supply chain management software covers a wide range of software functionality – various modules and tools can be used to carry out supply chain transactions, manage suppliers and control all aspects of supply and delivery. They help manage storage and movement of parts, components, raw materials and finished goods, as well as work-in-progress (WIP), final despatch and customer delivery.

Supply chain management covers planning, execution and shipping – the two main categories of supply chain management software are supply chain planning (SCP) and supply chain execution (SCE). Supply chain planning software applications use algorithms to predict requirements and balance supply and demand, while supply chain execution software applications track the physical status of goods, the management of materials, and financial information involving all parties. Supply chain execution systems also address the many tasks involved in the physical supply chain including order fulfilment, procurement, warehousing and transporting.

Sales and operations planning

The roundtable discussion in *Manufacturing & Logistics IT* magazine (2014) pointed to the importance of sales and operations planning systems in contributing to a company's supply chain visibility and business agility.

Sales and operations planning (S&OP) recognizes that demand is not a constant but may change from moment to moment. Internally-driven factors such as sales promotions, product development and pricing will all affect demand, as will uncontrollable external factors such as trends, fashions, competition, new technologies and seasonal demands.

The technology in today's software solutions can facilitate better data analytics and faster demand trends than ever before. A fully collaborative S&OP system that is able to track changes in near to real time, ensures that management is better informed with improved insights and understanding to make good business decisions and will thus play a vital role in achieving supply chain visibility.

Warehouse management systems (WMS)

The warehouse management system (WMS) helps companies manage warehouse and distribution centre operations and provide the levels of visibility essential to running an efficient storage, picking and dispatch operation The WMS stores and manages the required information about all goods and materials passing through the facility – including transactions such as receiving, put-away, picking and despatch. Data is typically collected based on real-time information electronically linked to pallets, cartons, totes, containers or other unit-load types.

WMS software may also incorporate and be integrated with a variety of data identification and collection systems such as barcode readers, wireless devices, mobile computers, RFID identifiers, security access systems and PCs.

Voice-directed warehousing

Using technology to direct operations by voice and speech recognition is becoming increasingly widespread in warehouse and distribution-centre picking and order preparation. While based on audible rather than visual communications, voice directed technology can still be considered as an advance in visibility in the sense that it provides a clear, accurate and precise set of instructions to the operative – which are qualities that any visible system must display.

Voice-enabled operatives wear a headset connected to a portable computer that provides instructions in terms of where to go and what to store or pick within the warehouse. The user is required to confirm each task has been completed by saying certain pre-determined phrases together with the codes found displayed at different warehouse locations or on the packaging of goods. Potential benefits of voice-directed technology include the warehouse operators being hands-free and eyes-free, enabling a faster, more accurate picking methodology than using traditional paper systems.

Transportation management system (TMS)

The transportation management system (TMS) helps optimize transportation activities within an organization by maximizing the efficiency of resources and reducing operational errors. The TMS module includes functionality for tracking and managing every aspect of vehicle maintenance, fuel costing, routing and mapping, communications, cargo handling, carrier selection and management.

Mobile computing

Logistics and supply chain operations have taken great advantage of the advances in mobile computing and communications technology. Even small, portable devices for use on site or on the road now possess levels of computing power that would have been unthinkable just a few years ago. Mobile hand-held computers can provide hardware, software and wireless communications in a single, portable package. They also come with a bundle of extra features including a camera, barcode scanner, phone and internet access, bringing together in one unit what would previously have required several devices.

Commitment to integration is essential

The Supply Chain Insights study identified how large gaps remain in current supply chain visibility capabilities and highlighted three key conclusions businesses must recognize in their pursuit of supply chain visibility:

1 Outsourcing is here to stay – 90 per cent of respondents have some form of outsourcing and rely on external services for handling 40 per cent of their logistics by volume.

2 Supply chain visibility has many forms – few are being delivered well. Companies need to understand exactly what the concept means and how it applies to their particular business.

3 The gaps between aspiration and reality still loom large. Companies are generally satisfied with EDI but confidence in ERP systems to close the gap is low – the average company is dealing with seven different ERP systems.

Cross-functional internal collaboration with the IT function is a key enabler of visibility which in turn drives positive commercial results. Within the group designated above-average performers based on commercial results, 75 per cent of companies stated that their IT systems met total corporate objectives; and in 67 per cent of cases the supply chain management and IT departments share business planning and jointly select technology suppliers, based on vendor profile and systems functionality.

While the majority of companies claimed supply chain visibility was very important to their business, it was generally not seamlessly available across all facets of the business, with the biggest gaps occurring in the areas of co-ordination of orders, managing multi-tier suppliers and integrating of transport and logistics activities.

To succeed across the supply chain ecosystem which inherently involves multiple stakeholders, over and above technology integration, it is important to have managers representing each participating partner working diligently in building and nurturing organizational relationships, such that managers are individually and collectively responsible and accountable for collaborative projects – especially in the area of deploying technology solutions that enable supply chain visibility. These relationships need to be established and maintained for the long term so all parties can develop more efficient and productive ways of co-operating and that lessons learned in the good times will help during downturns.

Lessons learned from the study result in some pithy and practical recommendations:

1 Have a clear definition of supply chain visibility and how it applies to your business.

2 Align IT and functional department heads on a roadmap to close the gap.

3 Define priorities and align solutions – document requirements for supply chain visibility across the network.

4 Document clearly what you are doing today; understand the 'As-Is' whilst clearly defining in detail the 'To-Be'.

5 The goal is hands-free transactions and having the right data for the right person at the right time – as needed for their respective positions and roles in the supply chain ecosystems.

Where next?

The Aberdeen Group (2014) survey of chief supply chain officers (CSCOs) explored their priorities for the coming years ahead. Best-in-class companies are 50 per cent more likely to focus on visibility as important to understanding the customer and essential to planning.

Knowing where the customer is going can certainly reduce demand volatility and provide advance warning of any potential loss of volume, thus limiting its impact. Increases in volumes can be better planned in advance which would explain why best-in-class companies are much less concerned than others by increasing demand.

Visibility also plays a significant role in supplier management, with timely insights into raw material and component supplies enabling strategies to be promptly implemented to offset fluctuations in supply and demand – and allow for contingences.

Visibility across the supply chain ecosystem goes hand-in-hand with collaboration, whereby open communications increase the availability of information and reduce the time for decision making and problem resolution. Close technological and physical connections with customers and suppliers enhances sensitivity to changes up and down the supply chain, improving business agility and supply chain responsiveness.

Summary

There's little doubt that executives worldwide appreciate the importance of supply chain visibility – without it their businesses are less agile than they would wish, incur higher supply chain costs, are less able to identify and remedy faults in their supply chain execution, and are unable to identify and take advantage of opportunities to improve.

Despite prevailing economic uncertainties, global trade has grown hugely in the past few decades and with emerging economic powers, it will continue to do so. A suitable, productive and well-designed supply chain visibility platform is surely an integral and essential component of any business planning to benefit from the long-term growth in international commerce.

CASE STUDY   How technology enables supply chain visibility

Visibility is a vital component in building efficient and effective supply chain ecosystems.

Effectively managing the movement of information flows around such complex, multi-layered, globally connected and interdependent networks is an ever-increasing challenge for businesses and one that most admit they have not yet fully mastered.

In simple terms if you cannot see where you are going, the chances are you won't get where you want to go. This applies just as much to managing the supply chain as it does to driving a car or planning any other type of journey – the scenery may suddenly change, new data is continuously available and obstacles may unexpectedly appear that cause you to change direction.

Achieving supply chain visibility is vital for the business agility that enables competitive advantage – the ability to build and manage strong, customer-focused distribution models, to respond and adapt to changes in demand, component supply, routes, modes of transport and the many other often unexpected events that can affect even the most well-planned supply chain ecosystem.

The logistics industry has in general been very aware of the many advances in telecommunications systems and information technology – and the role they can play in improving productivity, managing costs and providing high-quality customer service. In terms of achieving real-time visibility, the latest generation of data collection and recording devices and associated software tools can be fully integrated to provide a comprehensive and seamless picture of the status throughout the supply chain – anytime, anywhere.

Multi-platform technology solutions can combine and process inputs from multiple devices and systems – such as personal computers (PC), laptops, notepads, bar-code scanners, global positioning systems (GPS), stock management applications, warehouse management systems (WMS), in-cab proof of delivery (POD) tools and other mobile devices – thereby putting information integration and supply chain visibility at the heart of managing the ecosystem. Cloud computing has provided an additional dimension for data collection and information sharing that provides yet further integration, speed and security to connect all the various stakeholders throughout the supply chain.

Along with the growth of world trade, any global supply chain ecosystem may now involve hundreds or potentially thousands of suppliers and partners, with each stakeholder possibly using different platforms or technologies, presenting a range of obstacles to collaborative information sharing and communications, inevitably leading to blind spots.

Technology can overcome these barriers and enable supply chain visibility, in even the most complex of ecosystems, with key input and output features being that data is entered only once and that information provides a single version of the truth that can be shared collaboratively amongst all stakeholders.

Leveraging a cloud-based information technology solution, featuring a shared hub, platform or portal through which every partner in the network could connect with any other supply chain participant, will allow everyone to track, monitor and report on events in the supply chain.

With all ecosystem participants sharing the same system – suppliers, carriers, 3PLs and other trading partners – data duplication is minimized, increasing efficiencies and reducing errors – and the principal and their chosen business partners obtain a holistic view of all the activities across the supply chain, thereby enabling collaborative execution and gaining competitive advantage.

According to Aberdeen Group, a robust collaborative execution solution will include:

- The ability to share new plans and monitor exceptions on a single, global platform.

- Real-time multi-party or multi-tier demand and supply data.

- Internal integration across functional departments, operating divisions, and geographies.

- Rapid resolutions and what-if support in order to 'make the plan' so it can respond intelligently to supply/demand/transport shifts or disruptions.

- Dynamic resolution of the majority of exceptions and shipment events quickly and cost-effectively, while reducing cost, noise, and latency.

A successfully deployed technology solution has the potential to help improve supply chain performance in three key areas of visibility:

- *Visibility for planning and forecasting:* data gathered on factors such as demand, movements, costs, different modes and stock levels – which in themselves provide companies with hour-by-hour and day-by-day operational visibility, also provide an invaluable record to enable senior management to make more informed and intelligent plans and forecasts.

- *Visibility for storage and transport:* more and more standard cloud computing applications are becoming available for functions such as network strategy, inventory management, warehousing, route planning, order processing and transportation.

- *Visibility for open sourcing and procurement:* as cloud-based systems are essentially collaborative and accessible, they are of great benefit for companies who deal routinely with a great many suppliers. Collaboration allows multiple parties to jointly develop supplier contracts and improve contract management.

One leading technology solution that enables supply chain visibility is CargoWise One from WiseTech Global. The CargoWise One system provides a global platform that simplifies and improves integration and communication between supply chain partners, customers and suppliers. Their technology solution is testament to how supply chain management software that provides end to end visibility will improve productivity, lower costs, increase standards of customer service and ultimately deliver greater profitability from a seamless supply chain operation.

The system is specifically developed with the functional capabilities for logistics and supply chain applications can be scaled to individual business demands for any company from a small business start-up to a multinational operation. Modular design allows the user to select the most appropriate system tools with the ability to upgrade as circumstances change.

The ability to integrate in-house functions with those of supply chain ecosystem stakeholders is essential to any Cloud-based system. Users should therefore ensure that any other relevant process such as accounting, document management or e-commerce, as well as the more obvious logistics functions, can be fully integrated into the platform.

Where a fully integrated Cloud-based system really comes into its own is when managing international trade and the many complexities that arise when moving merchandise from one jurisdiction to another. CargoWise One features an integrated online tariff classification tool that helps enable regulatory compliance with customs, quarantine, supply chain security and dangerous goods authorities – in an ever increasing number of countries across the globe.

The software has been implemented at more than 5,000 locations across 105 countries with users confirming powerful and positive results in terms of increasing visibility and helping their businesses successfully compete in the international market. CargoWise user Senator International, a Hamburg-based international carrier and logistics supplier, say that the software helps them meet their clients' visibility expectations and has improved their internal and external systems.

DJS International in the USA switched to WiseTech Global's software to increase productivity through reduced paperwork and other business efficiencies. Instead of re-keying information, printing data, using calculators and handling high volumes of paperwork, staff now only need enter the relevant incremental data once and the automated system does the rest, giving the company and client full visibility on all shipments around the world.

Conclusion

From the technological interfaces to the organizational relationships, integration of all the participants is essential to provide the visibility required to empower efficient and effective performance in the collaborative execution of your global supply chain ecosystem. This again reinforces the need for robust technology platforms, efficient data collection channels and information-sharing protocols to ensure successful collaboration between and amongst the multiple business partners coexisting within the supply chain ecosystem. A single, shared version of the truth is the elusive goal, whilst being 'only as strong as your weakest link' is the harsh reality.

Sustainability and green supply chains

03

Positive environmental strategies for a sustainable supply chain

In recent years, environmental considerations have become part of mainstream policies and strategies for business, government and consumers.

The consequences of past behaviours are now with us – including global warming from CO_2, health risks from pollution, rising sea temperatures, melting glaciers, finite fossil fuels, renewable energy sources and the rising tide of waste products – so doing nothing is no longer an option.

Similar to the concept of Corporate Social Responsibility which gathered momentum during recent years, environmental concerns and building a sustainable supply chain – covering all aspects of the business from sourcing and manufacturing through to final delivery – are now rapidly rising in significance on the corporate agenda.

The good news is that the strategies required to develop a sustainable supply chain make sound business sense. Using fuel and resources more efficiently reduces costs and therefore increases profits, whilst also strengthening the organization's position in selling to both industry and government – and increasing the company's appeal to the environmentally aware consumer.

Implementing a sustainable supply chain involves operating, managing and monitoring every function with a continuous improvement approach, seeking to use less energy, to use energy more efficiently and to operate the supply chain in such a way that the corporate environmental impact and carbon footprint are as low as possible. Such a strategy will reduce costs, protect the company from the worst effects of inevitable rising energy costs over the long term, and ensure the business is well prepared to meet ever-tougher legislation. Companies with green supply chain strategies will be more attractive suppliers to other businesses and consumers, ultimately driving business growth in market share, revenues and profits.

Website thegreensupplychain.com reported that a study by George Serafeim (2014), an associate professor of business administration at the Harvard Business School, concluded that stocks in companies with high sustainability credentials are now outperforming the average stock by up to 50 per cent over the long term. The survey covered the period from 1993 to 2010. Serafeim explained: 'The long-term approach is consistent with sustainability strategies enhancing the brand of a firm, raising employee morale, attracting better talent, gaining better access to finance, and securing a licence to operate. All these effects are built slowly and require a continuous commitment by a firm.'

The result was a classification of 90 firms as having 'high sustainability' and another 90 characterized as 'low sustainability'.

At high sustainability firms, the 'notion of sustainability' appears to be embedded in a holistic and multi-dimensional manner within and throughout the organization. Serafeim added that in the early 1990s, there were fewer than 30 companies producing and publishing a report relative to their environmental or social activities. Two decades later, more than 6,000 companies in the world produced such reports.

Few sectors are as dependent on environmental concerns as today's global supply chain ecosystems, whose performance, efficiency and profitability is inextricably linked to the price and availability of energy in all its forms. In the warehouse, on the road, by rail, sea and air, businesses need to continuously review how energy is used throughout the supply chain – which in turn relates to how efficiently they use costly equipment, staff and other resources. Equally critical, is how supply chain decisions are measuring up to customer expectations – whilst always maintaining a close watch over the bottom line.

In search of a definition

Whilst there is no industry-agreed standard definition for 'sustainable supply chain management', we should consider the key fundamentals in providing a green supply chain to include the logistics and supply chain management processes that incorporate environmentally sustainable strategies to minimize the effects of particulate emissions and pollution, including management processes to mitigate climate change. Ultimately the best way to understand green supply chain concepts and practices is to explore the various aspects involved and to point out the practical ways in which a sustainable supply chain can be constructed, managed and deployed to deliver maximum value to all stakeholders.

Today's global supply chain ecosystems have adopted complex logistics networks featuring elongated transportation linkages that consume expensive oil and other fuel sources while serving globalized markets. The combination of shifting production landscapes together with the dramatic rise in consumerism across emerging and developing markets is resulting in unprecedented international flows of products around the world, contributing to pollution and the ongoing depletion of natural resources such as oil and gas – with all the consequent effects on climate, habitat and depletion of fossil fuels.

A green supply chain will have an effective and well-integrated sustainability strategy in place that addresses multi-dimensional issues pertaining to the economy, the society and the environment. It ensures that the economy benefits in terms of promoting growth, efficiency, employment, competitiveness and choice, and that the welfare of society is protected in terms of ensuring that safety, health, access and equity are safeguarded. As for the environment, a sustainable supply chain will employ the best practices that have at least minimal, if not positive, impact on a number of factors, including:

- the climate;
- air quality;

- noise levels;
- land use;
- biodiversity;
- waste.

The important areas of supply chain sustainability are being able to measure your footprint and implement suitable strategies that reduce carbon or particulate emissions, which are crucial in meeting the increasingly stringent legislative expectations of governments and environmental committees. Furthermore, such emission reduction strategies directly correlate to health improvements amongst communities which are located close to major highways and ports, two of the most prevalent areas where respiratory, heart and lung diseases are most commonly diagnosed – resulting from exposure to high levels of roadside pollution or shipping emissions.

Drivers of a green supply chain

As identified by Stuart Emmett and Vivek Sood (2010) in their book *Green Supply Chains: An action manifesto*, there are five primary categories of environmental stakeholder groups that drive green supply chain initiatives within an organization:

1 Regulatory stakeholders – who either set regulations or have the ability to convince governments to set standards.

2 Consumers – who seek emotional resonance alongside the cost and convenience factors of where and when they buy a particular product.

3 Organizational stakeholders – who are directly related to an organization and can have a direct financial impact on the organization.

4 Community groups – environmental organizations and all those other potential lobbies, who can mobilize public opinion in favour of, or against, an organization's environmental policies.

5 Media – who have the ability to influence society's perceptions.

FIGURE 3.1 Green supply chain drivers – Stuart Emmett and Vivek Sood (2010)

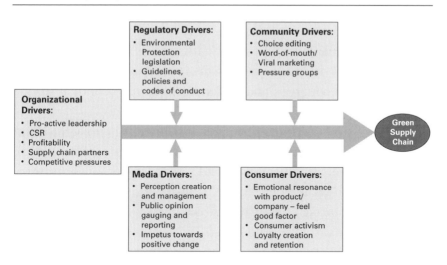

Public opinion – why sustainability matters

Today's consumer is increasingly aware of the environment and ready to some degree to favour the greener option, even if it costs more. Organizations that develop green strategies will therefore enhance their brand profile and generate competitive advantage. The most important issue from a business perspective is that they understand that consumers now really care. Consumers are increasingly educated and are making their purchasing preferences and choices based on their perception of sustainable business practices.

Gaining a strong reputation for environmentally responsible supply chain management can be achieved through embracing new elements of business processes, incorporating sustainability strategies and integrating these processes into daily operations.

The consumer perspective

Consumers today are taking far more notice of green issues and are conscious of the impact on all our lives. They see that sustainability and the environment are not just abstract concepts but have a direct effect on daily life, health, well-being and living standards – and that modern lifestyles could be in danger if we allow present trends to continue unhindered.

The Green Brands study conducted by the WPP group (2011) is one of the largest global consumer surveys of green brands and corporate environmental responsibility. It explores consumer attitudes and perceptions towards green issues, surveying over 9,000 people across eight countries and ranks more than 370 brands around the world.

The 2011 study revealed that consumer interest in green products had expanded across categories and that consumers are intending to purchase more environmentally friendly products across the automotive, energy and technology sectors. Consumers across the globe are already well informed about how green choices in their purchasing of personal care, food and household products directly affects them and their families, and are expanding their green purchase interest to higher value items, such as cars and technology.

For brands, the findings emphasize how they must not only develop sustainability strategies to address their environmental impact, but they must also connect with consumers in a compelling and relevant way – and on a market-by-market basis.

Globally, more than 60 per cent of consumers want to buy from environmentally responsible companies. Respondents in all countries indicate that they are willing to spend more on green products. In developed countries such as the US and the UK, 20 per cent of those surveyed would spend more than 10 per cent extra on a green product. In developing countries, consumers say that green products have a higher inherent value – in China, 95 per cent of consumers say they are willing to spend more on a product because it's green.

The green purchasing survey for Organizations and Individuals conducted by the Green Council of Hong Kong (2010) reported that 72 per cent of respondents had purchased environmentally preferable products, with paper products the most commonly identified product category; 77 per cent said they would include environmental considerations during future purchasing activities; while 88 per cent expressed interest in getting more assistance about green purchasing and in receiving information on green products. Some 94 per cent stated that they would definitely consider practising green purchasing if there was a comprehensive database of environmentally preferable products.

The Green Council also runs its own Green Label Scheme which sets environmental standards and certifies environmentally preferable products, employing a product information database to identify and select the appropriate product categories. A concerned product category must not cause threats to human beings or environmental quality and cannot be fully replaced by other environmentally benign alternatives; in addition, the concerned product category must be commonly used in Hong Kong.

Back in 2010 the UK-based grocery home delivery company Ocado offered its customers the option of choosing a delivery slot when a green delivery van would be in the area, helping to minimize travel distances. It was a good experiment because there was no price differential – therefore no financial incentive either way. Evidently, many people just want their groceries on, say, Thursday morning and don't mind precisely when. Logistics and price being equal, they're happy to select a more environmental option. This is a much better indication of their interest and tolerance than hypothetical questions. In addition, Ocado's revenues grew from $1,030 billion in 2012 to $1,112 billion in 2013, confirming that going green can indeed have a positive effect on the financial performance (Global Cool Foundation, 2010).

The online system from French organization Noteo enables consumers to understand the health and environmental impact of products they buy, using the company's app or by visiting their website. The Noteo organization has evaluated around 60,000 products widely available across the country according to their health, environmental, social effect and budget, with a ranking from 1 to 10. The scheme covers almost anything the consumer might need within the four categories, such as readymade foods, soaps and shampoos, cheeses, washing powders, breakfast cereals, drinks and cosmetics. Currently a brand of aloe vera body-lotion was marked down to a low point of 1.9 out of 10, while a spinach and tomato meal with pasta received 8.9 marks. By logging on and scanning the selected product's bar code, users can easily find out how chosen products perform, enabling them to make a more informed environmental choice.

Business perspectives

Eurobarometer carried out a 2013 survey of small- to medium-sized companies in Europe and the USA to determine their stance on sustainability and environmental issues. Among respondents 93 per cent, including almost all of those in the USA, said they are taking at least one policy initiative towards a more resource-efficient business, with 88 per cent of them saying this was just the first step (European Commission, 2013).

Cost was the biggest driver for 60 per cent of respondents, followed by environmental concerns and customer demand. One in five claims to be exceeding current legislation, while 40 per cent stated that resource efficient steps have cut costs in the past two years and 68 per cent were satisfied that their strategy had been successful.

At the other end of the scale, retail giant Walmart introduced its Supplier Sustainability Assessment throughout its supply chain ecosystem. Buyers and suppliers are evaluated based on their performance in reducing energy costs and greenhouse gas emissions, waste management, responsible sourcing and ethical production methods. Each buyer's annual performance review is based on the sustainability of products with smaller pay raises or lower bonuses for those who do not perform to the required standards.

When one of the world's largest and most profit-focused businesses places such importance on sustainability and environmental concerns in its supply chain, we can be sure it is confident such policies will result in more sales and bigger profits. Its corporate reputation will also be enhanced and shoppers will feel the benefits of a keenly priced shopping basket whilst also playing their part in protecting the environment.

According to its 2011 North American Environmental Report, Honda has made considerable progress in its environmental strategies. One of the most impressive statistics from the report is the estimated 5.6 million miles of truck travel and the 6,743 metric tons of carbon dioxide emissions that were avoided thanks to careful logistics management, procurement planning and supply chain strategies. The company also took a more eco-friendly approach to the manufacturing side of the supply chain. Honda has reportedly cut waste to landfills by 91.9 per cent since fiscal year 2001. In addition, 10 of its

14 plants in North America currently operate without creating any landfill waste.

Another example is General Motors (GM), which has reduced disposal costs by $12 million through establishing a reusable container programme with its suppliers. This initiative not only contributes to the bottom line but also provides a highly positive marketing message.

The 'Buy green and make a difference' guide launched by the UK Office of Government Commerce (2008) outlines how every spending decision a commercial buyer makes has an impact on the environment. It urges buyers to consider green issues such as carbon emissions or waste in each contract negotiation and to make early decisions on how their purchasing decisions can minimize environmental impact. This could involve an innovative approach to procurement, for example considering options to re-use or re-cycle products, and exploring alternative packaging solutions. It is also critical to ensure that once the contract is in place, the suppliers are performing their environmental obligations as agreed. The OGC has already set mandatory sustainable procurement targets, including buying timber from legal and sustainable sources and purchasing low emission cars.

Media and community

Mainstream media, pressure groups and non-government organizations (NGO) as well as the community at large are also exerting pressure for sustainable supply chains. As the media expand their coverage about the environmental impact of manufacturing operations, concern is growing among consumers, advocacy groups, health professionals, and other sectors of society over the perceived exploitation of their community's natural resources. Public concerns go beyond environmental concerns to embrace broader social issues, such as human rights, child labour, liveable wages, working conditions, economic inequality and other issues.

As a result of this increasingly public vigilance and scrutiny, further fuelled by social media, companies are compelled to establish systems and controls that monitor environmental performance, and develop sustainability reporting mechanisms to demonstrate to external audiences the steps they are taking to live up to green and ethical standards in their supply chain management practices.

Regulations and incentives

Governments and international regulatory organizations are also stimulating the requirements for more sustainable supply chains, with mounting pressure to comply with environmental legislation and to take advantage of incentives on offer. With this increasing pressure from all dimensions, it's not surprising that more and more companies worldwide are starting to provide evidence of reducing carbon footprints and implementing strategies for reducing greenhouse gas emissions.

Countries and organizations in various parts of the world have put a variety of policies, procedures and regulations in place to encourage, and in some cases force, those in the supply chain sector to use resources more efficiently. One of the most important governmental agreements is the consensus from the G20 nations to work on reducing emissions by 80 per cent by 2050. This may seem a long way away but to achieve this goal, companies need to now be embarking upon measurement and benchmarking programmes that will gradually reduce particulate levels to a point where climate change can be controlled. Both China and India, countries with significant pollution challenges, have put measures in place to contain spiralling levels of CO_2 emissions.

On the positive side, carbon trading schemes allow better performing firms to buy carbon credits, and subject to meeting their agreed emission goals – can subsequently sell these credits to poorer-performing firms. Cap-and-trade schemes, together with carbon taxation programmes, are expected to be predominant trends in the future.

There is no doubt, therefore, that monitoring and reducing CO_2 emissions is required to improve the environment, but there are many more reasons why supply chain stakeholders are creating an emissions inventory for their businesses. As businesses implement appropriate monitoring systems, they are able to manage energy and fuel consumption more effectively, adopt methods to improve operational efficiency, make progress in measuring carbon footprint and progress towards acquiring environmental accreditation. Any and all reductions in fuel consumption will not only reduce emissions but will also save money, and is therefore good for both the environment and for the business!

Stricter government regulations and stiffer penalties for polluters are becoming the more common approach and in many jurisdictions, carbon reporting for large organizations is likely to become mandatory within the next couple of years.

In China the initial decision to adopt a carbon tax for polluting industries was announced in early 2013 – the country's carbon emissions are already the largest in the world and continue to rise. In India, radical changes in policy have resulted in the first ever carbon tax programme coming into effect, initially aimed at the most heavily polluting sectors such as the coal industry, which is likely to be extended in the future to the transportation sector (China.org, 2013).

Specifically impacting the global logistics sector we are seeing several developments in terms of both regulatory and voluntary programmes, across all modes of transport, especially shipping.

Green shipping

In North America, the maritime sector has established 'Green Marine', a voluntary environmental certification programme supported by ports, terminals, ship owners, seaway corporations and shipyards along the US west coast and Canada. The programme encourages its participants to reduce their environmental footprint by taking concrete actions, including developing best environmental practices, acting responsibly to minimize environmental impacts, develop and promote voluntary protection measures and to collaborate with all interested groups supporting the Green Marine environmental programme. To receive their certification, participants must benchmark their annual environmental performance through Green Marine's exhaustive self-evaluation guides. Their results also need to be verified by an accredited external verifier and all participants have to agree to publication of their results.

In California, the Port of Long Beach's ambitious Clean Trucks Program has reduced air pollution from harbour trucks by more than

90 per cent in a little over three years. Effective from 2012, the programme permanently banned the last remaining older, more polluting trucks from port terminals. Virtually all of the 11,000 drayage trucks that service the port terminals are now 2007 or newer models.

In Hong Kong, the world's fourth busiest port, the industry has adopted the Fair Winds Charter. This is a voluntary industry framework under which participating shipping lines agree to switch their vessels to cleaner fuel whilst at berth in Hong Kong waters. In this particular case, industry is lobbying government for legislation, which will enforce cleaner fuel requirements on all port users. Neighbours Shenzhen are implementing a similar program, which bodes well towards eventually establishing an emissions control area for the whole south China port cluster.

Practical steps to a green supply chain

Green supply chain management is now evolving into a company's core business strategy, as pressures to reduce environmental impacts are coming from investors, supply chain partners, customers and institutional purchasers.

For most companies a sustainable supply chain is no longer just an option but a must-have if they are to increase the odds of success in a perilous world. Nowadays the majority of global companies are pursuing sustainability initiatives, and those with a dedicated and comprehensive strategy are more likely to achieve supply chain sustainability.

Getting accreditation

Many companies have directed their attention to achieving a globally recognized environmental standard certification such as the International Standards Organization (ISO) or the Global Reporting Initiative (GRI). Industry leaders have pursued ISO 14001 accreditation to demonstrate that they are environmentally responsible and keep ahead of the competition. By investing in these globally recognized standards, which include regular audits to ensure their business practices conform to agreed standards, they are committed to continually improving their environmental footprint. Such international certifications provide high levels of assurance to companies who wish to work with vendors who meet their environmental expectations.

Fuel efficiency

From the tactical perspective, the biggest and most obvious starting point is reducing the fuel bill. In logistics, there are enormous opportunities from the trucking perspective for fuel efficiencies and emission reductions. Trucking around the world, particularly in developing and emerging markets, is inherently inefficient – the majority of trucks are travelling only at 50 per cent utilization and therefore 50 per cent of the capacity is being wasted.

The majority of back-haul is massively underutilized, especially in emerging markets. So if we can get better truck assets on the road, and if we can get better fleet management systems in place, we can take a massive amount of trucks off the road, easing congestion, reducing fuel which is good for the environment as it reduces emissions and saves money which is good for the business.

One example of improving utilization is to consolidate low and high density freight on to the same vehicle. For example, combining small and heavy products together with bulky but lightweight products all onto the same truck – thereby optimizing the truck load weight capacity whilst maximizing the use of the vehicle space. Logistics service providers and trucking companies are best placed to identify and explore such collaborative arrangements as the intermediary amongst non-competing shippers.

Who can apply green supply chain and logistics programmes?

Contrary to the popular belief that only large companies can afford to be environmentally friendly, implementing and operating a green supply chain programme is equally applicable for small, medium and large companies alike – including local players and multinationals.

Tony Wines, CEO of Turnkey Group, has worked on sustainability initiatives with many medium-sized businesses and believes 'sustainable supply chains are not just for the global giants'. He says: 'There are many different green supply chain initiatives that can be undertaken by small and medium sized companies. Businesses of any size can adopt green supply chain initiatives that will improve efficiencies, reduce costs and deliver competitive advantage, whilst also increasing compliance regulatory requirements, meeting customer expectations – and providing branding benefits generated from market perceptions of green leadership.'

Educating staff on environmental awareness

Integrating sustainability topics into employee training helps solidify an organization's commitment to sustainable practices and get employees on the same page. The US National Environmental Education Foundation (2014) reports that employee engagement and education on environmental awareness has become an emerging trend in the business community.

This growing movement sweeping through establishments ranging from giant conglomerates to microenterprises to teach employees to conserve, recycle, improve efficiency and reduce waste is reaping numerous benefits for employees, companies and communities. By cultivating workers' knowledge in energy conservation and environment preservation, companies can save resources, energy and money as well as boosting their green reputation.

Industry leadership

The supply chain sector is one of the leaders in embracing concepts of green programmes for sustainability. Numerous companies have embarked on the implementation of eco-rating systems whereby vendors are monitored and measured on a range of enviro-metrics. Such systems provide the principal with the ability to rate their suppliers, with options to downgrade or de-select those that are underperforming against defined scorecard measurements for environmental standards. This is becoming widespread in Europe and North America, and now gradually filtering into markets across Asia.

According to Dexter Galvin, head of Supply Chain at the Carbon Disclosure Project (CDP), a non-government organization helping industry to reduce greenhouse gases, 'Logistics companies' environmental performance in terms of CO_2 emissions data has become so important to large customers (shippers) that it can win or lose major contracts.' (Loadstar, 2013)

The resulting trend is also impacting on the role of freight forwarders, logistics service providers, transportation companies, shipping lines and cargo airline carriers. It is clear that the dynamics are changing – a global survey by Eye for Transport (2008) found that 82 per cent of logistics firms consider green supply chains to be an important part of their business while 12 per cent considered it their number one priority.

In future, companies that do not take the role of green supply chain seriously will be financially penalised by having to pay for carbon credits to offset higher levels of emissions. In other words the worse you perform, the more you will need to pay, with the potential of additional negative consequences impacting customer loyalty and market perceptions of brand and reputation. Therefore, companies need to ensure that they have suitable monitoring and reporting tools to meet these exacting requirements. As governments seek to establish legally binding environmental targets that can be implemented globally, it is clear that companies must act now.

Summary – it makes sense all round to go green

Introducing green working is now a natural progression for the supply chain industry to seriously consider. In addition to improving productivity and cost savings, using an electronic proof of delivery system, mobile field service management or real-time job scheduling and route optimization systems for instance, have been shown to have a significant impact on reducing CO_2 emissions and the carbon footprint of logistics operators.

Companies that embrace green supply chain programmes benefit not just from improved environmental performance and regulatory compliance, but can also generate cost savings if they implement programmes and strategies effectively. Furthermore, businesses adopting green strategies also gain competitive advantage and improve their brand image. As well as global multinationals these benefits extend very much to small- and medium-sized companies which can avail themselves of external expertise as appropriate to support and assist in the development of green logistics strategies.

CASE STUDY   Green supply chains depend upon accurate and complete data collection and analysis

The environmental agenda is becoming one of the most pertinent supply chain issues of the modern age, with both fuel consumption and pollutant emissions at the forefront of the industry challenge.

In our highly competitive world of complex, connected supply chain ecosystems, it makes sound commercial sense – as well as demonstrating high levels of corporate social responsibility – to minimize fuel usage, reduce CO_2 emissions and align with international environmental standards.

How carriers and shippers are working together to save fuel and reduce carbon emissions

While the sea-freight industry is a major consumer of fuel, water-borne freight actually uses proportionately less fuel than aircraft or road vehicles. In recent years, leading supply chain ecosystem participants – carriers and shippers – have come together to combine efforts and resources to achieve further improvements, thereby helping make ocean freight supply chains much more environmentally responsible.

The Clean Cargo Working Group (CCWG) is a business-to-business initiative that comprises leading ocean freight carriers and their customers. Established more than a decade ago by the global NGO Business for Social Responsibility (BSR), CCWG now comprises 40 members, including cargo carriers ('carriers'), and their customers (freight-forwarders and 'shippers'), who together represent 85 per cent of ocean container cargo.

Dedicated to improving environmental performance and enhancing industry standards in the maritime sector, CCWG's mandate is to encourage and support members to cut fuel consumption and reduce emissions.

CCWG initiative to enhance data quality

Recognizing that their data gathering, monitoring and reporting procedures had room for improvement, CCWG established a collaborative project with Turnkey Solutions, the leading industry software provider of sustainability reporting, data collection and cost optimization technology. The Turnkey system measures impact within the supply chain, highlighting opportunities to save cost and reduce environmental impact.

Prior to CCWG implementing Turnkey Solution's online platform, data was collected using manual processes including complex Excel spreadsheets, involving extremely time-consuming and labour intensive data consolidation processes.

With 40 different data points being collected individually from more than 2,900 ships operated by 23 of the world's leading ocean container carriers, errors can easily occur. Furthermore the old spreadsheet system involved many complexities at management level, in particular cross-referencing multiple sources and validating calculation methods.

'When you work on multiple complex spreadsheets, you have people sitting for days, ploughing through the data, pulling numbers, trying to make them fit. We've seen some of the most creative and beautiful spreadsheets, but it takes days and days to administer,' explained Ian Catley, Business Development Director of Turnkey Solutions.

The project also highlights the importance of implementing a greener supply chain and demonstrates how leveraging e-commerce technology platforms can provide time and cost benefits, improve processes and develop competitive advantage.

'Adopting the Turnkey online platform service has helped overcome existing inefficiencies in data collection and management, whilst enabling the participants to benchmark and monitor their environmental performances against competitors,' states Tony Wines, CEO of Turnkey Solutions.

Common data challenges for supply chain practitioners

Data challenges are by no means unique to CCWG. Seeking to consistently use accurate, complete and timely data is an ongoing challenge throughout today's global supply chain ecosystems – for customers, suppliers, collaborators and competitors alike.

There are three primary contributing factors that make it essential to achieve accurate collection:

1 Scale and scope – handling large amounts of data is an arduous process; switching between screens or Excel sheets easily leads to errors and confusion of data transparency.

2 Inefficient resource utilization – manual data collation involves higher operational costs and introduces inaccuracies, rather than focusing time for strategic improvements and innovation.

3 Extended ecosystem – for organizations with global suppliers, data management becomes complicated due to non-standard methods of data collection and inconsistent metrics.

CCWG selected Turnkey Solutions for its logistics sector management experience as well as its proven expertise in developing technology platforms with strict and secure controls that ensure data integrity and protect confidentiality.

The Turnkey system validates and consolidates all the data inputs, compiling summary reports and score-sheets for each carrier that benchmark their performance against peer averages, together with comparisons to the CCWG baseline – all readily available in downloadable pdf format. Individual carriers can choose whether or not they want to share their ranking data with their customers.

The end result is a greatly enhanced and much more user-friendly experience for the participants, requiring considerably less time and effort, resulting in CCWG members becoming even more willing to participate in the project, with resulting benefits for all the stakeholders.

The Turnkey solution has been configured to support the logistics and supply chain sectors. Developed in collaboration with CCWG management, the system delivers valuable and cost-effective tools that help members implement greener supply chain ecosystems that reduce costs and improve productivity.

For the carriers and shippers involved, participating in this initiative helps promote their green supply chain credentials throughout the industry – reflecting the increasingly important aspect of sustainability that differentiates companies and delivers competitive advantage in a complex world.

Green supply chain has become strategically important

Sustainability strategies of leading companies now include targets to reduce CO_2 emissions within their global supply chain ecosystems, focusing on optimizing transportation and logistics networks. Businesses increasingly favour working with like-minded supply chain partners to support best-in-class green supply chain practices.

'When implementing green supply chain initiatives, e-commerce tools, especially cloud-based technology, will substantially increase efficiencies, reduce costs, particularly in labour hours, as well as significantly improve the credibility of sustainability reporting,' stated Tony Wines, CEO of Turnkey Solutions.

The motivation to both achieve and portray sustainability initiatives in green supply chain strategies by reducing emissions and cutting fuel consumption is fast becoming a business imperative – from both commercial and legal perspectives.

Conclusion

Proven reduction in emissions confirms the success of the CCWG project. As a measure of its success, the CCWG 2014 report confirmed that average CO_2 emissions per container per kilometer for global ocean transportation routes have declined by more than 7.7 per cent year on year – and by over 22 per cent since 2009.

Angie Farrag-Thibault, Associate Director of the BSR Transport & Logistic Practice, summed up the successful CCWG and Turnkey collaboration: 'We are delighted to be working more closely with Turnkey Solutions; they offer us a level of industry experience in sustainability and supply chain with strong emphasis on the ocean sector. We undertook a rigid due-diligence process in selecting our strategic partner for this important role and Turnkey ticked all the boxes for us. It is part of Clean Cargo strategy to create lasting partnerships with third-party service providers that can help support these industry leaders improve their reporting capabilities.'

Risk and supply chain resilience

04

Risk – building supply chain resilience for competitive advantage

Almost every business venture ever undertaken has had some element of risk – from the early seafaring traders who faced storms, enemy ships and Barbary pirates, to thwarted attempts by the European powers to open up trade with the Far East.

Risk is simply the other side of opportunity and will always be present in any commercial venture, even though the cause may vary.

Graphic reports of natural disasters, terrorism, political upheaval and other big impact events have helped drive supply chain risk towards the top of the agenda in many boardrooms, alerting chief executives to the hitherto less obvious vulnerabilities in many parts of their businesses.

However, the big change is that as supply chain ecosystems have become more complex and, almost inevitably these days, extend across international boundaries, they have become progressively more vulnerable and are exposed to occurrences that are seemingly random and difficult to foresee.

The trend towards leaner supply chains with lower stock holdings has also contributed to supply chain vulnerability, with companies less able to turn to inventory of goods or materials in hand to provide a buffer against sudden shortages.

Catastrophic risks are those unpredictable but inevitable events that cause massive and immediate disruption to the supply chain ecosystem, often with tragic consequences to human life – for example extreme weather conditions, traffic accidents and acts of piracy.

Executives increasingly appreciate they have to try to identify where their supply chain ecosystems are most vulnerable, what can be done to mitigate the risk and the likely costs to the business of sudden disruption. However, it's never easy to convince the Board to budget for what may never happen – and cannot be predicted or easily identified.

What can help win the day however, are the increasingly frequent real-life examples of what has happened to many leading global concerns – such that the 'it could not happen to us' mindset can be overcome more readily.

However, as we have experienced in recent years, floods, earthquakes, volcanic eruptions, terrorist attacks, ship hijackings and plane crashes all do happen – with massive and immediate disruption to the supply chain ecosystem; so every organization should take notice and plan accordingly – prepare to expect the unexpected!

When London was hit by the terrorist bombing on its passenger transport system on 7 July 2005, mobile phone networks, railways, highways and other services were very quickly overloaded, making a bad situation even worse.

At the other end of the spectrum are the somewhat lesser, routine business risks that impact the supply chain ecosystem, for example issues such as supplier failures, shipping delays, product shortages, cargo crime, strikes, corruption and other hindrances that eat away at business efficiency. And again if supply chains are lean, then any sort of interruption can have far-reaching consequences that negatively impact the company's production activities or customer services.

Today's supply chain ecosystems are not only vulnerable where and when goods are being physically stored or moved. They also depend on a huge number of inter-related networks including information technology systems, finance, energy supplies, telecommunications, transport and other networks of services, any of which could fail, causing severe knock-on effects within the supply chain.

After reading this introduction the supply chain executive might feel somewhat helpless, but there is hope. The reality is that – considering the volatile nature of the world today – companies regularly and routinely deliver goods across the world, on-time and in an efficient manner that most consumers take for granted, which is down to the way in which today's supply chain ecosystems have been constructed.

In this chapter we will look at the various types of risk, what they involve and most importantly, what steps companies can take to build supply chain resilience for competitive advantage, so that when and if the unexpected does arise, they have adaptable business models with the tools, the systems and the organization in place to respond swiftly and positively to keep any damage to the business to the absolute minimum.

A resilient supply chain ecosystem will provide the best defence against risk whilst also delivering competitive advantage. So, how do we arrive at that position? In this chapter we consider:

- Evaluating the potential for risks in the supply chain.
- The main types of risk and their potential effects.
- Expect the unexpected – example of catastrophic risk.
- Pitfalls of culture, standards and regulations.
- Cargo theft, piracy and disruption.
- Hacking – the new threat from cyber-criminals.
- The qualities of a risk-resistant supply chain ecosystem.
- How to build a resilient supply chain ecosystem.
- Choosing your supply chain partners.
- Protecting your reputation.
- Best practice examples.

Evaluating the potential for risks in the supply chain

The dictionary definition of risk is 'a factor, thing, element, or course involving uncertain danger; a hazard'. The Supply Chain Risk Leadership Council (SCRLC) (2014) adopts the definition 'any factor or event that can materially disrupt a supply chain – whether within a single company or spread across multiple companies.'

A more succinct version from the Sourcing Innovation (2014) blog is 'If you're counting on it, it's a risk'!

Bearing this in mind, we can see how supply chain risks are common and widespread – not just within our own organizations but within all the other participants throughout the ecosystem.

Supply chains that were once local or regional are now truly global and have consequently become more complex, multi-layered, connected ecosystems – with numerous and profound interdependencies across and amongst multiple participating stakeholders. In our volatile world, these ecosystems have become even more vulnerable and we therefore need to build supply chain resilience for competitive advantage.

The myriad of supply chain risks include component shortages, product failure, supplier failure, quality defects, transportation breakdowns, systems malfunction, commodity price fluctuations, operational breakdowns, price increases, shipment delays and fraud – including counterfeiting and theft of intellectual property.

Some risks are easy to identify, others far less so and there are some that would have required a crystal ball and a fertile imagination to have foreseen!

Catastrophic risks are the known but unknown events that occur around the world, incidences that are almost certain to happen at some stage – except that the actual what, where and when remains very much elusive, posing indiscriminate risks to the supply chain ecosystem.

For example, the 2010 Eyjafjallajökull volcano eruption in Iceland resulted in the closure of much of European airspace for the best part of a week, causing havoc for airfreight-oriented supply chain ecosystems serving the electronic, fresh produce and pharmaceutical industries.

This volcanic eruption had far reaching implications and consequences beyond the direct impact to specific supply chain ecosystems, with the broad economic ramifications summarized by *The Daily Telegraph* (2011) as follows:

- Most European airspace closed progressively, during April 15–21.

- 100,000 flights cancelled in total, peaking at 19,000/day.

- Over 10 million people stranded or unable to board flights.

- Airlines lost $1.7 billion in missed revenues.

- Airports lost $300 million.

- 90 per cent of flights were cancelled in worst-affected markets: Finland, Ireland, UK.

- Low-cost carriers were worse hit than long-distance carriers, cancelling some 61 per cent of their flights.

- Travel by business jets was the least affected.

- 30 per cent of total worldwide airline capacity was cut.

- European airline capacity was cut by 75 per cent, Africa by 30 per cent, Middle East by 20 per cent, others 15 per cent.

- Airline kerosene demand fell by 1.2 million barrels a day, compared with 4.3m barrels consumed on a normal day.

- Emerging market currencies tied to tourism fell – such as the Kenyan shilling and Turkish lira.

- OECD said ash week cost the European economy $5 billion.

- Travel and tourism, including transport, lodgings and related investment were all impacted, which together comprise about 4 per cent of West European GDP, according to the World Travel and Tourism Council.

- PricewaterhouseCoopers estimated each week of disruption destroyed around 0.025-0.05 per cent of annual British GDP; the same would probably be true of other European countries.

- While hotels received fewer incoming tourists, some were able to raise prices to take advantage of stranded tourists.

- While one volcano wreaked havoc, the economy of the volcanic islands of the Azores, governed by Portugal, got an unexpected lift: traffic boomed due to flight diversions!

While such catastrophic risks capture global headlines, the smaller, routine business risks that may be more predictable and easier to identify can in reality be just as damaging to the business, although simpler to spot and resolve.

It is also important to note that one's perspective on risk depends largely on where one sits within the supply chain ecosystem – the positional perspective. For example, the finance manager is likely to have a different perspective on supply chain risk than the logistics or procurement manager. Likewise, the component supplier may well have a different perspective on supply chain risk to the high street retailer. Nevertheless, they could all be participants and stakeholders in a single supply chain ecosystem, susceptible to a whole variety of risks which are likely to impact many of the components and players within the ecosystem.

Types of risk

The better we understand the different types of risk, their likelihood and potential damage, the more effectively we can identify what strategies can be put in place to protect the company from their effects. Broadly speaking there are two main categories of supply chain risk:

Business risk – often foreseeable such as credit difficulties, suppliers being unable to deliver or having financial or quality issues, labour disputes either within your own company or elsewhere in the supply chain, rising fuel and energy costs, transportations breakdowns and delays, etc.

Catastrophic risk – events that are likely to occur but for which the where and when is extremely difficult to predict, consisting of three primary categories:

— natural disasters, such as floods, earthquakes and volcano eruptions;

— sabotage, including terrorism and political/social conflicts;

— accidents, including traffic collisions, airplane crashes, ships sinking, etc.

Such events often have tragic consequences involving loss of life but from the supply chain perspective inevitably cause massive and immediate disruption and disorder to the supply chain ecosystem.

In his book entitled *Supply Chain Risk*, (2014) industry expert John Manners-Bell describes how inventory reduction strategies have made supply chains more vulnerable than ever to a range of external threats, and identifies the 10 leading risks to supply chains:

1 Corruption.

2 Civil unrest and geopolitical security.

3 Demand shocks.

4 Terrorism and piracy.

5 Fire and floods.

6 Geo-physical disasters.

7 Extreme weather events.

8 Cargo crime.

9 Smuggling and counterfeiting.

10 Ethical and environmental practices.

Expect the unexpected

It would be easy to fill a book with examples of supply chain failures, because few if any organizations can say hand on heart that nothing has ever gone wrong. However, a few examples will illustrate just how vulnerable even some of the best run businesses can be to catastrophic risks, where their supply chain ecosystem spans the globe and embraces multiple partners and collaborators.

- Leading automotive manufacturers were taken unawares when the March 2013 earthquake in Japan shut down the sole provider of a glittery paint pigment for two months, halting production for companies such as Ford, Toyota, GM and Honda in North America and in Europe.

- When the monsoon rains flooded parts of Thailand in late 2011, industrial parks around Bangkok were hit hard with many factories becoming inoperable. Over 25 per cent of the world's hard-drive production capacity is located in Thailand, so the floods resulted in a global shortage of disk drives – which lasted well into 2012 – in turn impacting production and supply of desktop and notebook computers throughout Asia, Europe and the USA. Toshiba, the world's fourth largest hard drive producer, had 50 per cent of its capacity in Thailand; whilst Western Digital, the world's second largest maker of hard drives, had about 60 per cent of its global capacity there and suffered losses estimated at almost $200 million.

- A tragic fire at a Bangladesh clothing factory in late 2012 caused massive disruption to some garment supply chain ecosystems. The terrible loss of life amongst hundreds of low-paid workers resulted in several global brands issuing statements expressing regret. As well as the fire impacting the supply of products, many leading retailers such as Walmart, Asda, Tesco and Primark found themselves in the spotlight for not doing enough to protect low-paid workers following several safety incidents in Bangladesh.

Pitfalls of variations in culture, standards, regulations and local practices

While the world continues to become apparently more homogeneous, there are many nasty traps in wait for those who think that the ways in which companies do business and the laws that govern trade are universal. What may be accepted in one part of the world as normal can be the subject of a heavy prison sentence elsewhere, making even the company's employees vulnerable to an unwitting lack of judgement or knowledge.

Indeed, regulatory compliance is now consistently featured as a priority item on the risk agenda, reflecting the multi-jurisdictional nature of global supply chain ecosystems.

Executives may find themselves trying to reconcile corporate standards with cultures and environments that take a very different stance on issues such as the payment of commission or incentives – not to mention outright bribery – or what is considered legal in terms of information gathering. They will often be working in environments with established local business practices, across a range of jurisdictions, sometimes contradictory, and with poorly drafted or even ambiguous legislation, with varying levels of interpretation and enforcement at the local level.

Cargo theft, piracy and disruption

From the earliest days, traders have faced the threat of theft and piracy. Today's extended supply chain ecosystems that empower the enormous increase in the movement of goods around the world, are sadly providing fertile grounds for all kinds of illegality.

- The International Chamber of Commerce's International Maritime Bureau conducted a survey of piracy and cargo theft, with the results showing that in 2013, nearly one in 11 container ships had been attacked with worldwide losses of over $22 billion.

- Piracy continues to make the headlines with the number of pirate attacks against ships worldwide reaching 264 in 2013. Top of the vulnerable locations list was Indonesia with 106 incidents, followed by Nigeria, India, Bangladesh and Malaysia.

- In the USA, 41 per cent of all cargo theft incidents involved a parked truck, whilst in Russia, hijacking was the preferred technique, accounting for 25 per cent of all cargo theft; not surprisingly, small and high value products such as mobile phones, computer notebooks and tablets and other consumer electronic devices were the most popular targets.

Hacking – the new threat from cyber-criminals

Every advance in technology brings both good and bad to society. While the digital revolution has and continues to transform the way we work, shop and play, it has also provided new opportunities for every type of criminal behaviour.

Computer hacking is a breach of computer security that is increasingly affecting commercial companies, countries and organizations. Hackers may delete or manipulate sensitive information and put at risk data stored on the hacked company's IT system, depriving an organization of that all-important visibility into their supply chain ecosystem or the means to run their business.

Unexplained declines in computer performance, an unexpected increase in file size, unexplained modifications to files, sudden changes in network settings and frequent disk crashes are some of the warning signs. Reliable antivirus software is a first and essential step in combating hackers but the best protection is constant vigilance and awareness of the threat throughout the whole organization.

Prevention vs preparedness

The Centre for Transportation and Logistics (CTL) at MIT conducted a survey which found that 54 per cent of respondents considered risk prevention more important than response preparedness, while 16 per cent considered response preparedness more important, and 30 per cent gave them equal weighting. They reported that one reason for this is that it is easier to identify preventable risks than it is to identify potential required responses from an endless list of disruptions.

With resilience being defined in the Farlex online dictionary as 'the power or ability to recover quickly from change or misfortune and return to the original form, position, etc, after being bent, compressed, or stretched' – then supply chain resilience is about being prepared and being better able and equipped to handle risks within the ecosystem.

The low level of attention that was given to response preparedness can be linked to the slow recovery of the global economy since the global financial crisis. If more sense and response mechanisms had been developed within supply chain ecosystems, then a speedier recovery could have been expected.

Features of a resilient supply chain ecosystem

Every business will have – or should have – its own unique risk strategy to evaluate and counter potential weaknesses in individual supply chain structures and networks. However, a resilient supply chain will typically feature a soundly based risk mitigation framework structured around four key pillars: *visibility, collaboration, flexibility* and *speed*. Developing such capabilities will empower an organization with timely information that feeds into sense and response mechanisms that underpin the company's preparedness – harnessing its readiness, intelligence and resources to manage supply chain risk.

Visibility

In order to be aware of a problem it must be visible. Developing visibility is a process combining technology and partnership throughout the supply chain ecosystem. Technology is at such an advanced stage

FIGURE 4.1 Supply chain resilience for competitive advantage

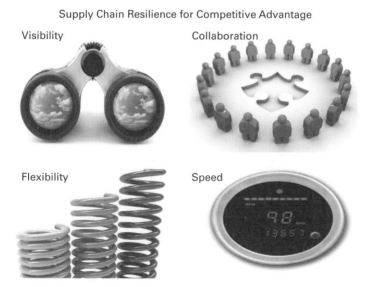

Supply Chain Resilience for Competitive Advantage

Visibility

Collaboration

Flexibility

Speed

that we can in theory see and measure virtually every aspect of the supply chain. To be used effectively, however, the available technology needs to be shared with openness and trust amongst partners up and down the supply chain. As we have explored in Chapter 2, supply chain visibility enables companies to deploy early warning systems that alert relevant participants when events are deviating from the plan.

Collaboration

As supply chain ecosystems have become increasingly complex, effective collaboration is essential to connect the multiple participants in a cohesive network of commercially engaged stakeholders. Collaboration is the open and cooperative sharing of information with constituent partners throughout the supply chain ecosystem on a need-to-know basis for the overall efficiency and performance of the supply chain, without compromising proprietary data.

For successful collaboration, over and above technology integration, it is important for senior managers representing the supply chain partners to work diligently on building and nurturing organizational relationships, such that the managers are individually and collectively responsible and accountable for collaborative projects. These relationships must be maintained throughout downturns so that when the upturn arrives, there is still a strong collaborative bond between companies.

Flexibility

Being flexible means being responsive to change, being adaptable – for example having alternative sources of supply ready to bring on-stream at short notice. Another example would be to have the appropriate flexibility within the supply chain infrastructure and resources to respond to fluctuations in demand. In fact, flexibility is one of the key supply chain performance measures adopted by the Supply Chain Council in their SCOR model (Hudson, 2004). Their agility metrics include supply chain adaptability – both upside and downside – defined as 'the sustainable increase or decrease in product quantities that can be achieved within 30 days (without back-orders, cost penalties or excess inventory) expressed as a percentage of current run-rate'. Such flexibility measurements help to determine the organization's ability to respond to changes in the market, such external influences being beyond the immediate scope and control of their own supply chain ecosystem.

Speed

Coupled with flexibility is the 'need-for-speed' – velocity is essential in order to enable effective rapid-response mechanisms. Trade and commerce now move at digital speed and therefore a key component of a resilient supply chain is the ability to communicate and act swiftly – in information gathering, decision making and in execution. This means being able to sense and respond quickly to changes in the marketplace, such as changes in customer demand, to supplier capabilities and to employee needs.

Visibility enables problems to be sensed and seen. It is then essential to act with speed in assessing, deciding and implementing corrective actions. One method to support speed in decision making and in implementing action is to match responsibility, authority and accountability at the same level within the organization.

Building supply chain resilience

Each and every business is different, so there is no single risk strategy that will work for all. The responsibility to produce, manage and implement the strategy lies with the company's senior management in their own particular way to reflect their own company's corporate structure, markets and supply chain ecosystem.

How top executives view supply chain resilience

An Accenture 2013 global survey of 1,000 senior executives collated key risk factors they judged to be the most critical and therefore the issues that deserved the most attention (Accenture, 2014). Top of the concerns was information technology systems that could give fragmented, insufficient, incomplete or inaccurate data thus inhibiting companies from having the agility to react quickly and decisively to unforeseen events.

What is abundantly clear from the many surveys and recommendations is that the first step in managing risk is to recognize that it exists, how it can arise and affect the business, and a determination to invest time and money into taking all reasonable steps to manage risk.

Successful companies ensure that risk management is a specific topic for regular review at meetings to instil a risk awareness culture into the company. Appointing a senior risk executive is a sound step to providing sustained focus on the subject and a focal point for spotting potential risk and counter-measures. As previously mentioned, however, the senior management team's decisions will only be as good as the intelligence they have to hand, so an efficient, accurate and suitably designed IT system is vital, as well as the organization being up-to-date with external events and developments that may affect the company's business.

A well-designed supply chain risk management plan will:

- Identify and prioritize potential risks, their likelihood and possible cost implications.

- Establish clear individual and personal responsibilities for action in respect of the various types of risks identified.

- Have a worst case disaster-management plan whose purpose will be to ensure that the business continues to function and can identify the steps and resources that lead to full recovery.

- Be under constant review, both as circumstances inevitably change and also to ensure that effective risk management is part of the day-to-day business operations and corporate culture.

A simple but effective tool for prioritizing risk management strategies is to plot – for each identifiable risk – the likelihood of it happening versus the resultant impact.

FIGURE 4.2 Risk analysis matrix

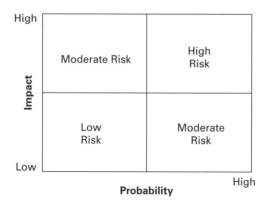

Choose your partners with care

Today's supply chain ecosystems inevitably involve numerous partners and stakeholders, often in other countries or continents, whose reliability and performance may have a profound effect on the business, for better or for worse!

During their 2014 supply chain briefing in China, Baker & McKenzie reported the sobering statistic that 90 per cent of actions brought before the US Department of Justice involve misconduct by third parties. And pursuing effective court action in other jurisdictions may prove to be a long and arduous process, ever more so as companies further extend their supply chain ecosystems across borders into emerging and developing markets, many with relatively underdeveloped, or in some cases unstable, political and legal systems.

More so now than ever before, is the need for detailed due diligence in the evaluation and selection of supply chain partners, processes that involve not just assessment of their capabilities, but also scrutinizes their reputation, track record and background.

Checks should also include the financial health of any potential partner – a sound balance sheet and strong cash flow means the supplier can withstand variable revenue streams and support higher levels of business.

If the potential partner is part of a larger group, it is important to ensure there are no potential conflicts of interest that could affect the external perception of the relationship in a negative way.

With so much potential for supply chain disruption it's even more important to clearly identify and agree in the pre-contract stage precisely what sub-tier suppliers are expected to provide, including key performance indicators and suitable parameters and measurements that will help assess their activities.

Key questions to consider during discovery and due diligence would include:

- Can the supplier handle the volume of activity proposed and where it will take place?

- Do they conform to their own domestic or other states' laws, standards or commitments, such as environmental and labour laws?

- What do their own business partners and customers say about their performance – do they have a sound reputation in the industry that may provide either reassurance or a warning sign?

Suppliers with a high level of business integrity, well financed, flexible and eager to build strong, long-term partnerships are to be valued and will play a vital role in building an efficient, cost-effective supply chain ecosystem. So it's well worth taking the time to assess and review relationships that could make or break the business.

Protecting your reputation

When disaster strikes or a major disruption occurs, it's understandable if management attention is focused on solving the problem as quickly and effectively as possible. However, stakeholder communications are as important as problem resolution.

With the lightning speed and omnipresence of modern communications, bad news these days gets around even faster. A company's misfortune or misjudgement may be quickly picked up by print media and online social networks and rapidly shared across the world to customers, partners, suppliers, shareholders, competitors and regulators.

In today's world of billions of netizens – all permanently hot-wired and super-connected – the power of social media can destroy in seconds the diligently developed and carefully nurtured reputations of companies, brands and products!

So an essential part of the corporate risk management strategy must be to defend its reputation in the eyes of all its stakeholders and others whose perception and response could make a bad situation worse.

Every business small and large is vulnerable to a loss of reputation and trust, so a well-structured, planned and implemented public relations strategy will play a powerful role in presenting the facts of the case, to explain the positive steps the company is taking, and to protect the integrity and authority of the business.

Summary

Risk is a certainty. Perhaps Robert Burns was not entirely accurate when he said that the most carefully prepared plans may go wrong. The reality is that things will almost certainly go wrong – somehow, somewhere and sometime for every business – we just don't know what, where or when our turn will come! Operating in today's volatile and unpredictable world, our global supply chain ecosystems are exposed as never before to risks and danger from all quarters.

Dick Jennings, senior vice-president and general manager, supply chain solutions, for end-to-end supply chain logistics management company Ryder Systems Inc, neatly summed up many of the key issues: 'Because of the increasingly global nature of supply chains, addressing risk has become a more complex exercise. To take advantage of lower labour costs many companies have off-shored manufacturing and sourcing to Asia. However, the longer the supply chain the greater the risk. Risk in this case could come in the form of a spike in fuel prices or a change in consumer demand.

'New risks that companies face include disruptions from political instability and even security-related risks like terrorism. As a result, having a comprehensive supply chain security and risk reduction programme has significantly increased in importance.'

While we have raised and reviewed the many issues that surround supply chain risk to help those responsible be aware of the multitude of threats and possible solutions, each and every organization has its own unique structure and constantly changing set of circumstances. The only place where a truly effective risk management strategy can be developed is inside the company itself at the highest level.

The biggest risk is the unknown, expect the unexpected – and be prepared!

CASE STUDY   Examples of supply chain risks and contingency planning

General guidelines and principles are helpful in directing the thought processes. However real world examples and experiences from those in the firing line provide practical and valuable lessons on how risk and contingency strategies function in practice.

A structured and practical process for management teams to complete for supply chain risk management and contingency planning embraces a three-step process of assess, prioritize and mitigate:

1 Engage a multi-functional cross-disciplinary group of managers to assess the company's risks. In reality, it's not possible to eliminate them all – but you can mitigate and reduce them.

2 Prioritize these risks from the most to the least important. The same management group should go through the list, assigning a value to each item based on its likelihood and on its impact – potentially plotting each risk on the probability vs impact model above.

3 Having established the priority rankings, specific sub-groups can then review an item and develop a set of mitigation steps that the company could and should take if the risk occurs.

What-if scenario modelling greatly assists in developing preparedness, as does exercises and simulations to stress-test risk mitigation strategies. Of course the amount of effort deployed in developing supply chain resilience will reflect the level of the company's commitment to the idea of the entire organization taking responsibility for risk contingency planning.

Dave Zamsky (2014), Vice-President of UPS Capital explained how the company had organized to prepare for Superstorm Sandy that hit the north-east USA in 2012: 'With limited notice we worked with clients to move critical freight ahead of the storm and to identify alternative locations and suppliers to divert shipments where feasible. For one retail customer we repositioned inventory and shipped 90 truckloads of fast-selling hurricane supplies such as bottled water and gas cans; and for a major auto manufacturer we identified critical inventory and began to pull ahead materials from suppliers before the storm.'

Dick Jennings (2014), Senior Vice-president and General Manager, supply chain solutions, Ryder Systems Inc, confirms and extends Zamsky's advice: 'The [risk] programme would identify supply chain risks. Crisis management plans are critical and must be reviewed, practiced and updated on a regular basis... companies need to consider outsourcing, distribution networks and transport alternatives for their supply chains. Partnering with an outsourced provider that has the infrastructure, engineering expertise, technology and purchasing power can help mitigate supply chain risk.'

On the topic of the logistics and distribution network, Jennings added: 'Consider regional or near-sourced distribution centre networks incorporating alternative energy solutions that will function in the event of power loss; investing in technology to help increase supply chain visibility to improve fast decision-making, rethinking inventory positions and working with a transportation management partner who has the scale to procure alternative carriers and modes in the event of disruption.'

Jeffrey Karrenbauer (2014), founder and President of business analytics and supply chain consultant Insight, suggests taking a close look at suppliers: 'Supplier management is an area companies should be looking at and planning for when it comes to risk management and business continuation in their supply chains. If you analyse your supply base you should be able to identify those that are providing raw materials for more than 50 per cent of the product, or any single supplier in an unstable part of the world where you have a sole source agreement in place... spreading contract awards across several suppliers – even if you have one that is decidedly primary – also provides flexibility of supplier choice that enables you to switch to another supplier who already knows your product.'

Arthur VanGervin (2014), Senior Director of Business Development at European company Menlo Logistics, not surprisingly but quite reasonably puts the case for using fourth-party logistics (4PL): 'A 4PL provider is an orchestrator of the supply chain that provides strategic support, assembling best-in-class supply chain elements to facilitate a continuous flow of value and operating only where it brings most value to the customer. 4PLs focus on optimizing the processes that lie upstream and downstream within the enterprise… and provide robust project management and governance processes to ensure that rapid change can occur to optimize delivered value. In this way, service levels increase, costs go down and supply chain knowledge in the shipper's organization increases.'

Conclusion

So what matters as much as the risk itself is how well prepared the organization is – to sense and respond, spot, react and counter the worst effects of whatever mishap has occurred. In the view of most employees, such events are unlikely to happen or are peripheral to their daily tasks. It therefore falls to the company's senior management to take responsibility to ensure the organization has the vision, imagination and determination to protect the business in every way that can be reasonably envisaged.

Free trade for all – navigating the FTA landscape

05

Free trade agreements – economic necessity or political minefield?

Supply chain ecosystems cannot begin to function effectively without recognizing and dealing with the myriad of free trade agreements (FTAs) now in operation across the globe.

The concept is simple and goes back to the origins of world trade, and in particular the ideas of 18th-century economists Adam Smith and David Ricardo. Observing how Great Britain's growing empire and industrial revolution were about to usher in the modern world, Smith concluded that the fewer obstacles in the way of international trade, the richer nations and individuals could grow. Cartels, monopolies, tariffs and other restrictions on the other hand would all inhibit trade.

Ricardo expanded and developed the free trade concept by explaining why international trade is essential. As each nation has a competitive advantage, everyone has something they do best and if they trade with each other, both parties will live better.

The reality was never quite that simple as it ignored the fact that organizations and nations will seek to protect their interests and try to tip the scales of trade in their favour.

As we have seen in Chapter 1, today's global supply chain ecosystems reflect the enormous complexity at the heart of international trade, involving a diverse range of manufacturers and suppliers, shippers and freight companies, dealing with multiple layers of stakeholders in other countries or continents. We saw how many modern devices such as laptops and smart phones – and as an example the automotive sector – typically involve components and operations from 15 to 20 countries – with a vital role being played by ever more complex and far-reaching supply chain ecosystems.

However various attempts to establish free and unfettered commerce have come up against vested interests, political resistance and of course a mountain of red tape. Even the latest attempts in 2014 by the World Trade Organization (WTO) to liberalize world trade continued to face opposition and a lack of agreement among its members.

It is no exaggeration to conclude that the WTO faces a crisis, seemingly unable to reach an effective consensus, whilst an ever-increasing number of regional, bilateral and cross-regional preferential trade agreements and free trade areas are being established – in many ways as a direct response to the lack of progress at WTO.

These local and regional agreements may help the individual countries involved, but are leading to an even more complex and challenging business environment, whilst making the conclusion of full international agreements even more difficult.

We now need to look in some detail at recent events, current developments and the latest agreements – to help guide supply chain and logistics executives through one of the more challenging and potentially costly aspects of the industry.

How can companies keep abreast of the hundreds of existing and proposed FTAs, both WTO approved and others? How can they navigate around the many elements that can be affected by FTAs such as tariffs, labour costs, local and regional legislation while still running efficient, productive and competitive businesses?

It's not an environment for the faint-hearted, but it is an inevitable factor in international trade and an integral component of today's global supply chain ecosystems.

Who's who in free trade?

The World Trade Organization provides a global forum for governments to negotiate trade agreements and to settle trade disputes. As at 2014, the WTO had 160 countries as full members – with a further 17 observer countries waiting for accession.

The WTO's role is to oversee and encourage far-reaching preferential trade agreements, negotiated and signed by the bulk of the world's trading nations. These documents provide the legal ground rules for international commerce – in effect contracts that bind governments to keep their trade policies within agreed limits. Although negotiated and signed by governments, the goal is to help producers of goods and services, exporters, and importers conduct their business, while allowing governments to meet social and environmental objectives, partly by removing obstacles and also ensuring that individuals, companies and governments know what the trade rules are around the world, giving them confidence that there will be no sudden changes of policy.

To quote from the WTO website – 'At its heart are the WTO agreements, negotiated and signed by the bulk of the world's trading nations. These documents provide the legal ground rules for international commerce. They are essentially contracts, binding governments to keep their trade policies within agreed limits. Although negotiated and signed by governments, the goal is to help producers of goods and services, exporters, and importers conduct their business, while allowing governments to meet social and environmental objectives.'

However, whilst trying to maintain and extend a more liberal and open system of world trade, the power of the WTO is necessarily limited by its democratic structure. The WTO approach includes the need for consensus across all 160 members – with veto powers that can easily stifle progress. Multilateral negotiations on trade liberalization issues therefore move very slowly with inevitable limits on how far trade reform agreements can go.

While multilateral efforts have successfully reduced tariffs on industrial goods, it has usually been a long and difficult journey to free-up trade in agriculture, textiles, apparel and other areas of international commerce, including the services sectors.

International support for FTAs

The European Commission strongly believes in the power of free trade, claiming in early 2014 that if the EU were to complete all its current free trade talks, it would add 2.2 per cent to the EU's GDP – equivalent of $346 billion. That is equivalent to adding to the EU's economy a country as big as Austria or Denmark. In terms of employment, these agreements could generate 2.2 million new jobs, or an additional 1 per cent of the EU total workforce.

There are of course other FTAs and bilateral agreements in force or under negotiation that involve individual nations or regional groups as well as those organized and approved by the WTO.

Predicted to add 0.5 per cent to the EU's annual economic output, the Transatlantic Trade and Investment Partnership (TTIP) under negotiation between the EU and the US, encompasses half of the world's GDP and almost a third of global trade flows. Designed to drive growth and create jobs, talks first started in July 2013. When negotiations are completed and the agreement is ratified, it will become the biggest bilateral trade deal ever concluded, with projections that the TTIP would provide economic improvement worth $151 billion for the EU, $113 billion for the US and some $126 billion for the rest of the world.

The two parties are already huge trading partners, with total US investment into the EU being three times higher than US investment in all of Asia, and investment from the EU into the US being eight times the amount of EU investment in India and China combined.

Given that tariffs are already relatively low – average under 3 per cent – the key to unlocking this trade agreement's potential lies in tackling non-tariff barriers, consisting mainly of customs procedures and behind-the-border regulatory restrictions.

As far back as 1994, the North American Free Trade Agreement (NAFTA) was formed, with the United States, Canada, and Mexico agreeing to phase out all tariffs on merchandise trade and to reduce over the subsequent decade restrictions on trade in services and foreign investment.

The United States also has bilateral agreements with Israel, Jordan, Singapore, and Australia and has or is working on bilateral or regional preferential trade agreements with countries in Latin America, Asia and the Pacific.

In the Asia region, three major multilateral trade agreements are coming into play, illustrating an almost universal acceptance of the vital role that FTAs can play in facilitating world trade and global prosperity. These three agreements will further drive substantial progress in facilitating and empowering growth in international trade for all Asian economies.

AEC 2015 is the ASEAN Economic Community (AEC) agreement to adopt regional economic integration commencing from 2015 of the ten ASEAN (Association of South-East Asian Nations) member states – Brunei, Cambodia, Indonesia, Laos, Malaysia, Myanmar, the Philippines, Singapore, Thailand and Vietnam – into a single economic community, harmonizing tariff-free flows of goods, services, people and funds across 10 jurisdictions comprising over 600 million people.

TPP – the Trans-Pacific Partnership will provide Asian economies – Australia, Brunei, Japan, Malaysia, New Zealand, Singapore and Vietnam – with preferential-tariff multilateral access to the huge markets in Canada, Chile, Mexico, Peru and USA.

RCEP – the Regional Comprehensive Economic Partnership joins the 10 ASEAN nations together with trading partners Australia, China, India, Japan, Korea and New Zealand, forming a trading block containing almost half the world's population, with $21 trillion GDP and a 27 per cent share of global trade.

Many other trade groups have proliferated in recent years including the Organization of American States, comprising the Andean Community, Caribbean Community (CARICOM), Central American Common market (CACM) and MERCOSUR.

A valuable South-east Asia perspective

A 2014 survey from HSBC and the Economist Intelligence Unit (EIU) on attitudes to FTAs in Singapore, Malaysia, Vietnam and Indonesia, highlighted and reaffirmed two vital aspects to FTAs.

Namely the almost universal belief in the essential role that nations as well as private companies have to play in international trade, and on the other hand the reasons why most businesses struggle to take full advantage of such agreements.

While the respondents came from just four countries, the arguments put forward are likely to be echoed in other economies. As Asia is at the heart of the trend to develop and take advantage of FTAs both within the region and globally, their experience is likely to echo that of other regions.

When asked whether exporters are using FTAs and if not, why not, the replies were quite clear. Only one in four exporters actually took advantage of the applicable FTAs in force, although 85 per cent of those that had, agreed that doing so had helped their businesses.

Half of all respondents avoided using FTAs because they found the agreements and requirements were so complex that the difficulties and costs of adhering outweighed the advantages.

As previously raised, negotiating rules of origin provided the prime example of the kind of red tape and complex administration that inevitably deters all but the most experienced companies.

For many would-be exporters some FTAs do not go far enough and are limited simply to cutting tariffs, whilst behind-the-border issues such as trade in services, e-commerce and other kind of business are only tackled in a very limited manner.

Despite their reservations, those polled had high hopes for the next generation of trade deals as 81 per cent of ASEAN exporters see it as vital that governments sign up to FTAs. The regional pacts referenced above, such as Regional Comprehensive Economic Partnership (RCEP), the Trans Pacific Partnership (TPP) and the ASEAN Economic Community (AEC) 2015 were all cited as positive steps.

What's gone wrong with the WTO's mission?

While there is no doubt that world trade could not have grown at such a pace over the past two decades without the efforts of the WTO encouraging a more open and free international trading environment, its critics say it has not achieved as much as it might have done and now needs a different approach for the future.

Events came to a head in the period following the various meetings from late 2013 to 2014 with India's failure to meet the deadline in July 2014 to ratify the deal that was agreed in Bali in December 2013.

As far back as 2001 the Doha Round, known semi-officially as the Doha Development Agenda, was launched in Doha, Qatar, with the intention of achieving major reform of the international trading system through the introduction of lower trade barriers and revised trade rules. Despite dozens of meetings and conferences across the ensuing decade or more, by 2014 many commentators believed it had strained its credibility to breaking point.

The real power of any organization claiming to fully represent the global community lies in its ability to reach a consensus, with countries naturally defending their corner, either openly or covertly. Therefore in a forum such as the WTO with so many members, little or nothing can happen without compromise. This has always been the case and inevitably throws up barriers and obstacles to the more ambitious and far reaching proposals.

The Bali Accord

The most significant event in the struggle to implement free trade in recent years, the WTO's Bali Accord, was concluded in December 2013 to mixed reactions. While some – mainly the industrialized countries – saw it as a fully binding multi-lateral agreement, others were more sceptical about the promises made to less-developed countries, thinking that all such promises may not be kept.

For over 15 years, the industrialized countries and some advanced developing countries such as South Korea, Chile and Mexico had been pushed hard for rapid liberalization of customs procedures as part of the trade facilitation agreement, so as to enable their exports to rapidly penetrate the developing and least developed countries without undue hindrance.

In return, the developing countries managed to secure only best-endeavour agreements on some issues of their concern in agriculture and most of the issues relating to trade-distorting farm export subsidies and export credits.

The Bali package included multiple agreements. They comprised a binding agreement on trade facilitation and four descriptive items in agriculture such as general services, public stockholding for food security purposes, understanding the tariff rate quota administration provisions of agriculture products, and export competition.

In the development dossier, the Bali package offered non-binding best-endeavour outcomes on preferential rules of origin for least developed countries, organization for the waiver concerning preferential treatment to services, duty-free and quota-free market access, and a monitoring mechanism on special and differential treatment.

India steadfastly pushed hard for strong language to ensure that the public stockholding programmes for food security continued without interruption until a permanent solution could be reached.

Following the failure to ratify the Bali package, the WTO consensus through compromise approach may no longer be on the table, to the deep and long-term disappointment and frustration of many members and observers. In a sharp criticism of the WTO, Robert J Bowman (2014) of SupplyChainBrain, summed up the general reaction to the Bali package: 'For years, the WTO has struggled to standardize international customs rules and in the most recent setback it failed to endorse a FTA as part of the Bali package from December 2013. This time the obstacle was India, which at the last minute demanded concessions on the right to subsidize and stockpile food grains, dashing hopes for an agreement that would have sharply lowered the cost of doing international business and bring predictability to global customs procedures.'

WTO's director general Roberto Azevêdo even described the setback as not just another delay which can simply be ignored – 'this will have consequences'.

Whilst India had little support, the WTO's convention of consensus decisions enabled India to use the pretext of farm subsidies linked to food security, to block any agreement. Leading WTO members tried to find a compromise but short of unravelling what had been agreed in Bali, there was no workable solution.

In his October 2014 statement, WTO Director-General Roberto Azevêdo was ready to admit that despite intensive consultations 'we have not found a solution to the impasse' more than two months after the deadline for the Bali Trade Facilitation Agreement had passed. 'This could be the most serious situation that this organization has ever faced,' he said, and while members should keep working for a solution to the current impasse, 'we should also think about our next steps'.

Fortunately in November 2014, a meeting of the WTO's General Council confirmed that all members had adopted decisions related to public stockholding for food security purposes, the Trade Facilitation Agreement and the post-Bali work – 'By agreeing these three decisions we have put ourselves back in the game. We have put our negotiating work back on track — that means all the Bali decisions: trade facilitation, public stockholding, the LDC issues, the decisions on agriculture, development, and all of the other elements. And we have given ourselves the chance to prepare the post-Bali work programme.'

The challenge of red tape

Sadly it's not just the failure of the world community to support WTO's efforts to create an open and free world market. Even where there are WTO-approved free trade agreements in place, they often fail to meet the real-world needs of businesses and in particular those in the newer and emerging economies.

In a paper published in August 2014, Harvard University Asia Centre Senior Fellow William H Overholt (2014) pointed out that regional and bilateral trade negotiations tend to focus on the country of origin, by definition a single state or preferential grouping.

As a result it's not uncommon for such bodies to produce hundreds of pages of country of origin rules in a single trade agreement. With each state having potentially numerous agreements, companies can find that the rules are so complex that it is easier to pay the higher tariffs – with the consequent knock-on effect on price and competitiveness – than to tackle the mountain of paperwork involved.

This discriminates disproportionately against the smaller, more open economies such as Singapore and also discriminates against smaller companies who do not have large accounting departments to handle the paperwork.

In defence of the WTO

It would be wrong to condemn the WTO without recognizing what it has achieved in the past – and to some extent continues to do – in helping to create a more open international marketplace.

Its 2014 report argues that the organization has enabled developing countries to take advantage of international trade and to mitigate the risks involved. It has done so by ensuring that countries make binding commitments which increase the levels of security in trading, provide greater flexibility to allow developing countries to make commitments and – by facilitating technical assistance – build trading capacity.

Those countries that had implemented substantial reforms to achieve WTO accession had grown 2.5 per cent faster for several years afterwards and illustrate the potential for further growth. They have been able to open up new and emerging markets, integrate into the world market at lower cost and reap the rewards of higher world commodity prices. The WTO has underpinned this progress by providing certainty and a more predictable environment allowing economic activity to flourish.

What now for the WTO and FTAs?

After further rounds of meetings and negotiations among the WTO members to find a post-Bali way forward, Director-General Azevêdo summed up the situation at a formal meeting of the trade negotiations committee, reflecting on the various members' comments and possible steps forward. He stated: 'We have not found a solution to the impasse and the deadline on the trade facilitation agreements passed more than two months ago.'

He raised several key questions – how do the WTO and its members move forward to overcome the current paralysis and mistrust? What will happen to the other Bali decisions including agriculture, the monitoring mechanism and the package of measures for less-developed countries (LDCs)? What should be included in the post-Bali programme? Finally and most importantly, what does it mean for the WTO organization itself?

He continued: 'Once again the negotiating track is stuck. Of course this is not new to us – deadlock has unfortunately become a familiar position. But that doesn't make it any more acceptable. And it is not often that we have been able to overcome situations like this. We have seen this situation too many times. So we can't continue in such an inefficient and ineffective way that is so prone to paralysis.'

One idea being aired is what has been called a plurilateral approach, allowing those who want to make progress on agreed issues to do so without hindrance from those opposing the move. This would allow those willing partners to make progress where there was partial agreement, unhindered by opposition from those who do not.

Such plurilateral decisions in turn raise the question whether the agreements reached could discriminate against non-participants. It would weaken the power of the veto and in some sense the spirit of the organization, but further compromise may be the only way forward.

Only the coming years will tell whether the WTO can work through its challenges and find a more productive way to resolve the issues that have dogged it for many years. But trade is a continuous and dynamic process, and the world economy cannot wait for the WTO to find its salvation. Successful companies never stand still and trends that evolved over the past few years are set to accelerate to fill the void.

Local and regional FTAs

For several years bi-lateral, regional and multi-lateral trade agreements have co-existed alongside WTO treaties, several of which have been mentioned earlier in this chapter. However, the number of preferential trade agreements is rapidly increasing with over 300 such agreements in place – and a further 100 in the pipeline.

Proponents of these preferential trade agreements (PTA) argue that the advantage of such bilateral or regional arrangements is that they promote greater trade among the parties to the agreement. They may also hasten global trade liberalization if multilateral negotiations run into difficulties. Recalcitrant countries excluded from bilateral agreements, and hence not sharing in the increased trade these bring, may then be induced to join and in turn reduce their own barriers to trade.

But these advantages must be offset against a disadvantage: by excluding certain countries, these agreements may shift the composition of trade from low-cost countries that are not party to the agreement to high-cost countries that are included.

Critics of bilateral and regional approaches to trade liberalization suggest that these approaches may undermine and supplant, instead of support and complement, the multilateral WTO approach, which is to be preferred for operating globally on a non-discriminatory basis. Hence, the long-term result of bilateralism could be a deterioration of the world trading system into competing, discriminatory regional trading blocs, resulting in added complexity that complicates the smooth flow of goods between countries. Furthermore, the reform of some issues such as agricultural export subsidies cannot be dealt with effectively at the bilateral or regional level.

So, in the world of complex global supply chains, how can companies keep abreast of the smorgasbord of trade agreements, how can they determine which are relevant and how can they best adopt them to benefit their own supply chain ecosystems?

Can trade barriers be justified?

Despite the universal support – at least in public – for free and unfettered international trade, many if not most countries either do, or still try to, impose some form of trade barriers to bolster their own economies. The most common trade barriers are tariffs, import quotas, and non-tariff barriers.

Trade barriers are designed to discourage imports – which improve a country's balance of trade by effectively increasing net exports – and also to protect the domestic economy and local businesses.

So, despite all the advantages of free trade, what are the main reasons used to justify trade barriers?

One of the most powerful arguments is that carefully constructed trade barriers protect domestic employment against imports, often coming from low-cost labour economies that could be seen to unfairly undermine established local wage structures. As imported goods substitute goods produced domestically, they displace jobs in the importing economy, and therefore restricting imports is seen to be a popular way to protect local employment – and invariably goes down well with voters and taxpayers.

In addition, local wages could also be driven down as local producers attempt to defend their markets against low-cost imports. However, by restricting access to imports and keeping domestic prices high, such trade barriers are also harmful to domestic consumers.

Protectionists may also argue that trade barriers can help protect new businesses that are not yet mature enough or large enough to hold their own in competing against established international players, who enjoy the benefits of economies of scale and strong international branding.

The case for defending national security and state sovereignty can provide strong justification for some form of trade protection. Barriers are often claimed to protect firms or industries that produce output vital for the security and the defence of the nation, such as energy sources or advanced technology.

Each of these arguments provides logical, reasonable, and necessary justification for the imposition of trade barriers. However each is also commonly misused, especially by politically powerful domestic producers that seek little more than to limit foreign competition, charge higher prices, gain greater market share and increase profits.

Most importantly, such moves inevitably mitigate against the greater long-term benefits of global free trade which are proven to build a more stable and wealthy world economy.

Tariff engineering, the new supply chain discipline

With so many FTAs already in force or under negotiation, it is almost certain that in configuring a global supply chain ecosystem major stakeholders will need to ensure that their strategy is designed to take advantage of the lower tariffs and preferential treatments the various trade agreements can offer.

While this adds a further dimension to the configuration and structure of what may already be a complex supply chain ecosystem, leveraging preferential trade agreements to reduce costs is the primary and most tangible benefit for most businesses.

The concept of tariff engineering means structuring and organizing the business and its supply chain ecosystem to take maximum advantage of the relevant FTAs in order to lower costs, improve margins and reduce shipping delays.

To take advantage of the benefits of almost any FTA, the goods manufactured and shipped must be either wholly or largely produced from raw materials and components within the territories embraced by the particular FTA. However, with many of today's supply chain ecosystems this may well involve a complex network of manufacturing and assembly locations across the globe, some of which are in the relevant territories of the FTA with others being outside its scope.

In addition, behind some primary suppliers may lay several layers and tiers of sub-suppliers around the world which in some cases may be difficult to identify.

It's a fact of today's economic environment that in many sectors such as automotive, electronics, fashion, pharmaceuticals and cosmetics, globalized sourcing is the norm. Successful FTAs therefore will reflect not just geographical or political relations but the pragmatic world of economic interdependencies and realities of trade-driven relationships.

All this information – and in considerable detail – needs to be included in the certificate of origin required by any FTA, which is one of the reasons why some companies judge the task so complex and onerous that it makes more business sense just to pay the higher tariffs.

Critical factors when considering location

Let us assume however that the FTAs on offer provide a sufficiently attractive revenue incentive to make the effort worthwhile. In this case, the locations where the materials, components and assembly processes take place add a further dimension to the cocktail of supply chain complexities. Existing suppliers, subcontractors and stakeholders may find their position weakened or strengthened according to whether they are located in the FTA's territories or outside, although this may not necessarily include or exclude them from future business.

The most favourable supply chain ecosystem will be the one constructed around the most productive configuration of a number of critical factors that will impact on the overall effectiveness of the project.

Labour costs

Often the single largest cost element in supply chains, the price of labour – whether at the point of manufacturing and assembly, or in the transport and logistics activities – can fluctuate due to market forces, with significant impact to the business model. For example, we have experienced continuing wage inflation in China – which is impacting businesses around the world that have configured their supply chain ecosystems around a fulcrum of low-cost labour-intensive production activities in China. Any decision to relocate specific functions into alternative FTA territories needs to consider the impact on labour costs and whether such potential increases would be sustainable in the long term.

Fuel and transport costs

Likewise, in considering alternative geographies, companies need to assess how the decisions they make will affect transport costs, whether by road, rail, sea or air. Additional transportation legs mean extra fuel, the possible impact of emission controls and the potential for slower customer shipping times.

Suppliers and stakeholders

Is it worth the risk moving from tried, tested and trusted partners in the supply chain ecosystem if they are located outside a specific FTA zone, and would it be wiser to consult them to see if there are possible solutions such as sourcing materials or components from more favourable locations across the supplier's network?

Customers

Before any changes are made to comply with the requirements of the FTA, it is essential to consult existing customers about any possible changes. They may themselves have strict rules about where products are sourced from – for commercial, political or ethical reasons – which may materially affect any decisions on the table. Losing a major customer would be a large price to pay for lower tariffs.

Summary

There is unanimous agreement worldwide that open and liberal world trade, unhindered by tariffs and various forms of protectionism, has played a vital role in boosting the world economy and in raising living standards across the globe. Despite the current crisis within the World Trade Organization, much of this success is down to what the WTO has achieved in recent decades.

However the global business environment continues to change and the WTO may now be, even by its own admission, no longer fit for purpose as it is being supplanted and disintermediated by a plethora of regional and multilateral FTAs around the world.

The challenge for those operating and managing global supply chain ecosystems is to determine how best to take advantage of the many preferential trade agreements that are in force – and those that are in the pipeline – in order to help keep their businesses competitive and profitable in the medium and long term.

Companies need to take into consideration all the elements and components that comprise the modern supply chain ecosystem, but with the added dimension of the various demands and requirements of the relevant trade agreements for their industries and territories. As more companies become actively involved in using FTAs to their advantage, it may no longer be a question of whether to join in, but simply how.

CASE STUDY Best practices in effective customs duty management

Navigating the complex landscape of more than 300 free trade agreements is an increasingly important factor in optimizing global supply chain ecosystems.

Having established the cross border trade flows and supporting logistics networks that best support your business, it is essential to then ensure your company is maximizing the benefits of the trade agreements whilst ensuring full compliance with the relevant rules and regulations, in particular dealing with customs – the implications for 'getting it wrong' are often severe.

Some of the main complexities that companies generally need to navigate include:

- Customs valuation methods.

- Harmonized system (HS) code classifications.

- Duty drawback, waiver and exemption.

- Preferential duty rates.

In most countries, importers are, under the law, assumed to be both knowledgeable in customs matters that are often technically complex, and to have a thorough understanding of customs requirements. Most global supply chain ecosystems will involve dealing with emerging and developing markets where customs are notoriously bureaucratic and processes can be extremely convoluted and complex.

Here we present 10 best practices in effective customs duty management:*

1 Consider duty minimization and customs compliance collectively

Any customs duty management strategy should have two simple objectives:

i Aim to achieve minimum duty exposure.

ii Ensure maximum regulatory compliance.

These two objectives are mutually supportive and complementary to each other, and should not be considered separately from each other.

2   Understand the fundamentals of customs duty management

Essentially, duty liabilities and risks are a function of four factors, the exact dynamics and comparative weighting of which will vary from company to company and between individual supply chains:

- Product customs valuation.

- Product tariff classification (specific HS code used).

- Free trade agreement – coverage, eligibility and conformance.

- Customs regimes and special incentives.

Effective customs duty management strategies will always aim to achieve the appropriate best practices construction of these four fundamentals and depending on size and business diversity, different products or supply chains within the same organization could have different dynamics and weighting.

3   Work with professionals who understand the specific country's customs environment, customs audits and penalty regime

In many markets, customs clearance processes are based upon self-assessment principles, such that the majority of import shipments are cleared with minimal intervention at the time of importation into the country. The downside of this policy is that most importers can expect to be audited by customs every couple of years. During the audit, the company's level of compliance with the various customs regulations will come under scrutiny. Particular attention is typically paid to multinational companies and also to transactions involving special duty facilities, such as duty waivers on items shipped out of, or into, the country for repair purposes. Given revenue collection targets set by governments, these audits generally focus on recovering import duty and taxation in relation to short payments. To compound this situation, in some customs organizations auditors are encouraged to maximize revenue recovery through incentive schemes under which the auditors personally share in the proceeds from administrative penalties that are imposed. It is essential therefore to be working with experienced, knowledgeable and professional business partners who are familiar with local market conditions.

4   Establish clear customs duty management responsibility

Companies should establish clear demarcation of strong, senior and committed management responsibility for duty management and customs compliance.

Whilst some companies have taken a more progressive approach with dedicated departments, there is no natural or generic home for this function. Regardless of where this responsibility resides, companies must ensure that the customs duty management is given the attention it deserves, together with the appropriate resources and authority to fulfil the responsibility.

5 Understand existing risks

Companies are seldom aware of ongoing exposure to previously unidentified liabilities and are often caught unawares when such a situation arises. Being prepared is the best and most sound approach to take. By understanding any potential liabilities, making adequate provisions and having robust risk mitigation strategies in place, companies will be more effective as and when a customs audit is initiated or queries are raised – much preferable to being in reactive mode. During an audit, any refunds or drawbacks could be delayed which could impact cash flows. Shipments could also be delayed pending further investigation, with knock on ramifications throughout increasingly complex supply chain ecosystems.

6 Accurate knowledge of annual duty and tax costs

Whilst this may seem glaringly obvious, many businesses do not have clear knowledge and information on hand concerning their annual costs of duties and taxes. In order to effectively manage customs duties and compliance risks, we must first know what our activities and expenditures are in this area. Complete, accurate and timely data should be readily available information, with the ability to segment and segregate reports by product, region or country.

7 Seek and apply customs rulings wisely

When a customs ruling has been applied for – or imposed – such rulings can play an invaluable role in providing clarity and certainty of treatment – especially the case in relation to many complex tariff classification issues – specifically HS codes. Rulings can be an effective tool to minimize possible penalties as well as for supporting duty management strategy planning and ensuring submission of correct declarations. In many countries, the customs authorities are quite willing to work with importers to determine correct product classifications. Although in some more complex jurisdictions, such rulings may be considered non-binding or expressed in ambiguous terms.

8 Avoid grey areas and 'benefit of the doubt' situations

Customs duty declarations are and should be based on absolute fact rather than self-interpretation of the law. This means that in principle, all declarations made by the importer must either be right or wrong, correct or incorrect. In other words, there is little room within customs laws and policy in most countries for grey areas or benefits of doubt to be exhibited. This is fine in theory but when working in some emerging economies this can prove challenging – good corporate governance and supply chain ethics are not as prevalent in some markets as others. Additionally, in some markets, the laws and regulations themselves are not always as precise or clearly defined as in developed markets, making this an area for cautious due diligence in ensuring fact based and fully compliant declarations.

9   Understand the key differences between duty and corporate tax

Important to appreciate three key differences between customs duty and corporate tax:

- First, customs duty, unlike corporate tax, is not driven by national fiscal laws. It is a trade policy measure underpinned by international agreements and protocols such as WTO, WCO and the International Chambers of Commerce (ICC). Misunderstanding of this basic premise is the reason why some companies assume that an acceptable transfer price for tax purposes is also acceptable for customs valuation purposes, and vice versa – which is generally not the case.

- Second, customs duty is not technically a self-assessed charge. Rather it is determined by the respective national authorities, based upon transaction-specific declarations of absolute fact submitted by the importer of record.

- Third, unlike effective tax management or 'tax avoidance' strategies, which have high levels of accounting transparency and controls, customs duty costs are invariably deeply embedded within Cost of Goods Sold (COGS), which leaves little room for variation.

10 Monitor operations

Another obvious initiative; however, in reality this is a practice often overlooked. Borrowing from Edward Deming's cycle of plan–do–check–act (2015), once the optimum customs duty management strategy is established, the company needs to ensure that each and every customs import declaration properly reflects the facts to be presented.

Conclusion

Adopting these best practices will help companies adopt and implement effective customs duty management. Businesses also need to keep updated and abreast of changes and developments in national and international trade policies and regulations, and continually seek opportunities to fine tune duty management practices – to optimize business benefits, whilst at the same time ensuring full compliance. In this respect, companies are encouraged to leverage expertise from within their supply chain ecosystem, in particular through the diligent selection and management of appointed logistics service providers (3PLs) and customs brokers.

* *Adapted with kind permission from Raymon Krishnan, President of the Logistics and Supply Chain Management Society.*

The Asian Era

06

The workers have become the shoppers

Any review of global supply chains – whether manufacturing, distribution or retail – would not be complete without considering what is happening in Asia.

Over the past three decades, the region emerged as the factory of the world, driving the need to transport vast quantities of merchandise all the way from Asia to the developed markets in Europe and North America, which in turn gave birth to complex, far-reaching and economically vibrant global supply chain ecosystems.

In more recent years, the employment created by this outsourcing and offshoring of production to Asia has increased economic prosperity across the board, such that now the region is home to numerous domestic consumption markets that are very large and expanding rapidly.

The workers have become the shoppers – and economies in Asia are morphing from net exporters into consumer societies. Asia is rapidly becoming the powerhouse of the world economy, with over half of global GDP growth to 2050 expected to come from the region.

During 2014, China was producing and shipping over one million mobile phones per day – 400 million for the year – the majority of which were exported to overseas markets; whilst in the domestic market, at the beginning of 2015 there were over 450 million smart phone users in China; just one example of the critical mass of volume production, economic power and digital consumerism in Asia.

What is happening in Asia is either already affecting or will soon be impacting on most businesses in the west, so it is essential for every business executive to have a grasp of the complex dynamics of the region.

Whether companies are already importing goods from the Far East, facing stiff competition from low-cost producers, planning to source merchandise from Asia or intending to provide supply chain or 3PL

FIGURE 6.1 Asia – geographical sub-regions and selected economic groupings

Eastern Asia	South-Eastern Asia	Western Asia
China	Brunei Darussalam	Armenia
China, Hong Kong Special Administrative Region	Cambodia	Azerbaijan
China, Macao Special Administrative Region	Indonesia	Bahrain
Democratic People's Republic of Korea	Lao People's Democratic Republic	Cyprus
Japan	Malaysia	Georgia
Mongolia	Myanmar	Iraq
Republic of Korea	Philippines	Israel
	Singapore	Jordan
	Thailand	Kuwait
Southern Asia	Timor-Leste	Lebanon
Afghanistan	Viet Nam	Oman
Bangladesh		Qatar
Bhutan	**Central Asia**	Saudi Arabia
India	Kazakhstan	State of Palestine
Iran (Islamic Republic of)	Kyrgyzstan	Syrian Arab Republic
Maldives	Tajikistan	Turkey
Nepal	Turkmenistan	United Arab Emirates
Pakistan	Uzbekistan	Yemen
Sri Lanka		

SOURCE United Nations (2013)

services into the region, the first step is to be aware of the kaleidoscope of different countries and economies, what they can offer and equally important, their limitations and potential pitfalls for the unwary. The nuances can be difficult to read and expensive to ignore.

From the start, it is essential to recognize and appreciate that what is generically called 'Asia' in fact comprises multiple countries at vastly differing stages of economic development – spanning the full spectrum of developed, developing and emerging markets – within which the two worlds of production and consumption are interconnected and converging.

From a geographic perspective, Asia can have a different meaning for different people. As per Figure 6.1, the United Nations (UN) outlines five geographical sub-regions of economic importance in Asia: central, eastern, southern, south-eastern and western.

This chapter will focus on a selection of key markets in Asia and explain the complexity and diversity across the region; examine China's future role in servicing global supply chains; look at Vietnam, Indonesia and the Philippines – the rising stars of ASEAN; and in the case study, explore the opportunities and challenges in Myanmar.

The Asian Era is here and now!

As the traditional strongholds of consumerism – the western markets of Europe and the United States – suffer from a range of economic woes, consumption growth has slowed down, causing revenue and profitability challenges for multinational corporations (MNCs).

With the developed economies still experiencing low or no growth, companies are increasingly looking to Asia for market expansion, revenue growth, and increased profits – and therefore need to revisit and reconfigure the structure of their supply chain ecosystems in order to serve these local markets.

As growth shifts to Asia, significant supply chain complexities arise for companies as they venture into new territories, seeking to establish effective and efficient logistics networks for domestic distribution into the emerging and developing consumer markets.

Centre of economic gravity has shifted eastwards

One of the overwhelming drivers of the need for change is that the centre of economic gravity has shifted east – we are now firmly in the 'Asian Era' and will remain so for the foreseeable future.

In keeping with the principle that future economic competition will be between cities rather than between countries, the *McKinsey Quarterly* article by Dobbs *et al* (2011) entitled 'Urban economic clout moves east' graphically projected how by year 2025 more than 20 of the world's top 50 cities – as ranked by GDP – will be located in Asia, up from just 8 Asian cities in 2007 (see Table 6.1). They project that during that time more than half of Europe's top 50 cities will drop off the top 50 list, as will 3 in North America.

Christened the 'Dropouts' – 16 of the world's leading cities from 2007 that will not retain their top 50 place by 2025 include many familiar names – see table below. By 2025 they will be replaced in the top 50 by 16 'Newcomers', predominantly Asian cities including many names that are currently unfamiliar to many people and including some 12 cities in mainland China.

This shift is being driven by the rapid pace of urbanization in developing countries – in particular China. With large-scale migration of people from the rural villages into the cities, even the poorest people are becoming better off, whilst many are becoming quite affluent – all of which is engendering continuing economic growth.

McKinsey point out that in this new world order, from an 'urban economic power' perspective Shanghai and Beijing will outrank Los Angeles and London, while Mumbai and Doha will surpass Munich and Denver, with profound implications for companies' growth priorities.

To capitalize on the resulting new business opportunities emerging around Asia, it is essential for companies to reconfigure their supply chain ecosystems. But throughout the region, the various countries are at vastly different levels of maturity and sophistication in their supply chain capabilities, logistics networks and transportation infrastructure – all of which of course are especially critical for consumer product markets.

TABLE 6.1 Newcomers and Dropouts in World's Top 50 cities in 2025

World's Top 50 Cities, ranked by GDP	
Newcomers in 2025	**Dropouts in 2025**
Bangkok	Athens
Beijing	Barcelona
Chengdu	Denver
Chongqing	Detroit
Delhi	Hamburg
Doha	Lille
Foshan	Melbourne
Guangzhou	Minneapolis-St Paul
Hangzhou	Munich
Mumbai	Nagoya
Nanjing	Oslo
Shenyang	Rhein-Main
Shenzhen	Rio de Janeiro
Tianjin	Stuttgart
Wuhan	Taipei
Xi'an	Vienna

SOURCE McKinsey

Consumer market potential

The low-cost labour-intensive production outsourced to Asia during recent decades has gradually expanded economic prosperity, thus creating rapidly emerging consumer markets. In Asia, there are significant numbers of predominantly young people who now have disposable income – many for the first time – and who are technologically enabled, permanently connected and globally aware. The Asia region has millions of digital natives with money to spend!

The Organization for Economic Co-Operation and Development estimates that, globally, the size of the middle class (defined by the Economist Intelligence Unit as those who can afford to spend money on non-essential items) will increase to 4.9 billion by 2030, more than two and a half times the 1.8 billion people in 2010.

Asia will deliver 85 per cent of this growth, with spending by the region's middle class expected to account for almost two-thirds of middle class spending globally.

At the same time, urbanization is accelerating – China is forecast to create more than 200 new cities with a population greater than 1 million people by 2025. Projections also predict that in the next decade some 500 million people in Asia will have access to electricity in their homes for the first time, which will drive exponential increases in demand for a whole range of consumer household products.

Demand for fast-moving consumer goods (FMCG) is also forecast to rise, but as MNCs rush to capitalize on this consumer market potential, they may discover that the most attractive markets are also likely to have challenging logistics environments.

Logistics challenges

It is easy to generalize and consider Asia to be one market, but in fact Asia is a collection of very different markets that vary widely in their maturity and complexity, especially when it comes to logistics networks and supply chain ecosystems. The Logistics Performance Index (LPI), compiled by the World Bank (2014) on average every two years, vividly highlights these substantial differences.

The LPI measures the trade logistics profiles of 160 countries based on six key performance criteria: customs, infrastructure, international shipments, logistics quality and competence, tracking and tracing, and timeliness. The resulting rankings for a selection of Asian economies are summarized in Table 6.2 and reflect the wide disparity throughout Asia, which of course embraces the full range of developed, developing and emerging markets.

While developed economies such as Singapore, Japan, Hong Kong and Taiwan achieve high scores and are all ranked within the top 20 worldwide, among other Asian economies there is a significant spread in the rankings from India at 54th position globally all the way to Myanmar which is ranked 145th out of the total 160 countries measured worldwide.

The complex, fragmented and inefficient nature of the logistics sector can present many challenges for those doing business in Asia. The region's dynamic economies span developing, developed and emerging markets – all at different stages of maturity and sophistication.

The top three key challenges for MNCs are likely to be infrastructure, bureaucracy, and talent. Companies also need to deal with multi-modal distribution into the hinterland regions, for which they will need partners with local market knowledge. Different consumer markets may also require product localization, adding an extra layer of complexity to supply chain operations.

Additionally, Asia's diverse geographies – for example the massive land masses of China and India, or the substantial archipelagoes of Indonesia and the Philippines – together with the heavy traffic congestion in major cities, all add to the complexity of logistics operations, impacting supply chain effectiveness and efficiency.

A key factor for businesses to consider – for their logistics and distribution activities in Asia – is whether they will be best served by a global 3PL or a local service provider. There is no one-size-fits-all solution. In making their decision, companies must evaluate a number of factors including local market knowledge, sector specific expertise, information technology systems, international best practices – and of course price.

The rapid emergence of the Asian Era will require companies to adapt and adjust their business models accordingly – reconfiguring

TABLE 6.2 Selection of Asian economies, 2014 Logistics Performance Index (LPI)

Asia rank	Economy (total 160)	2014 global rank	Customs	Infra-structure	International shipments	Logistics quality and competence	Tracking and tracing	Timeliness
1	Singapore	5	3	2	6	8	11	9
2	Japan	10	14	7	19	11	9	10
3	Hong Kong	15	17	14	14	13	13	18
4	Taiwan	19	21	24	5	25	17	25
5	Korea	21	24	18	28	21	21	28
6	Malaysia	25	27	26	10	32	23	31
7	China	28	38	23	22	35	29	36
8	Thailand	35	36	30	39	38	33	29
9	Vietnam	48	61	44	42	49	48	56

Asia rank	Economy (total 160)	2014 global rank	Customs	Infra-structure	International shipments	Logistics quality and competence	Tracking and tracing	Timeliness
10	Indonesia	53	55	56	74	41	58	50
11	India	54	65	58	44	52	57	51
12	Philippines	57	47	75	35	61	64	90
13	Cambodia	83	71	79	78	89	71	129
14	Laos	131	100	128	120	129	146	137
15	Myanmar	145	150	137	151	156	130	117

SOURCE Adapted from World Bank

their supply chain ecosystems to focus on the multiple markets throughout the Asia region. Businesses that successfully address this challenge will become empowered to gain competitive advantage and drive profitable business growth during the coming years ahead.

China at the crossroads?

There is little doubt that China will continue to outgrow both the established western economies as well as those of its neighbours – due to its sheer size, population and steely determination on the part of the government to direct and manage its growth.

Statistics and various forecasts showing how economic and industrial power will steadily swing further towards China over the coming decades are available from a number of respected organizations and companies. Just a few examples will serve to underpin the profound implications these changes will have throughout the world.

China contributes 13 per cent of global GDP and has an 11 per cent share of world trade – and will soon take over the number one spot from the US. Seven of the world's top 10 container ports by volume are in China and the country has consistently posted annual GDP growth rates above 7 per cent – way ahead of any other developing economy. It sends over one third of all its exports to the US and the EU and its new generation of consumers has taken to online shopping with fervour.

Demand from the Chinese consumer is now supporting many markets across the world. The country is credited with reviving the European luxury goods market, the Australian mining sector and global car manufacturers – more than a million cars were imported in 2014, compared with just 42,000 imports in year 2000. Two thirds of automobile imports are from luxury motoring brands.

New challenges for China supply chains

China now finds itself faced with a number of challenges that to a considerable extent result from its own massive success. The Pearl River Delta, the heart of the country's manufacturing phenomenon, faces rising costs and labour shortages. In an effort to ease pressure on its eastern coastal regions, the Chinese government is encouraging businesses to move inland to the mid-west provinces where labour is plentiful and cheap. However, the infrastructure there is not as advanced and exporters face big time and cost penalties to move goods up to 2,000km from inland locations to the main deep-sea container ports on the eastern seaboard.

In a drive to balance the country's dependence on exports, China's latest five-year plan mandated the minimum wage to increase by an annual average exceeding 13 per cent – to stimulate domestic spending and create a stronger home market. As a result, factory wages in traditional production locations have been rising by 15–20 per cent per annum in recent years, an inflationary challenge for manufacturers only exacerbated by the Chinese government's confirmation of their intention to see wages rise at similar levels for a further five years. At the same time, the low-cost, labour-intensive manufacturing sector is experiencing increasing dissatisfaction amongst factory workers who – with higher expectations and louder objections – are seeking better benefits and improved working conditions, such that the total labour costs are increasing at unprecedented levels.

Challenges for China's eastern manufacturing zones?

The big hit for companies with established manufacturing bases is the rapidly rising cost of labour and a shrinking pool of blue collar workers, many of whom are disgruntled and generally unhappy with their lot. Originally coming largely from the underdeveloped and rural inland provinces, some 220 million workers toil in what by most standards are harsh conditions, doing repetitive and boring tasks, often working in huge factory campuses with tens of thousands of workers, living in vast company dormitories and only being able to go back home to see their families once a year. In 2014 in Guangdong province – source of more than 30 per cent of China's exports – there were over one million vacancies for factory workers, with 10 per cent of factories reporting a 30 per cent shortfall in shop floor labour.

As job opportunities are being created in new factories further west, some migrants are returning from the east coast back to their home towns and cities in the inland provinces, where they can find employment in areas where the living costs are lower, live with their families and overall have a better quality of life, often supported by the savings they have put by during their time working in factories in the east.

In contrast, the new generation of better-educated young Chinese workers have higher expectations than their parents and grandparents, and those do not include manual labour in factories working for long hours at boring and routine tasks and for low pay.

The issues over labour supply run deeper and could well put a brake on China's growth plans. As imports and exports grow and domestic consumers start to increase spending, more volumes of merchandise need to be produced, stored and transported, which means increasing demand for logistics and supply chain services, in turn requiring more people to manage and run larger supply chains. But the talent pool is neither large enough nor suitably trained to fill the looming gap. Many potential employers in the logistics sector believe that the education system is not delivering the skills the industry needs and is often reluctant to take on board graduate trainees who will expect higher salaries than the previous wave of workers. In the face of the economic success driven by private company initiatives, some consider the public sector is not playing enough of a role in providing the right skills the industry needs in the quantities required to keep pace with forecast growth.

Moving inland lowers costs, but still plenty of challenges

Moving production operations inland is not necessarily the panacea to increasing labour and land costs on the coast. While many western companies have jumped at the chance to bring down the key components of their manufacturing costs – land and labour – some may have overlooked the implications of being so far from the main transport and logistics connections on the coast. Big brands – and their first- and second-tier suppliers – have been attracted by favourable terms offered to establish operations inland, including tax-breaks, where compared to the coastal areas, land costs are some 40 per cent cheaper and factory wages potentially halved, at least for the time being.

There may be a plentiful supply of low-cost blue-collar workers but the inland locations have limited trained, experienced and skilled workers for the supervisory roles so essential to harness the scale and power of large-scale manual labour. Meanwhile, educated and experienced white-collar staff tend to be reluctant to relocate inland from the big eastern cities, where they may have put down roots and are enjoying a new middle-class lifestyle.

The tyranny of distance is such that moving products for export from an inland factory typically involves a journey of some 2,000km to get to the container ports on the east coast, which by inland waterway can take more than two weeks – longer than it takes to transport the same goods from Shanghai to Los Angeles!

Inland supply chain challenges include the fact that large container vessels are unable to navigate into the centre of the country, even along the great Yangtze river, which runs over 2,000km inland to the province of Sichuan and municipality of Chongqing – just one third of the river's total length of 6,300 kilometres.

Road vehicles are still generally old and unreliable, operated by owner-operator drivers or small companies, and the vast new highway infrastructure, impressive as it is, comprises all toll roads, with the tolls representing some 30 per cent of domestic road transportation costs.

The country does have a well-developed and extensive rail network. However, the priorities for the railway are to move the military, the people (passenger transport), bulk commodities (coal, steel, iron ore) and foodstuffs such as grain and rice – and finally general cargo, for which containerized rail freight is not yet widely deployed.

The new high-speed passenger rail system being built out across the country will free up some capacity on the current rail network, which will then be adapted for containerized freight, but with the current level of just 7 per cent of freight transported by rail, it will require a major switch in traffic mode to make a noticeable difference.

However, this does not mean that companies should not explore moving westwards, as there is little doubt that the country has the funds and the determination to make the inland regions a viable alternative to the long-established and successful coastal zones. In particular, third- and fourth-tier cities in the inland provinces are home to the fastest-growing consumption markets.

Alternative production locations

Companies are of course also pursuing their China-plus-one strategies – usually seeking additional, rather than purely alternative low cost manufacturing sources. With abundant labour pools – at least in quantity if not necessarily in quality – there are several options to explore – particularly India, Vietnam and Indonesia – and more recently Myanmar.

Martin Holme, Chief Operating Officer, North Asia Region, at Damco – one of the first global logistics companies to establish operations in Myanmar – said: 'More than 40 years into the megatrend of moving production to Asia from Europe and North America, we see Myanmar as one of the last frontiers in Asia. While the overall megatrend is almost coming to an end we still expect significant growth in exports from Myanmar over the coming decade. This will be driven by production moving primarily from other Asian countries with higher labour costs to countries such as Myanmar, Cambodia and Bangladesh; and as usual the 'first mover industry' is the garments industry, which has relatively low factory investment costs and high labour intensity. With a population almost the same size as Vietnam and the continued drive towards reforming and opening up the economy, we believe Myanmar offers a significant potential to our customers in the retail and lifestyle industries.'

But each alternative option has its own supply chain challenges. Companies considering manufacturing in alternative locations should consider the maturity and capability of their chosen market and assess the supply chain challenges they may face, including three critical aspects:

● The regulatory environment, including bureaucracy and administrative overheads, and its implications – for example, India's state-level tax system often leads to operating multiple distribution centres across different states.

- Infrastructure – in many Asian markets the transportation infrastructure is underdeveloped which can lead to damage and delays resulting in costly inefficiencies in the supply chain.

- Talent shortages – more than 70 per cent of businesses are now affected by the industry's ongoing skills shortage, according to the Logistics Executive Employment Market Survey Report (2013).

Such supply chain developments involving the relocation of offshoring to lower-cost labour environments also has the knock-on effect of helping the economic development of these emerging markets, with the result that many of these Asian countries with large populations are now becoming very attractive consumer markets.

The rising stars of ASEAN

Ten nations make up the Association of South East Asian Nations (ASEAN) – Indonesia, Malaysia, the Philippines, Singapore, Thailand, Vietnam, Cambodia, Laos, Myanmar (Burma) and Brunei. Together they have a population in excess of 600 million, GDP of over $1.5 trillion and recent economic growth rates of 5 per cent plus.

While China will continue for some time to be the dominant economic force in Asia, the ASEAN groups a potentially powerful new group of countries which – while in vastly different stages of development – either have or could become significant regional or even global players in their own right. They represent a commanding bloc of potential consumers and producers to rival many more established but less dynamic economies elsewhere.

ASEAN has a young and growing population with the potential to create significant new consumer markets, boosted by the ASEAN Economic Community (AEC) regional integration which commenced in 2015. The AEC's aim is to build a single market and production base with equitable economic development, fully integrated into the global economy. Areas of cooperation will include human resources, trade financing measures and more regional sourcing to establish an integrated economic community with free movement of goods, services, investment, skilled labour, and freer flow of capital.

Within this diverse group of 10 countries, three are considered to be the 'rising stars' of ASEAN, namely the 'VIP' nations of Vietnam, Indonesia and the Philippines, which together have a combined population of over 450 million, similar to that of the 28 countries in the European Union, offering vast pools of labour inextricably linked with large potential consumer markets.

Vietnam

After experiencing some economic bumps and hurdles in the last couple of years, Vietnam appears to be bouncing back and is once again one of the up-and-coming rising stars in the Asia region.

PricewaterhouseCoopers forecast that Vietnam may be the fastest of South-east Asia's emerging economies by 2025, with a potential annual growth rate of about 10 per cent in real dollar terms.

With a young, well-educated and highly motivated population of almost 100 million, Vietnam has recovered from its turbulent past to become one of the most exciting and promising economies in the region. Its early growth stemmed from the successful apparel and textile sector, which continues to prosper as the industry announced an additional 200,000 new jobs in 2014.

The country's GDP is growing above 5 per cent but GDP per capita at $9,600 is still outside the world's top 100. According to Dezan Shira & Associates' Vietnam Briefing (2014), consumer confidence was rising in late 2014, but with inflation levels nudging 20 per cent the government is raising the minimum salary in 2015. The government is also working to create a more open and business friendly environment and is attracting major multinational companies such as Samsung, Mitsubishi and DHL to invest in the country's future.

As is typical in emerging and developing economies, infrastructure remains a huge challenge, with inadequate transportation networks resulting in substantial inefficiencies throughout both international and domestic supply chain ecosystems.

It is estimated there are $171 billion dollars' worth of infrastructure projects planned or currently underway in Vietnam's transport sector. The government actively encourages public-private partnership (PPP) models in order to attract private sector investment in infrastructure projects. Twenty-four specific PPP projects have been identified and it's expected this approach will generate investment of $70–$80 billion within 10 years.

However, like many emerging economies, Vietnam's progress has not been without its problems in infrastructure development. Despite a programme to improve road links and to help a fragmented 3PL logistics sector, several manufacturing zones and ports continue to lack modern highway connections. In 2013 the government allowed provinces to advance $250 million to accelerate progress of the numerous projects underway to upgrade the national highways 1 and 14, some of which are five years behind schedule.

An initiative to develop port infrastructure in south Vietnam seemed to overlook the scale economies of modern container shipping by allocating parcels of land only 500m in quay length, with concessions awarded to a myriad of joint venture organizations, resulting in over half of the new port infrastructure projects being either on-hold, abandoned or mothballed.

Whilst the capital Hanoi is the centre of government and politics, Ho Chi Minh City (HCMC) – formerly Saigon – remains the primary commercial hub of Vietnam's economy. As the epicentre of trade and commerce, an estimated 80 per cent of all goods move through the city, thereby making HCMC the most critical logistics hub in the whole of Vietnam. The vast majority of logistics providers – both domestic and foreign – have therefore established a presence in HCMC.

Indonesia

With over 250 million inhabitants, Indonesia is the fourth most populous country in the world – and by far the largest in ASEAN. It has an increasingly well-educated workforce, where English is widely spoken amongst the white collar sector. At the end of 2014, the rupiah currency was appreciating and the country was reporting a trade surplus, which combined with low inflation, puts the country in a good position to continue to further develop and expand its economy.

The 2014 change in political leadership is widely expected to accelerate commercial initiatives and ease pathways for foreign investors. The new president campaigned on the basis that development of maritime infrastructure would be a top priority for new government and work has already begun in evolving Indonesia into 'a maritime axis of the world'.

A massive archipelago comprising over 17,000 islands in total, Indonesia has six economic corridors with related waterborne logistics networks that link and connect the country's 6,000 inhabited islands. The centre of economic gravity is firmly focused on the island of Java, responsible for 60 per cent of Indonesia's GDP and home to the two largest cities being Jakarta the capital (population over 10 million) and Surabaya in east Java (population over 3 million).

The National Logistics Blueprint, a collaborative initiative between the government and the private sector, plans to improve sea ports, airports, railway lines, roads and IT infrastructure to improve transport connections and support more advanced track and trace technology for goods flows across the country. The logistics sector grew by 16 per cent in 2013–14 and the industry's improvements in recent years have been recognized in the World Bank's Logistics Performance Index, where Indonesia has risen dramatically from 75th place in 2010 to 53rd place in 2014.

Tanjung Priok container port in Jakarta is the country's primary international cargo gateway and a major maritime hub serving the island nation. After years suffering from heavy congestion, operating almost at its full capacity of 7.5 million twenty-foot equivalent units (TEU), the port's massive expansion project, named as New Priok involving large-scale reclamation and dredging to draught of 20 metres, commenced construction in January 2013. The first phase – costing over $2.5 billion – opening for business in 2015 with Container Terminal 1, providing an additional 1.5 million TEU's of capacity. When finally complete in 2023, the New Priok expansion will include seven additional container terminals, increase capacity by 12.5 million containers to a total of 20 million TEU per annum.

The other major maritime development that will enable more efficient supply chain ecosystems is the Pendulum Nusantara project – 'Pendulum of the Archipelago' – comprising a shipping corridor running from the east to the west of the country. The pendulum system utilizes larger vessels to connect the six major ports of Belawan, Batam, Jakarta, Surabaya, Makassar, all the way to Sorong, which are supplemented by localized shipping loops to reach the surrounding areas – serviced by feeder vessels of smaller sizes. This pendulum system approach is designed to reduce logistics costs by using larger vessels for the main inter-island shipping routes, creating a balance between east and the west of the country as well as minimizing return journeys by under-utilized or empty vessels.

According to Dr Mark Yong, Business Development Director at BMT Asia Pacific, 'The pendulum service will focus on the major ports accounting for 70 per cent of Indonesian domestic cargo throughput. Cargoes will be transported like a "bus stop" system which will provide significant efficiencies and savings. Actual cost reductions will vary depending on the port pairings, but as an extreme example, from $2,000/TEU to $375/TEU.'

Minister of Transportation, Bambang Susantono, in 2013 summarized the four critical steps involved in successfully adopting the Pendulum Nusantara to increase efficiencies and reduce costs:

1 Improve the port infrastructure.

2 Deploy bigger vessels for improved efficiencies.

3 Build information technology systems that connect all the major ports.

4 Improve human resources capabilities.

FIGURE 6.2 Indonesia's Pendulum Nusantara maritime corridor

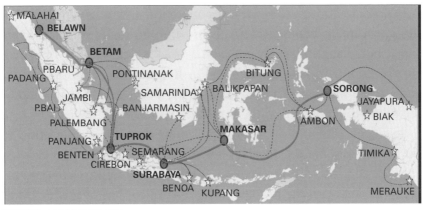

SOURCE 4.bp.blogspot.com

Overall, the government's total infrastructure master plan calls for $60 billion of investment in port infrastructure, with more than half the funding being sought from international investors.

The Philippines

With strong economic growth in the Philippines driving demands on the logistics sector in the capital Manila, supply chain capabilities and infrastructure have been coming under pressure.

Congestion at almost every level is the biggest barrier facing the Philippines as its infrastructure struggles to keep pace with continued economic expansion. In recent years, the country has enjoyed GDP growth above 5 per cent putting it among the fastest growing economies in Asia.

The economy has weathered global economic and financial downturns better than its regional peers due to lower dependence on exports, relatively resilient domestic consumption, minimal exposure to troubled international securities, and remittances from millions of overseas Filipino workers – including around a third of the world's seafarers.

Congestion challenges impact all modes. To ease congestion at Manila's Ninoy Aquino International Airport, the Civil Aviation Authority had to limit corporate jets and small planes.

Two of the country's biggest ports, the Port of Manila (POM) and the Manila International Container Port (MICP), consistently experience heavy congestion, further compounded by the Manila truck ban, introduced for most of 2014.

In order to address heavy traffic congestion downtown, the Manila city government banned trucks from being on roads between 5 am and 9 pm. That effectively prevented trucks from leaving or entering the country's busiest port for 16 hours a day, resulting in an undisclosed number of import containers being delayed indefinitely according to an official of the Bureau of Customs.

President Aquino is on record confirming that severe congestion at the Philippines' main seaports is hurting the economy. Import growth has slowed reflecting the economic impact of the port congestion. To try to deal with the problem, the government has opened a 'trade lane' into the port area that is always open. This has cut the backlog of containers to load and unload, but far from ending the delays altogether, trucks still face long waiting lines. Meanwhile, the authorities have urged shipping firms to use under-utilized seaports outside Manila, where it has opened container yards in economic zones where empty containers can be moved.

The government's Department of Transportation and Communications (DOTC) has published plans for improving and expanding transport infrastructure. The DOTC blueprint is a five-year, multi-billion dollar Transport Infrastructure Build-up Plan that will upgrade the country's transportation networks – covering land, air and sea infrastructure and multi-modal connectivity. To implement this strategy, the government is actively seeking more participation from the private sector, including foreign direct investment. The various government transport infrastructure programmes will be implemented through a combination of public-private partnerships (PPP), government capital outlays and official development assistance (ODA).

Such government and private sector support for infrastructure developments, together with active industry and stakeholder engagement, will further strengthen the well-established but somewhat fragmented local logistics sector. This will empower Manila to adopt a more holistic and integrated approach to the capital's transportation networks and thus enable multi-modal cargo interchanges with hinterland connectivity that will better balance cargo flows, optimize asset utilization thus easing congestion, reducing delays and driving supply chain efficiencies.

Summary: where next for Asia?

There is little doubt that the Asia region will continue to play a larger and even more influential role in the world economy, both as a huge pool of labour resources producing for global supply chains, and as a growing army of consumers eager to purchase home-grown goods and imports from the West.

But on top of Asia's geographic, economic, and political complexity, there are significant supply chain challenges resulting from developing regulatory environments, inadequate infrastructure, and talent shortages.

Acquiring the insights and knowledge of the issues in each country, together with capabilities to develop appropriate supply chain solutions will be key enablers of competitive advantage for organizations seeking to capitalize on the groundswell of opportunities in these exciting markets.

However, with informed insights and the right business partners together providing deeper understanding about the region, businesses can benefit from both production and consumption opportunities in Asia – and ensure that they are in a position to capitalize on that growth during what is becoming known as the 'Asian Era'.

CASE STUDY   Myanmar enters the world of global trade

After nearly 40 years of military rule and international isolation, Myanmar (Burma) took its first steps into the modern world when the first general elections were held in 2010. After some setbacks on the road to democracy, May 2013 signalled the country's return to the world stage when the US President, Barack Obama, welcomed Myanmar's President, Thein Sein, to Washington DC.

In just a few years, Myanmar has undergone a number of dramatic and positive changes, moving from harsh rule under a military junta to an open, democratic state. Now accepted and welcomed by the global community, during 2014 Myanmar assumed the role of chair of ASEAN – the Association of South-East Asian Nations.

Myanmar has a young and growing population of some 60 million with high literacy levels – above the global average at 92.7 per cent, on a par with countries such as Malta, Mexico and Peru. Thus Myanmar offers a huge pool of labour – and in the medium term, the potential for a substantial consumer market. The combination of a generally literate population with low wage costs – and a willingness to work to improve their economic position – provides the country with a potentially valuable human resource for its development. Strict sanctions are now being replaced by development capital, partnerships and political support from some of the previous regime's critics.

The country is one of the least-connected in the world in terms of telecommunication, transportation and logistics. The road density in Myanmar is less than one fifth of the average in ASEAN countries. The country's inland waterways network, which is important for freight traffic, is also underutilized due to an ageing fleet of vessels and neglected ports facilities. Myanmar has nine ports along the western and south-eastern coast of the country, with the principal port, the Port of Yangon, handling about 90 per cent of the country's cargo throughput; the other port facilities are mainly coastal ports with limited cargo handling capabilities.

Now that there are hopes that Myanmar's economy will start to grow with the potential to become a major exporter, especially of agriculture and food products, some observers have suggested that Myanmar could become a trade hub on the crossroads of Asia.

The country has designated three coastal Special Economic Zones (SEZs) for development – Dawei, Thilawa and Kyaukpyu – so port terminal developments and deep-sea freight facilities will play a large part in the new infrastructure investments.

At the beginning of 2013, a huge and unprecedented debt restructuring with Japan, the Asian Development Bank (ADB), the World Bank and Paris Club members, cleared over $6 billion, or 60 per cent of the total owed by Myanmar. Japan's leading stance in the debt cancellation has put it in a good position to enhance cooperation with Myanmar, with giant corporates such as Mitsubishi, Marubeni and Sumitomo all actively involved in the Thilawa developments.

The US and EU were somewhat slower to react in terms of development aid and political and business cooperation. However, in February 2013, US sanctions on financial transactions were lifted for four Myanmar banks that had been restricted under US law. In April 2013, the EU agreed to lift all remaining sanctions on Myanmar and re-instate the generalized system of preferences, demonstrating its commitment to long-term cooperation with the new pro-democracy government.

In late 2014, the Asian Development Bank (ADB) approved a loan of up to $100 million to Singapore-listed Yoma Strategic Holdings Ltd to improve infrastructure connectivity needed for sustainable economic growth in Myanmar. The loan will be made available in two tranches, with Yoma engaging partner companies to work with it on individual infrastructure sub-projects. The first tranche will be used to build telecommunication towers, develop cold-storage logistics, and modernize vehicle fleet leasing; and the second will fund sub-projects in transportation, distribution, logistics and other sectors.

Connecting Yangon to London

UK headquartered global logistics company Claridon has become the first privately owned British logistics company to open a wholly owned subsidiary in Myanmar. The company is working closely with both the Myanmar and UK governments and chambers of commerce to help promote business links for European manufacturers and exporters to this newly emerging economy, which represents long-term opportunities for almost all business sectors.

Claridon Group was the first British company to be invited to meet the country's transport minister for private talks. The meeting focused on raising awareness among British exporters of the opportunities in Myanmar and included a session with a Myanmar ministerial delegation to discuss and advise on such matters as regulatory impacts, private sector development, private-public partnership and anti-corruption issues.

Claridon opened its South-East Asia headquarters in the capital Yangon as a local base for its range of specialist international logistics services including sea, air and surface freight, leveraging their experience in operating in remote and politically unstable regions. From Myanmar's perspective, Claridon's commitment to the country will bring in much needed inward investment and create employment. The company views this opportunity as a long-term partnership, ensuring responsible trade to help support jobs within Myanmar and the UK.

Claridon Group works with the UK government and British chambers of commerce in an advisory capacity on various aspects of international trade matters, and CEO Chris Scott serves on the Bank of England's Monetary Policy Committee for the South-East region of the UK. As a member of the Essex chamber of commerce, Claridon advises members on developing business with Myanmar, providing opportunities for local companies to explore this exciting emerging market.

Conclusion

Myanmar started its new journey to economic prosperity from a very low base. The economy is one of the least developed in the world, following decades of stagnation, mismanagement and isolation. However, while Myanmar is one of the world's poorer nations – the effect of decades without an open and democratic regime – the country's new status is generating a great deal of interest among governments and investors from around the world. Its rich natural resources – both mineral and agricultural – and its location in the most dynamic part of the globe, make the country a highly attractive investment opportunity.

The New Silk Road connecting Europe and Asia

07

An historic trade route revived for the 21st century

For more than two millennia the Silk Road has provided a trade route between China in the Far East through the Middle East to Europe, starting from Xi'an (formerly Chang'an) in central China and reaching all the way into the Mediterranean. Trade along this ancient route began in the third century and over the years has extended beyond just the transportation of goods, also providing a means for the exchange of ideas and culture between China, India, Persia, Arabia, Greece and Rome. The Silk Road reached peak activity in the 13th and 14th centuries, after which trade gradually declined as the Mongol and Byzantine empires faded and the powers along the route became more separated culturally and economically. The name 'Silk Road' itself does not originate from the Romans but is a 19th century term, coined by the German scholar, Ferdinand von Richthofen.

Historically, the term Silk Road meant a network of different routes which, while all running generally from east to west and vice versa, were in reality a network of roads connecting trade centres across the entire continent. The northern route ran from Shangdu across the grasslands and north of the Caspian and Black Seas into central Europe; the main central route ran from south of Beijing through Xi'an and Samarkand into Damascus; a shorter journey linked Chendgu with India, and the marine Silk Road followed the same routes as today from the east coast of China south through the straits of Malacca to Egypt.

Explorer Marco Polo travelled the Silk Road to reach China and in his writings described in detail Chinese politics, economy and culture. His exploits generated considerable interest in the region from the courts of Europe and had a powerful effect on the growth of European navigation.

After centuries of neglect, the Silk Road is now being rediscovered and has become the focus of considerable political interest and financial investment to provide an economic and efficient conduit for the huge growth in trade between Europe and the Far East – principally China.

Following a 2011 conference in London, the New Silk Road (NSR) Forum was formed with the remit to act as a medium for all participants – including governments, institutions, corporations and professionals – to meet, discuss and understand the opportunities that the New Silk Road provides including lower costs compared with alternatives such as deep-sea traffic, faster and more direct road and rail links and a more integrated transport structure.

Its 30 members representing countries from Turkey in the west to China in the east provide information and support to organizations that could benefit from New Silk Road initiatives to promote consensus-building on issues of broad importance to participants involved in related business opportunities. Partners include the Middle East Association, the China-Britain Business Council, KPMG, UK India Business Council, PWC, Deloitte, Sumitomo Banking Corporation and the International Project Finance Association.

Having already attracted a number of global giants such as Hewlett Packard, Apple and several car manufacturers, this New Silk Road option has the potential to once again become one of the world's leading trading routes; however, there are many obstacles and challenges for the modern supply chain ecosystem.

The sheer length and complexity of the journey provide a major challenge for even the most advanced transport and logistics service providers; the route travels through some of the world's most inhospitable landscapes; it crosses numerous countries with differing cultures, languages and customs; in many parts of the region political instability poses a significant risk; finally bureaucracy, corruption and theft add further risks and dangers to the development of a successful, reliable and efficient trade route.

What the New Silk Road offers to commerce

Given so many drawbacks, there must be some powerful arguments in its favour to attract new users and governments seeking to invest billions in this ambitious project. Following dramatic increases in recent years, the China-Europe trade flows now represent a significant proportion of global commerce, and are the major driving force behind the revival of this historic trading route. Now the world's second largest economy, China is Europe's second largest trade partner (after the USA) and is the EU's fastest growing export market. From almost zero in the mid-1990s, China-Europe trade is now running at over $1 billion dollars per day and in 2013 reached $428 billion. However, there is a major imbalance in the bidirectional trade flows – China exports $280 billion worth of goods to the European Union, almost twice the value ($148 billion) of goods travelling in the other direction from Europe to China. This obviously results in a lot of empty containers and under-utilized transportation vehicles, adding to the overall cost of logistics.

Deep-sea ocean freight

International trade and certainly trade from China to the rest of the world has been – and will continue to be – dominated by ocean freight. Container trade volumes leaving the main Chinese and Asian ocean ports continue to grow and far outstrip those in the West. Only Dubai breaks the stranglehold on the top 10 ports with Shanghai, Singapore, Hong Kong and Shenzhen at the top of the table.

However, the long-haul ocean routes from these ports via the Straits of Malacca between Singapore and Malaysia then on to the Suez Canal can take at least three weeks, so companies are increasingly seeking alternative options for Asia-Europe cargo flows.

Furthermore, in recent years many of the long haul deep-sea routes have been impacted by piracy attacks – 231 worldwide incidents during 2014 according to the ICC International Maritime Bureau (IMB) – with the cost of warding off pirates estimated by US Merchant Marine to be $5–$8 billion per annum (Kemp, 2014).

Today, as a result of globalization and the advent of maritime container transport, about 80 per cent of world trade is carried out through some 30 increasingly saturated ports – which in 2013 processed over 350 million containers – causing bottlenecks and delays which in turn, increase costs all along the supply chain to the end consumer. Given these developments, Eurasia land-bridges via road and rail along traditional Silk Road trading routes are now being viewed as a viable option for overland transport.

Before we delve too deeply into the advantages the New Silk Road can provide, we need to keep a sense of proportion about the practical capacity of such a route and the extent to which it can replace deep-sea freight. The latest generation of container ships can carry around 18,000 TEUs; the top six Chinese ports in 2012 shipped around 125m TEUs with a total length (as if on a train) of 760,000km annually, or trains hauling around 2,000km of containers a day. So the reality is that even a highly successful New Silk Road could only hope to handle a small percentage of total freight.

The new routes are likely to be most attractive for companies shipping smaller volumes or in niche markets where time is important, such as specialized electronics and the fashion industry where items may need to be on shelves quickly to catch the season or a particular short-lived craze.

The latest developments of feasible and practical land links by road and rail provide traders with alternative transportation options that are faster than ocean freight and cheaper than air cargo, appealing to companies that are seeking to optimize their supply chains.

New transport links being developed today reflect the same concept of a network of routes, but which now connect modern centres of trade and distribution both at the start and end points but also at various commercial and distribution centres located along the route. The New Silk Road links Chinese provinces and cities such as Chongqing, Jiangsu and Hong Kong with St Petersburg and Moscow

TABLE 7.1 World's top 30 container ports

Rank	Port	Country
1	Shanghai	China
2	Singapore	Singapore
3	Shenzhen	China
4	Hong Kong	China
5	Busan	South Korea
6	Ningbo-Zhoushan	China
7	Qingdao	China
8	Guangzhou Harbor	China
9	Jebel Ali	Dubai, UAE
10	Tianjin	China
11	Rotterdam	Netherlands
12	Dalian	China
13	Port Kelang	Malaysia
14	Kaohsiung	Taiwan, China
15	Hamburg	Germany
16	Antwerp	Belguim
17	Keihin ports*	Japan
18	Xiamen	China
19	Los Angeles	USA
20	Tanjung Pelepas	Malaysia

(*Continued*)

TABLE 7.1 (*Continued*)

Rank	Port	Country
21	Long Beach	USA
22	Tanjung Priok, Jakarta	Indonesia
23	Laem Chabang	Thailand
24	Ho Chi Minh	Vietnam
25	Bremen/Bremerhaven	Germany
26	Lianyungung	China
27	New York-New Jersey	USA
28	Hanshin Ports	Japan
29	Yingkou	China
30	Jeddah	Saudi Arabia

SOURCE *Journal of Commerce* (2013)

*KEIHIN ports is Japan's superport hub on the Tokyo Bay and includes Yokohama, Kawasaki, and Tokyo.

in Russia, Lithuania, Lodz in Poland and through to Duisburg and Hamburg in Germany.

Will economic shifts boost the New Silk Road?

Ongoing economic developments may have the effect of reducing the attractiveness of the traditional ocean route, whilst at the same time favouring the New Silk Road's land based links from Asia to Europe.

Half of China's exports are generated by foreign companies that have invested in China, mainly from other Asian economies – companies from Japan, Taiwan, Hong Kong and South Korea play a dominant role in supplying parts and components for final assembly in China. The role of European companies is more limited as they tend to mainly invest in China to serve the Chinese market. Every year, 20 million Chinese households reach the threshold of $13,500 annual income – the point at which middle-class families have the disposable income for discretionary spending on key consumer products, including household goods and motor vehicles. China's importance will therefore increase over time, with greater potential for more exports from Europe, particularly for consumer products companies.

The Chinese authorities are encouraging companies to invest in manufacturing in the centre of the country, to take pressure off the eastern coastal cities and to develop a more balanced economic base across the country. In addition, labour costs in China's coastal cities have surged in the last decade, so manufacturers are seeking to reduce production costs by relocating operations inland and taking advantage of incentive packages to go west and establish manufacturing centres in the nation's interior.

China's Premier Li Keqiang confirmed in 2014 that there is some industrial shift from the developed and expensive cities on the eastern seaboard to landlocked inland central and western regions, with the government vowing to build on this to boost and balance the economy. Li said that the industrial shifts will help improve urbanization in central and western regions and enrich less-developed areas, enabling employment and growth and empowering the overall upgrading of the Chinese economy. Enterprises are attracted to move inland by lower land and labour costs as well as welcoming business environments. Thus the source of many export products destined for European markets is gradually moving inland and further away from the container ports on the coast.

Meanwhile, in Europe, as the European Union has expanded to 28 member states, there has been a gradual shift eastwards in the economic centre of gravity. While the western states including UK, Germany and France are still far larger economies than the newer EU members, their sluggish economic performance in recent years may allow some of the eastern countries to begin to close the gap.

While the present trend in Eastern Europe is one of patchy but identifiable growth, those economies have the advantage of faster growth from a smaller base; and despite the present downturn, some states such as Latvia and Poland could point to improvements over the previous five years. While it may take some years before they return to stronger growth, leading companies have and will continue to invest there for the long term. Therefore, many of Europe's fastest-growing consumer markets are now in the inland countries – further away from the coastal ports at the western end of the European continent.

These trends are resulting in both the production sources and consumer markets being further away from coastal ports, making the overland connection considerably shorter, whilst the ocean freight option becomes longer, due to the additional inland transportation moves at both origin and destination.

What this means for supply chain ecosystems across Asia

With manufacturing in China gradually developing westwards and the European markets moving slowly eastwards, ocean freight-based supply chains will take longer and land-based road and rail links through central Asia will be quicker.

For example, the journey for a container from the municipality of Chongqing – in the mid-west of China – to Shanghai's major container port on the east coast, involves more than 1,600 km, taking several days by barge, adding considerable cost and time when compared with coastal manufacturing locations.

At the other end of the journey, transporting goods from the western European coastal ports inland to Poland and other eastern European states will add another day or two to the overall transit time.

This adds additional days of transit time – together with the related financial implications for inventory and working capital – onto ocean freight-based journeys that have become on average 20 per cent slower due to slow-steaming. Adopted in recent years by the container shipping lines in order to reduce operational costs by saving on fuel consumption, the now industry-standard practice of slow steaming can mean a 40-day ocean journey from the mainland Chinese ports through to Europe.

Asia-Europe by land transport

To help stimulate regional trade and better connect their economies, China, Russia and Kazakhstan have established a new ground transportation corridor that stretches from eastern China's Jiangsu province to St Petersburg in Russia.

After nine years of negotiations, the three countries have reached agreement on a construction plan for the Asia-Europe road expected to be completed by 2017. The length of this new transport corridor will be 8,445km, with 2,233km in Russia, 2,787km in Kazakhstan and 3,425km in China.

Once completed, this new highway is expected to help attract foreign investment into Russia and Central Asia, with strategic locations along the route benefiting from expanded commercial activities such as distribution hubs and service centres, generating employment and economic prosperity.

New Silk Road rail hubs

As companies seek to optimize the time and cost of transporting cargo between Asia and Europe, containerized rail freight is becoming an increasingly viable option. At the heart of China's ambitions to develop the New Silk Road rail infrastructure sits the ancient city of Chengdu (once called the Brocade City for its silk production). Lying some 1,700km inland from China's east coast, it is the starting point of a 10,000km rail journey that passes through Kazakhstan, into Russia and on to Eastern Europe. Chengdu is already the country's fourth largest air cargo hub and an important inland focal point for increased investment in logistics hubs and supply chain services.

Chengdu is the starting point for a 9,800km rail service opened in 2013 through to Lodz in Poland. The weekly service carries electronic products such as laptops for Dell or iPads for Apple. The development is part of the city's efforts to change from a purely domestic logistics centre into an international transport hub, reducing overall time in transit by up to one month, compared with sea transport. It is estimated that some 50 per cent of the world's laptop chips and 65 per cent of the world's iPads are produced in Chengdu and this new rail service will help support further growth for the region. In its first year of operation the line carried 45 trains and over 8,000 tonnes of goods.

Since 2013, another cross-border rail route has become available that can transport made-in-China products from Zhengzhou, capital of Henan Province, to Hamburg in Germany. Named the 'Iron Silk Road', the journey takes only 15–18 days to cover the 10,214km, making it especially suitable for goods with relatively high value or which need to be delivered in a short period of time. Recently announced plans from the joint venture between Deutsche Bahn and Russian Railways are for yet another Eurasia rail route, this time running from Chongqing municipality in China via Kazakhstan, Russia, Belarus and Poland through to Duisburg in Germany.

Chongqing is the production hub for a number of global technology companies such as Apple, Hewlett-Packard and Acer – and is also home to many parts manufacturers in the automobile industry. This rail connection linking China to Duisburg runs three times a week with the intention to expand to a daily service. Despite the vast 11,000km distance the journey only takes 16 days – less than half the time of ocean freight.

Multi-Modal Silk Road

A multi-modal road-rail overland service connecting Asia and Europe has been launched by DHL Global Forwarding – delivering a reliable service that offers a competitively priced alternative, which provides significant cost savings compared to air freight.

The weekly China to Europe train service departs every Friday from Chengdu, travelling along China's west corridor rail line, through Kazakhstan and via DHL's intermodal hub in Malaszewicze, Poland. The multimodal service also promises delivery time reductions of between 10 and 21 days compared to sea freight, depending on origin and destination.

This new weekly service from Chengdu comes as an addition to DHL's established daily service – departing from Shanghai and running along the trans-Siberian north corridor – with a transit time difference of up to eight days. In turn, the new service also offers greater cost and CO_2 emission reductions.

Governmental and organizational investment and support

Developing a new and efficient supply chain system based on rail freight is welcome news to those keen on protecting the environment. As mentioned in Chapter 3, environmental issues and minimizing the corporate carbon footprint are now core values for most businesses, with governments and customers alike focusing their attention on a company's green credentials. Rail transport is proven to be less polluting than road freight, with lower particulates and CO_2 emissions, as well as being safer and with greater carrying capacity. So the new Silk Road Rail service should not face significant opposition; indeed, it should be welcomed as boosting economic growth by bringing jobs and investment to many nations along its 10,000km route.

There is no doubt that there is strong political will in many countries to develop these new Silk Road transport corridors into significant commercial and economic zones. Such transport linkages will attract new business and encourage further growth in east-west trade by providing a faster, lower cost and more efficient transport network compared with the current deep-sea ocean route. For the many countries and zones along the route it will provide additional impetus to manufacturing, assembly and distribution services providing employment and growth in some of the region's poorest states. During recent years, several international organizations, countries and various associations have given their support to the new Silk Road concept.

Through its Special Programme for the Economies of Central Asia (SPECA) and Almaty Action programmes, the United Nations is providing landlocked and transit countries with access to global markets.

In Europe, the Organization for Security and Cooperation (OSCE) has focused on adopting international best-practices in border-crossing governance throughout the region to improve trade facilitation capabilities and reduce supply chain barriers.

And since 1993 the EU has been implementing the Transport Corridor Europe-Caucasus-Asia (TRACECA) – an international transport programme involving the European Union and 14 member States of the Eastern European, Caucasian and Central Asian region – designed to further facilitate bidirectional Eurasia trade flows of goods and services.

The New Eurasian Land Transport initiative was launched back in 2008 by the International Road Transport Union (IRU) – seeking to effectively demonstrate that road haulage between Asia and Europe was viable, safe and cost-efficient. Emphasizing that no country is land-locked from the road freight perspective, the IRU advocate that trucking is the only transport mode capable of interconnecting all businesses throughout the central Asia region to major world markets.

In recent years the IRU has run a number of truck caravans to show the viability of various routes along the Silk Road economic belt. They included Islamabad to Istanbul, Beijing to Brussels, and the Black Sea ring from Belgrade to Istanbul, with all such projects collecting data and reporting on physical and non-physical barriers to transport.

Barriers to Silk Road trade

With a route running the best part of 10,000km across largely uninhabited, inhospitable terrain, through unstable states with a poor record for corruption and known for inefficiencies, it's no surprise that there is a great deal of work to be done to ensure that goods can move swiftly, safely and unencumbered.

The IRU's New Eurasian Land Transport Initiative (NELTI) collected data from users which revealed that vehicle delays and downtime at some border crossings accounted for up to 40 per cent of total transit time, while corruption could represent as much as 30 per cent of total transportation costs. Both these factors can provide a massive brake on the growth and success of the New Silk Road and need to be tackled by all countries and organizations involved.

Authorities must strive to reduce the scope of cross-border controls and inspections to the strict minimum, in accordance with their international obligations – for example adopting the UN convention on frontier controls – namely by moving export-import procedures upstream and downstream from borders to departure and destination points.

Accurate and timely information about real waiting times at borders is vital to monitor and check whether measures taken are being effective in reducing waiting times and improving logistics efficiencies. To help governments and competent national authorities meet their legal obligation of keeping all relevant parties informed, including fleet operators, the IRU has developed the Border Waiting Times Observatory (BWTO), a state-of-the-art web-based application which enables authorities, anywhere in the world, to report on border waiting times, free of charge, and enables drivers and transport operators to check these waiting times online and in real time.

As an example of successful cross-border collaboration, Kazakhstan, Russia and Belarus created a customs union that took full effect in January 2012. The trilateral agreement eliminated lengthy inspections at the borders in the zone between the three countries, which greatly reduced pilferage whilst eliminating several unproductive days from the total transit time.

A significant physical operational barrier is that countries along the route have adopted different rail gauges, meaning that trains and or containers have to be switched between gauges at national borders. Obviously this takes time and therefore incurs delays – and therefore additional costs – in the overall transit time. While Europe and China operate a 1.435m gauge, Russia, the Baltic States, Ukraine and Kazakhstan work with 1.520m tracks. To add to the confusion, India and Pakistan run on 1.676m tracks.

It would be prohibitively expensive to change entire systems so the rail freight industry needs to develop and deploy fast and efficient ways to switch over across different gauges. Investing in modern container and wagon transfer facilities will help to reduce delays when switching gauges. Heavy-duty lift trucks and overhead cranes equipped with container spreaders and other specialized lifting equipment provide fast, safe and efficient rolling stock transfer and should become the norm at border crossings.

Other regulations and industry practices may need to be harmonized to further reduce stoppages and delays. Trains carrying Hewlett Packard products from China to Germany had to be separated at the Belarus-Poland border because the length of the 41-wagon train exceeded European regulations for a freight train's maximum length. As a result, nine cars had to wait for a separate locomotive to arrive in order to complete the journey through to Duisburg.

An exceptional but not unique example of where the best laid plans can fall down appeared in the *New York Times* in 2013 (Bradsher, 2013). A 50-container train containing electronic products left Chongqing rail yard on a five-day journey to Kazakhstan. On the China Kazakhstan border, Chinese customs officers examined the sealed containers and inspected the documents, finding that for 49 of the 50 containers the paperwork matched the contents in every detail. However, for the last container, the documents showed a weight of 10,135kg whereas the actual weight was 10,153kg. A simple mistake with two digits transposed in error. Having crossed part of the Gobi and Taklamakan Deserts, where temperatures can hit 120 degrees, the train simply sat for 26 hours before the problem was resolved and the cargo could continue its journey.

One unavoidable factor in the development of the New Silk Road is that the region between China and Europe is not the most hospitable in the world. Much of it is taken up by the Taklimakan desert, one of the most hostile environments on our planet. There is very little vegetation, almost no rainfall and sandstorms are very common. Its climate is harsh with summer daytime temperatures between 40°C and 50°C, and winter temperatures down to minus 20°C. To the north-east lies the Gobi desert, almost as harsh in climate as the Taklimakan itself and on the remaining three sides lie some of the highest mountains in the world, including the Himalayas.

Such unforgiving conditions will add considerable cost to the construction of road and rail networks as equipment, materials and labour will need largely to be brought from neighbouring countries and centres. Repair, refuelling, servicing and repair facilities will need to be provided, as well as storage and intermodal hubs where parts of the Silk Road network meet.

Such wide fluctuations in temperature will also require temperature controlled rolling stock or containers for perishable foodstuffs and even for some electronic components which can be affected by excessively high temperatures. Modern electronics in vehicles and other transport equipment may malfunction without sufficient ventilation to maintain the required temperature, and even iPads and laptops can fail if subject to excessive heat.

Summary

Increasingly bi-directional trade flows between Europe and Asia are generating huge opportunities while revealing some challenges. However more than ever, organizations cannot go it alone. Collaboration is once again essential and requires ultra-diligent selection of business partners with a deep understanding of the complex, diverse and often unregulated markets across the Europe-Asia trading blocs. Companies should leverage independent expertise to help them navigate through some deep and dangerous waters to benefit from the substantial opportunities the new Silk Road offers.

There is no doubt that China will play an ever increasingly important role in the world's economy and will adapt and develop its products, services and infrastructure to meet its ambitions. As the New Silk Road develops it will also provide the opportunity for other central Asian states to develop their economies by taking advantage of local product assembly, storage and distribution, all linked to an effective and efficient transportation system between the East and West.

Leading technology companies and others from the West have already taken up the challenge but there will be room for many more to take advantage of the vast investment that China and other states are making into the new Silk Road.

CASE STUDY   China's $40 billion Silk Road Fund

Once the historic trade highway across much of Asia, the old Silk Road extended some 4,000km linking China, India, the Arabian Peninsula and Europe. Its role diminished as the Roman Empire fell in the 5th century but it was revived under the Mongol Empire in the 13th and 14th centuries.

China has for some time been promoting the idea of rejuvenating the ancient Silk Road – or roads, as there were in fact several routes running linking east and west – and in 2013, Chinese President Xi Jinping first announced China's plan to drive forward such initiatives with the intention to develop a Silk Road economic belt that would further boost trade between Asia, the Middle East, Europe and Africa.

In late 2014, concluding the 2014 APEC Summit (Asia-Pacific Economic Cooperation) in Beijing, President Xi Jinping pledged $40 billion for the Silk Road Fund to invest across the region as part of the country's 'One Belt, One Road' initiative. China's leaders see this as a key goal to create a more integrated economic mega-region that would include just about every economy across Eurasia – from the Philippines across East Asia, through Central Asia and into Europe and Northern Africa, all the way to Portugal at its farthest point.

The 'belt' on the land aims to promote greater connectivity between China and the central and western parts of Eurasia, whereas the 'road' at sea looks into closer linkage between the country and the economies in South and South-east Asia, as well as Africa.

The billions of dollars will be spent on infrastructure development investments, building ports, railways, roads, and airports across Central and South Asia, which will enhance opportunities for commercial, industrial and

FIGURE 7.1 Silk Road Routes

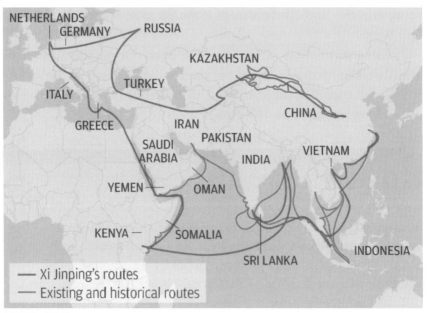

SOURCE SCMP

financial collaboration with the emerging and developing economies that lie along the routes.

- One Belt is the 'New Silk Road Economic Belt' which will pass overland through Kazakhstan, Kyrgyzstan and Iran through to Austria.

- One Road is the '21st Century Maritime Silk Road' – a maritime route that will link Chinese ports across the oceans and through to the port of Antwerp in Belgium.

President Xi Jinping told delegates at the summit that the construction of key infrastructure projects, as well as improvements in Asia's telecommunications systems, would help China enhance its trade ties with neighbouring countries and encourage overseas expansion of Chinese companies to tap markets in the region.

China's minister of commerce, Gao Hucheng said that if and when the 'One Belt, One Road' forms two new economic cooperation blocks, then they would together comprise over 60 per cent of the world's population and one third of the global economy.

In addition to the Silk Road Fund, China was instrumental in establishing the $50 billion Asia Infrastructure Investment Bank (AIIB) – also in late 2014 – which will help finance the region's infrastructure needs. Reflecting the strong appeal of – and need for – infrastructure developments across Eurasia, the AIIB initiative involves 20 other countries, including the other giant of Asia – India, and even two of China's South China Sea neighbours Vietnam and the Philippines.

Conclusion

Along the Silk Road regions, most goods are moved through sea routes, which take about 45 days. More rail links, roads and even airports could speed this up significantly. But while governments typically respond positively to the idea of more investments, the key to moving these projects forward is execution. This includes connecting the various modes of transportation involved in logistics, as despite huge investments, most of the economies along the Silk Road still have some way to go in terms of physical infrastructure, including an urgent need for new and improved roads, airports, water ports, telecom networks and energy grids.

Integrated logistics hubs

08

Integrated logistics hubs enable global supply chain ecosystems

International trade has increased massively during recent decades, enabled to a large extent by the development of more efficient, productive and cost-effective supply chain ecosystems. At the same time, logistics service providers have been able to take advantage of greater economies of scale and continued growth to justify the resources needed to upgrade, improve and develop better integrated services and facilities.

In this chapter, we will look at developments in integrated logistics services and how they connect the vital links in an effective supply chain ecosystem. Container port operations, integrated logistics hubs and logistics service providers are the pillars upon which the efficient movement of merchandise around the globe now depends – and into which companies and governments continue to invest as part of their own corporate and national macroeconomic expansion plans to facilitate trade and further commercial development.

Container ports as transit hubs

There is no question that containerized ocean freight is at the heart of the majority of 21st-century global supply chain ecosystems. However, infrastructure, regulatory and operational challenges both within and outside the port frequently result in congestion problems that adversely impact cross-border and multimodal trade flows, causing delays and adding cost for supply chain stakeholders.

The container shipping industry has continued to develop and expand across multiple dimensions, including traffic volumes, technologies, vessel design, container handling equipment and scale of operations. Today over 90 per cent of all global trade travels on the water – the majority in containers – so any obstacles or developments that impede the timely and cost-effective movement of millions of containers could have a profound effect on the health of the world's economies. Container port infrastructure is consequently an essential and critical component that empowers and enables global supply chain ecosystems.

Container ports have developed their infrastructure to become pivotal points in the supply chain ecosystem, with extensive land-side capabilities including container yards (CY), advanced handling equipment, container freight station (CFS) warehouse facilities and multi-modal transportation linkages to the hinterland.

Although they are often referred to as points of origin and destination, within a supply chain ecosystem, ports are a critical point of transit, rather than a final destination. Goods travel from their origin point of production (typically a factory) – transit through various container ports – to the point of consumption at their final destination, for example a retail store.

Therefore, in the context of the container port's role as a transit hub that facilitates cargo flows through the global ecosystem, there are many factors above and beyond pure capacity within the port that are equally important as critical enablers of the supply chain. These will include landside connectivity, overall throughput efficiency beyond the gate and the extended logistics network – involving multiple stakeholders across many operational activities.

Terminal operator one of many stakeholders in extended port operations

As the primary custodian of the container port facility and operations, the Port Operator manages a highly asset-intensive business model, requiring significant capital investment in 'hardware assets' such as

FIGURE 8.1 Extended port operations model

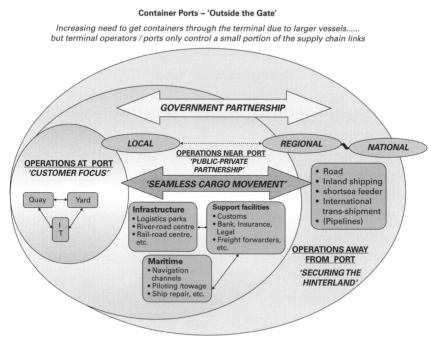

Container Ports – 'Outside the Gate'

Increasing need to get containers through the terminal due to larger vessels......
but terminal operators / ports only control a small portion of the supply chain links

GOVERNMENT PARTNERSHIP

LOCAL   REGIONAL   NATIONAL

OPERATIONS AT PORT
'CUSTOMER FOCUS'

OPERATIONS NEAR PORT
'PUBLIC-PRIVATE
PARTNERSHIP'

'SEAMLESS CARGO MOVEMENT'

Quay ⟷ Yard

I T

Infrastructure
• Logistics parks
• River-road centre
• Rail-road centre,
  etc.

Support facilities
• Customs
• Bank, Insurance,
  Legal
• Freight forwarders,
  etc.

• Road
• Inland shipping
• shortsea feeder
• International
  trans-shipment
• (Pipelines)

OPERATIONS AWAY
FROM PORT
'SECURING THE
HINTERLAND'

Maritime
• Navigation
  channels
• Piloting /towage
• Ship repair, etc.

SOURCE ICF

land, quay construction, container yard, machinery and handling equipment, not to mention the software aspects of sophisticated IT systems and the human capital resources to manage the whole operation.

However, the port operator is but one player – albeit a critical one – within an inter-dependent network of multiple stakeholders – including the all-important port authority or equivalent government body – that together enable the port's functionality as a critical transit point in the supply chain ecosystem.

As can be seen from the Extended Port Operations Model in Figure 8.1, the full extent of the port's operational activities embraces many organizations and functions that are literally and metaphorically 'outside the gate' of the port terminal – and therefore beyond the terminal operator's direct control of the operations within the port.

Nevertheless, all these different activities undertaken by the variety of organizations involved will impact the port's role as an effective and efficient transit point within a cargo owner's supply chain eco-system. It is essential therefore for all the stakeholders to work in harmony to positively impact the overall performance, economic viability and ultimately the port's economic contribution in the local, regional or national economy.

Integrated logistics hubs – leading examples

Over the years, many cities and regions have amalgamated what were previously standalone transport services such as shipping, road, rail and air freight, and connected them to establish multi-purpose transportation centres with inter-modal cargo exchange operations. Further development to include facilities for warehousing and light assembly activities combines all the various components into an inte-grated logistics hub.

This clustering effect gradually expands the critical mass of freight volumes, the scope and range of services and the number of service provider participants. In turn, integrated logistics hubs become net-worked with other cities, regions and countries, through strong and frequent multi-modal connections and thus develop into economic centres of gravity for cargo flows, trade and industry, and commercial development.

In the international context, whole economies such as Dubai, Sin-gapore and Hong Kong take advantage of efficient and transparent customs procedures, together with a light touch regulatory environ-ment, to further enable efficient cargo flows for import-export trade, with the result that these integrated logistics hubs become the essen-tial giant cogs that interconnect trading locations and nations, thereby enabling global supply chain ecosystems to function effectively.

Typically developing into major economic centres in their own right, these integrated logistics hubs are frequently found in strate-gically favourable geographic locations, such as close proximity to major shipping lanes. Seven leading examples from the USA, Europe, Middle East and Asia are examined in more detail below.

London Gateway

Located on the Thames river and to the east of London, the DP World London Gateway integrated port and logistics hub opened for business at the end of 2013, becoming the largest and most ambitious logistics infrastructure project in the UK for decades.

Modelled on the DP World group's flagship Jebel Ali facility in Dubai – which has been voted 'Best Middle East Seaport' for 19 consecutive years – London Gateway's container port can accommodate today's huge container ships up to 18,000 TEUs in its six deep water berths, alongside 2.7km of quay, with throughput capacity of 3.5m TEUs per annum.

With eight of the UK's largest quay cranes, the facility is well-equipped to service the world's largest container vessels. In late 2014 London Gateway welcomed the largest ship to ever enter the River Thames, the 397m long and 56m wide Edith Maersk, which has a draught of 16 metres and carries up to 15,500 TEUs.

Reinforcing the integrated logistics hub model that serves modern supply chain ecosystems, the site hosts an 836,000sq m logistics park providing a choice of warehousing options, including the 35,000sq m common-user facility coming on stream in 2015 for multi-tenant, multi-purpose, flexible logistics solutions. In explaining the value of the common-user facility, the Chairman of DP World, Sultan Ahmed Bin Sulayem, said: 'It offers customers a catalyst for collaboration and improved asset utilization, with occupiers sharing warehousing and transportation, saving costs whilst improving their own customer service with shorter replenishment cycles.' (DP World, 2014)

The all-essential multi-modal hinterland connectivity is enabled through on-site rail terminal and direct highway links into the UK's mainline motorway and rail networks for fast, direct access to London, the South-East, the Midlands and beyond.

With its central location, London Gateway's container port and integrated logistics facilities provide users with an efficient and flexible distribution hub from which to service the UK's major metropolises with cost-effective supply chain solutions.

Peter Ward, Commercial Director, DP World London Gateway commented: 'For so long ports and terminals have been seen as essential nodes in the supply chain that have traditionally added cost, but little value. London Gateway is a real game changer for UK supply chains. By combining a world-class deep sea container port with Europe's largest dedicated logistics park adjacent to the UK's primary consumer conurbation, designed to improve availability and speed to market whilst reducing costs and carbon emissions, exporters and importers have a new and unique opportunity to optimize international supply chain performance.'

Lille, France

It's not just the mega centres and wealthy new nations that see the economic advantages of clustering together the various transport, warehousing and supply chain services into an integrated logistics hub. Several cities and regions have seen this as a way to revitalize old industrial zones in response to new industrial and economic landscapes.

The north-east of France was once the country's coal, steel and textile heartland, which was badly impacted by factory closures during the 1970s and 80s. Seeking to respond to the economic downturn and rising unemployment, the region realized that with its location, natural assets and proximity to the Eurotunnel linking France and England, it had the opportunity to reinvent itself as a major distribution centre by adopting an integrated logistics hub model.

Over the past decade the region has invested in logistics infrastructure, equipment and skills development, thereby attracting leading international companies to locate their operations in the region – including clients such as DHL, FedEx, Michelin, Mercedes-Benz, Toyota, ArcelorMittal and Bridgestone.

With major local ports located close by, regular multi-modal transport services connect the region with the heart of mainland European transport networks, supplemented with Channel Tunnel links to and from the UK, and mainline container shipping connections at two of the world's biggest container terminals in Antwerp and Rotterdam, located just a few hours away.

Symbolic of the area's determination to develop and encourage logistics operators, the Lille region's Euralogistic cluster was founded in 2011 – and is now home to 6,000 logistics companies employing 60,000 people, ranking third overall in the industry in France.

Euralogistic brings together a regional cluster of complementary businesses – manufacturers and service providers, training and research services. Based in Henin-Beaumont south-west of Lille, the hub is financially supported by the EU and the regional government, and works with training and educational establishments throughout the region – involving more than 2,000 students – as well as all the major trade bodies, trades unions and logistics suppliers.

Dubai

Dubai is one of the Middle East's most dynamic and fast-developing states, with world class infrastructure, multi-modal connectivity and extensive air and ocean capabilities, which have enabled Dubai to become the leading Middle East trade and logistics hub servicing global supply chain ecosystems.

Dubai is widely viewed as the default distribution hub from which to serve the rapidly expanding economies in the Gulf Cooperation Council (GCC) region – the political and economic alliance comprising Saudi Arabia, Kuwait, the United Arab Emirates, Qatar, Bahrain and Oman.

Annual trade flows of goods through Dubai comprise $150 billion of imports and exports, 70 per cent of which is trans-shipment cargo, with the balance being goods serving the local and regional GCC markets.

The 21.5 square kilometre Dubai Logistics City is an integrated logistics platform providing all transport modes and logistics services, including light manufacturing and assembly, in a single customs bonded-free zone.

The Port of Jebel Ali is the Middle East's leading regional transshipment hub, where 180 shipping lines connect Dubai to 140 ports worldwide through 90 weekly services. The port handled 13.6 million TEUs in 2013, ranking it number nine in the world, the only global top-10 port outside of Asia. Jebel Ali's expansion plans underway for 2015 include adding six new berths and additional capacity of 4 million TEU, bringing the total handling capacity to 19 million TEUs.

Jebel Ali Free Zone (JAFZA) occupies 58sq km and is home to more than 7,000 companies, including one hundred of the Fortune 500. JAFZA offers a wide variety of benefits for both companies and their employees, including some very attractive tax incentives:

- 100 per cent foreign ownership;
- zero corporate tax for 50 years;
- no restriction on capital repatriation;
- zero import or re-export duties;
- zero personal income tax;
- no currency restrictions;
- no restriction on foreign talent or employees.

Chicago, USA

First named a city back in 1837 and conveniently located between the Great Lakes and the Mississippi watershed, Chicago became one of the United States' great trading centres during the 19th century. In 1848 the city got its first telegraph and railroad and two innovations – namely grain elevators and the Board of Trade's wheat grading standards – quickly transformed the way crops were sold. By 1854 Chicago was the world's largest grain port and had more than 30,000 residents, many of them European immigrants. Completed in 1848, the Illinois & Michigan Canal created a waterway connection between the Great Lakes and the Mississippi River. In the 1920s Route 66 started from the city's Art Institute and linked hundreds of predominantly rural communities across Illinois, Missouri, and Kansas to Chicago, thus enabling farmers to transport grain and produce for redistribution. The diagonal configuration of Route 66 was particularly significant for the trucking industry, which by 1930 had come to rival the railroad for pre-eminence in the American cargo transportation industry.

Today Chicago is one of the most important logistics and transportation hubs in the United States, with access to all major modes of transportation – rail, sea, road and air. It is home to one of the largest inland cargo ports in the USA, a leading container facility handling some 14 million TEUs per annum, and has more than 20 million sq m of warehouse space, making it one of the largest concentrations of industrial space in the United States. For air freight shipments, Chicago's O'Hare airport is the busiest in the United States and handles 1.6 million tons of cargo per year.

Road connections include six interstate highways reaching out east and west for more than 2,000 miles. This road connectivity places Chicago within one day's drive of 70 per cent of the country's population, a key reason why the country's leading logistics companies are represented in the city. In a nation where rail freight is well developed and deeply penetrated throughout the country, it is significant that Chicago is home to six of the seven major railroads and more than 50 railroads in total, accounting for a quarter of all rail traffic in the USA.

With rising costs of land and facilities in the heart of the city, companies are choosing to relocate their distribution centres to the suburbs, geographically extending the scope of Chicago as an integrated logistics hub.

Atlanta, USA

Atlanta is the capital of the state of Georgia which has the nation's fifth-largest concentration of supply chain companies, with over a million people employed in logistics businesses throughout the state. Atlanta itself is a global logistics hub, with one of the world's busiest airports and home to more than 130,000 supply chain jobs.

Well served with ground transport links by both road and rail to other parts of the USA, three major interstate highways connect Atlanta to more than 80 per cent of the country's commercial and consumer markets within 48 hours. Georgia has 4,900 miles of rail, the most extensive system in the south-east, and ranks number six in the country for inter-modal traffic.

Atlanta's Hartsfield-Jackson international airport is the world's most travelled airport with over 90 million passengers per annum and more than 2,600 daily take-offs and landings, with air freight shipments ranking Atlanta airport 12th overall in US air cargo traffic.

For container shipping, the Port of Savannah on the east coast, 400 kilometres away, acts as the maritime connection in Atlanta's integrated logistics hub. The port houses the largest single-terminal container facility of its kind in North America, with two modern, deep water terminals providing 9,700ft of berth space, together handling over 3 million TEUs per annum and ranking as the fourth largest – and claimed to be fastest growing – container port in the USA. Distribution centres are plentiful, accommodated at the 370,000sq m of warehousing facilities within 30 miles of the port, from where two major interstate routes and dual rail links connect to Atlanta, and onwards to the rest of the country. In 2014, the Georgia Ports Authority received final approval to proceed with a $700 million upgrade to the Port of Savannah that will extend, deepen and widen the port facilities, which will then accommodate larger vessels, increasing capacity and throughput.

Atlanta also demonstrates significant gravitational pull for developing both supply chain expertise and supply chain technology. Six of the top 20 supply chain management software providers – including Manhattan Associates and Red Prairie – have their headquarters in the city. Located in Atlanta, Georgia Tech is one of the top public universities in the United States and offers the industry renowned Executive Masters in International Logistics & Supply Chain Strategy (EMIL-SCS). This unique 18-month master's degree programme helps Fortune 500 companies design creative solutions for critical issues in their global supply chains by grooming their key executives, teaching them practical techniques for decreasing logistics costs and improving supply chain efficiencies.

As explained by Professor and EMIL-SCS Executive Director, Dr John H Vande Vate, 'Georgia Tech plays a pivotal role in fuelling innovation and providing talent. Tech's College of Engineering, the nation's largest and most diverse, is consistently ranked among the top programmes nationally and globally and is the largest producer of engineering degrees awarded to women and minority students. The H Milton Stewart School of Industrial and Systems Engineering, home of the EMIL-SCS programme, the Master's in Supply Chain Engineering and the Master's in Analytics, has been the top ranked industrial engineering programme for more than 20 years.'

Singapore

Singapore's strategic location in the heart of South-east Asia and at the focal point of major shipping routes has made it an important conduit for world trade. Despite its limited size and population, Singapore has developed into a world class integrated logistics hub, home to the world's number two container port (second only to Shanghai) and the 12th largest air cargo hub.

The maritime sector plays a significant role in Singapore's economy, accounting for 7 per cent of GDP and employing some 170,000 people in 5,000 companies. In 2014, it won the 'Best Seaport in Asia' award for the 15th time in the 25 years of the Asian Freight and Supply Chain Awards. From Singapore, shipping lines connect to 600 ports in 123 countries, with daily sailings to every major port of call in the world. Some 85 per cent of the containers that arrive in Singapore are trans-shipped to another port of call, making Singapore the world's leading trans-shipment hub.

For air freight, Singapore's Changi Airport handles almost 2 million tons of cargo per year, with flights connecting to 280 cities in 60 countries. Ranked the number one Logistics Hub in Asia by the World Bank's 2014 Logistics Performance Index, Singapore is a prime location for major multinational logistics companies – home to 20 of the top 25 global logistics players – many of whom have established regional headquarter offices.

From the human capital perspective, Singapore offers plenty of home-grown talent, including more than 8,500 graduates per year in science and engineering, as well as graduates of specialized supply chain management courses. However, concerns about the availability of talent have been raised by Raymon Krishnan, President of the Logistics and Supply Chain Management Society: 'In recent years, the government has had to balance population growth whilst keeping well-paying jobs in Singapore and at the same time keeping costs balanced for competitiveness. The supply chain and logistics sectors, like every other industry, are feeling the effects of this policy. There is a need to fine tune this further to ensure we have enough of – and the right mix of – supply chain and logistics professionals for Singapore to continue to maintain its leading role as a leading integrated logistics hub.'

Hong Kong

Hong Kong has taken full advantage of its geographical position, its longstanding role as an international trading centre, its unparalleled international access to China and the huge growth in global supply chain ecosystems to become one of the world's leading integrated logistics hubs.

With container volumes of 22.35 million TEUs in 2013, Hong Kong port is ranked number four in the world. Its nine container terminals are privately owned and operated, with total of 24 berths. Served by 80 international shipping lines, providing 450 container-liner services per week to more than 500 destinations worldwide, Hong Kong is well established as both a leading trans-shipment hub and the international gateway for southern China.

In the global air freight sector, Hong Kong International Airport (HKIA) is the world's largest air cargo hub, handling over 4 million tons of cargo per year, with almost 100 airlines flying to over 160 destinations, including 40 in mainland China. With substantial volumes of international trans-shipments, Hong Kong's logistics service providers have adopted e-logistics solutions that make it possible to submit road cargo information electronically, speed up customs clearance and facilitate cross-border trucking.

With its unique location on Lantau Island adjacent to HKIA – the world's busiest cargo airport – Tradeport is a purpose-built 30,000sq m logistics hub and regional distribution centre, providing modern warehousing and logistics services. Literally two minutes from the airport, twenty minutes from the container port and forty minutes from the border to mainland China, Tradeport provides logistics solutions for a wide range of customers needing cost effective multimodal logistics solutions to serve the whole of Asia. CEO Kenneth Bell reinforced Hong Kong's leadership role in serving global supply chain ecosystems: 'In today's world, connectivity is of paramount importance to facilitate safe, secure and efficient movement of goods between buyers and sellers. Regional distribution centres are key hubs for the storage and processing aspects within the supply chain. Hong Kong's logistics industry has long been a significant geographical cluster, underpinning its world-leading air cargo and sea port throughput as a logistics centre for not only the city itself, but its immediate hinterland in mainland China and beyond throughout the rest of Asia.'

South China connectivity will be further enhanced with the 2016 opening of the 29.6km Hong Kong-Zhuhai-Macau Bridge, which will further enable cargo flows between Hong Kong and the western Pearl River Delta – in the heart of Guangdong province's manufacturing base, which generates around one third of China's total exports.

Hong Kong's critical mass of cargo and extensive air-and-ocean connectivity enable the network effect that empowers its enviable position as the leading integrated logistics hub serving global supply chain ecosystems. Being strategically located in-between Singapore in south-east Asia and Shanghai in north-east Asia, Hong Kong is uniquely positioned to become the 'super connector' for the whole Asia-Pacific region.

Logistics service providers connect the dots

Logistics service providers (LSP) are the companies that join up the numerous dots between container ports and integrated logistics hubs by implementing and operating sophisticated transport and warehousing solutions which connect and enable the supply chain ecosystems that empower global trade.

Providing freight, transport, warehousing and planning services on an outsourced basis, third-party logistics providers – generally known as 3PLs – range from independent freight forwarding businesses, often family-owned, all the way through to giant global corporations with billions in revenues and thousands of employees.

The symbiotic relationship between 3PLs and their customers (generically called 'shippers') is another feature of the complex, connected world of global supply chain ecosystems. Differing perceptions of value provided, difficulty in conducting like-for-like price comparisons, and varying interpretations of total supply chain costs, all result in robust and regular discussions about performance and price.

The 18th annual third-party logistics study published by Capgemini in 2014 reported the continuing, positive overall nature of shipper-3PL relationships, with shippers reporting that their 3PLs helped achieve average cost reductions of logistics by 11 per cent, inventory by 6 per cent and fixed logistics costs by 23 per cent. The report summarized that shippers agree that 3PLs provide new and innovative ways to improve logistics effectiveness, and that they are sufficiently agile and flexible to accommodate future business needs and challenges. More than two-thirds of both 3PLs and shippers expressed themselves satisfied with the openness, transparency and good communication in their relationships.

Two developments were highlighted by the report. The first is that the IT capabilities of 3PLs are becoming increasingly important to shippers as they are seeing more opportunities to collaborate using Big Data. This reinforces the increasing need to deploy more sophisticated technology that can enable visibility across and throughout today's complex and interconnected supply chain ecosystems.

The second development is the increase in cross-border and inter-regional trade. As a result, shippers are now more likely to review their outsourced distribution networks to ensure that they have the most suitable partnerships in place. Respondents pointed out that with over 300 free trade agreements implemented around the world, they will increasingly seek advice and guidance from their logistics service providers on how to take advantage of trade facilitation arrangements and preferred partner programmes, the rules and compliance standards of which are increasingly complex.

The logistics sector itself is somewhat concentrated at the global level and massively fragmented at a local level. In late 2014, leading market research firm Transport Intelligence (Ti) reported an 'undiminished appetite' for mergers and acquisitions in the logistics industry and identified several reasons why M&A activity will increase in the years ahead (Manners-Bell, 2014a).

Improving economic progress and emerging market developments were key drivers – resulting in companies having increased confidence to invest in new markets, whilst new and expanding middle-class markets in Asia and Latin America drive the need for more complex supply chain networks.

New entrants, including investment institutions such as private equity companies, are seeking investment opportunities for their piles of cash, whilst economic progress in the developing world drives the need for more sophisticated logistics offerings, creating acquisition opportunities in these markets. Likewise, many Chinese and Asian logistics companies are now seeking to expand their inter-continental operations in order to serve their customers' global supply chain ecosystems and are therefore looking to establish a presence in the European and North American markets.

The shifting landscape of global sourcing operations, including near-sourcing of production activities to closer-to-market countries – for example Turkey to serve western Europe and Mexico to serve North America – will result in the need for improved international logistics networks to serve new geographic locations, whilst the exponential growth of e-commerce will continue to spur demand for specialist e-fulfilment services and last-mile delivery providers.

As a general trend in the sector of logistics service providers, in the years to come we will see increasing consolidation amongst and between logistics companies, both at global and local levels, as service providers seek to leverage scale economies, expand geographical footprints and further develop product and service offerings.

At the same time, within the customer base, we see a trend towards more rationalization of their supply base of logistics service providers – with companies reducing the number of outsourced partners to a handful of best of breed providers, likely specialized by geography, transportation mode or specific service offering.

Whilst they are simultaneously open to outsourcing more of their logistics activities, the net result is that the customers (shippers) will be outsourcing more activities to fewer providers, thereby driving both efficiencies and fierce competition.

Summary

Global supply chain ecosystems simply could not function if the various logistics networks that connect the systems' infrastructure were not fully integrated. From containerized deep-sea traffic and ports to inland dry docks and trans-shipment zones, in the air, on the road or via the railways, every stage from component sourcing through to final consumer delivery depends on integrating the physical movement of goods and related information exchange.

CASE STUDY SME freight forwarders connect integrated logistics hubs via membership networks

Freight forwarders are the conduit that connects various integrated logistics hubs, managing the transport of freight by road, rail, air and ocean. They connect the shippers that have the freight to be transported (cargo consisting of products ranging from shoes and toys to mobile phones, laptop computers and industrial equipment) with the carriers that have the transportation assets upon which to carry the cargo – the container ships and the aeroplanes.

Transport Intelligence (Ti) forecasts the global freight forwarding market – air and ocean freight combined – to grow at CAGR of 6.7 per cent through to 2017, when they project the market to be worth almost $200 billion. The top 10 global forwarders have 42 per cent market share, with the rest of the market being massively fragmented, comprising thousands and thousands of competitors.

Freight forwarders come in all nationalities and sizes. Ranked by Ti (2011) as the world's largest forwarder in terms of combined air and sea freight revenues, the German company Kuehne + Nagel has more than 900 offices in over 100 countries, with over 60,000 employees. Contrast that with the independent forwarder community where companies are frequently family owned businesses with less than 10 employees. The sector is massively fragmented – one global register has over 45,000 registered freight forwarders, whilst in Hong Kong alone there are over 4,000 forwarders, the vast majority of which are SME businesses, with less than 50 employees.

The multinational global giants of freight forwarding would appear to dominate the global industry with a level of resources that smaller, independent forwarders can only dream of. Yet in reality, a significant proportion of global freight is still managed by smaller independent forwarders – small- to medium-sized companies typically operating locally, without international offices.

How and why do the SME freight forwarders succeed?

In many cases they have the experience, organization and industry expertise in logistics and supply chain operations with the advantage of extensive local knowledge and contacts. This allows them to be flexible in selecting and contracting with the most suitable logistics providers for each project, including shippers, air freight companies, truck and railroad services – and finally, where required they may have overseas partners to help manage delivery to the ultimate destination. In this way such small-to-medium companies can operate with the minimum investment and risk, while providing a more individual and bespoke service within a limited geographical area.

Companies operating internationally will have additional expertise in preparing and processing customs and other export documentation and activities. While they may not have their own global networks to match the market leaders, they will have trusted overseas agents with their own contacts and networks.

One of the big challenges for freight forwarders is managing cash flows, including the need to make advance freight payments when sending shipments abroad, while depending on overseas partners to handle shipments and documents on schedule. Under the most widely used form of trade FOB (Free on Board), the seller pays for the transport and loading costs to the port of shipment. The risk for the exporting firm is not getting paid by its overseas counterparts – for example it pays the airfreight costs to secure the business but then does not get paid after the shipment has been completed.

Membership networks provide SME freight forwarders with global coverage

Numerous membership networks exist to provide SME freight forwarders with a platform through which they can evaluate, select and appoint business partners to develop the international capabilities to serve their customers, whilst benefiting from financial protection packages offered by the network.

One such example is Combined Logistics Networks (CLN) – a global network of proactive and reliable independent freight forwarder members covering almost 400 locations around the world.

To protect and enhance its integrity and reputation, CLN maintains the quality of its membership by undertaking due diligence on all prospective members.

The screening process primarily covers the applicant's financial standing, length in operation, reputation in market and sales strength.

Once accepted, members are entitled to the full package of membership benefits – see table below – whilst agreeing to conform to the CLN code of ethics and member guidelines. CLN also provides a standard network agency agreement template, which specifies expectations for communications and payment terms.

One of the major benefits is the CLN Safe Programme which provides a payment safety net for members. The programme pools a member's fund on an annual basis and provides payment security for members in line with tenure. CLN keeps its members informed with a regular security agency list, featuring colour coding to show which members are reliable and prompt payers and highlight those that have a payment issue pending. When unresolved payments arise, CLN management purchases the bad debt from its member and then pursues collection from the defaulting party.

CLN membership also provides forwarders with a cost-effective platform to develop their network of international business partners through CLN's regular conferences featuring business matching programmes. These international gatherings enable members to meet face to face, develop relationships and explore business opportunities, thus building networks of business partners around the world.

FIGURE 8.2 CLN network membership benefits

	CLN membership benefits
1	Only work with trusted and screened members
2	Immediate global network coverage
3	Meet partners face to face
4	Payment security within the network
5	Additional profit share – CLN cargo miles programme
6	Etihad cargo incentives programme
7	Avoid bank fees amongst CLN members
8	Global branding
9	Global partnership with WiseTech Global
10	CLN members exclusive information environment

Conclusion

Freight forwarding networks enable SME forwarders to provide an international freight forwarding solution to serve their clients' global supply chain ecosystems, by establishing business partnerships with fellow members around the world. Membership criteria and screening standards operated by the network provide the peace of mind for the members who will enjoy a range of privileges and benefits, depending on the specific network.

Human capital – the talent pool

09

Human capital – the fuel that drives supply chain ecosystems

Few if any other industry sectors are still so utterly dependent on people to design, operate and manage its systems and equipment as the supply chain. This quality however plays both ways. It is a powerfully effective industry for providing large-scale employment at all levels, from unskilled and semi-skilled roles up to experienced senior level management, ideal for developing economies. On the other hand finding, recruiting, retaining and organizing a large and disparate workforce from varying backgrounds and hugely different levels of education can provide a constant challenge. Levels of knowledge, skills, experience, expertise, attitude and motivation will vary and need to be understood and where necessary enhanced to complement what may represent huge capital investments by companies or even countries.

Add into the pot that modern supply chain ecosystems are or should be highly evolved service organizations functioning 24 hours a day, every day of the week all year round; managing such a vast and varied pool of human capital becomes even more of a challenge.

This could be considered the most important topic in the entire book, as every other aspect of operating a productive supply chain – organization, equipment and systems, IT, finance, risk management, marketing and sales, operations, administration and legal – are all utterly dependent on how well staff carry out their tasks.

While many of the issues are universal, the priorities and industry needs vary considerably across the globe, from the newly emerging economies with large pools of labour but poor levels of literacy to developed states where there is severe employment competition and high salaries on offer from other sectors.

Throughout the world, economic growth drives increases in freight and supply chain demand across all modes and geographies. Globalization had driven companies to continually expand their customer base into new markets around the world, whilst also seeking to extend their supply networks across continents in pursuit of lower cost production bases.

This in turn drives increasing volumes of freight with resulting demand for logistics and transportation services and capacity. However, the ongoing trends of location changes for both production and consumption activities result in uneven geographical distribution of the need for freight capacity, changing patterns of trade flows and associated logistics services.

Asia has for many years been the workshop of the world, deploying plentiful low-cost labour to manufacture goods for export to consumers in the West. In recent years, expanding economic prosperity, in large part fuelled by the success of the manufacturing sectors, is leading to the rise of increasingly prosperous consumers. It is estimated by OECD that by 2030 Asia will account for 66 per cent of the world's middle class, up from 28 per cent in 2009.

Thus we are seeing rapid expansion in markets throughout Asia and these continuing growth patterns are presenting multiple challenges in the area of human capital, where the supply cannot meet the demand, resulting in the battle for talent in Asia. Similarly, emerging and developing economies around the world are experiencing significant increases in consumption, in particular Brazil, Russia, India, China, Vietnam, Indonesia and others, which is fuelling accelerated growth in retail and fast-moving consumer goods (FMCG) sectors, which is driving more demand for experienced logistics practitioners.

In building a modern supply chain ecosystem the management team must ensure that the business has the appropriate levels of skills in place, with an active programme to both retain and motivate staff, to provide additional training as required and develop a cohesive, positive and customer-focused attitude throughout the business. In the Gartner 2011 survey (Millar, 2011), CEOs identified attracting skilled workers/talent as their number two priority after retaining existing customers.

Talent shortages in emerging markets

Supply chain ecosystems in emerging markets present a variety of challenges, with the top three consistently being infrastructure limitations, bureaucratic regulatory procedures and shortage of skilled experienced logistics professionals.

One of the key findings of the 2011 SCM World report (2011) was that 'talent acquisition and leadership development' represents a significant challenge in supply chain management, with 35 per cent of respondents listing it as one of their top challenges and a further 56 per cent agreeing that it is an important challenge.

The skills shortage is a significant logistics challenge common to the fast-growing consumer economies in the frontier markets of China, India, Indonesia and Vietnam – and indeed throughout all emerging markets. At the same time as their economies are rapidly expanding, logistics activity increases, which in turn drives demand for trained, skilled and experienced professionals.

In addition, as their logistics sectors have improved significantly over the last five years and continue to do so, we can expect to see a gradual reduction in the logistics costs as percentage of GDP, in line with maturing logistics sectors in developing and emerging markets. We will also see an increase in the level of outsourcing, which is good news for the 3PL logistics service providers.

In China the difficulty of recruiting skilled professionals is made more difficult because of the size of the country and also due to China's expanding role in global supply chains, leading to increasing demand for skilled logisticians. At the same time, the sheer size of the population gives it a larger pool of experienced workers than in other countries.

India's leadership role in global commerce has developed in areas such as telecommunications and business process outsourcing. The impact for supply chain management is a smaller pool of experienced talent to fill the expanding demand in the logistics sector. As India plans to modernize many sectors, in particular the retail trade, there will be further increasing demand for experienced logisticians.

In Vietnam, the majority of the population are young, well educated, with English widely spoken. Thus there is a large pool of potential workers for the logistics sector. However, as in many other countries, there are not enough young people choosing the logistics sector as their career path. Therefore in Vietnam, we are also seeing skills shortages.

Human resource challenges and opportunities in developed economies

Most developed economies have mature and sophisticated business structures, a generally well-educated and trained workforce and well-established supply chain structures.

In the UK, possibly like many more mature and other similar economies, one of the most pressing challenges is to replace an ageing workforce without losing the skills, expertise and experience that thousands of long-serving employees have acquired. In the UK over half the employees in the industry were over 45 years old, while a Logistics Management (2014) report for the US reported over two-thirds of workers were over this age. In these societies there is less appeal or need to work what are often anti-social hours and at tasks that, with the best will in the world, may seem somewhat routine.

One advantage the UK does enjoy is that of immigration – from a large and accessible hinterland, mainly of younger people from eastern European states, which is providing a fresh influx of skilled and enthusiastic staff ready to work in all sectors of the logistics industry. However, in other developed countries such as Japan, an ageing population and reducing workforce could undermine long-term economic growth.

The UK Skills for Logistics survey for 2013 found that of all recruiters who had experienced difficulties 47 per cent struggled to find applicants with the right skills with 20 per cent lacking in relevant qualifications. As a result they concluded in the case of 90 per cent of responding companies that this placed an additional burden on existing staff and in around half the cases, increased operating costs and adversely affected customer service.

In an effort to counter these problems some 75 per cent of companies have offered and provided funding for training, with around a quarter reporting improved productivity and efficiency, but this did little to ease the workload or improve staff retention.

Finding and retaining the best staff

Logistics Executive's employment market survey reports provide a detailed picture by region of the status of the industry, its growth, employment and challenges. The 2013–14 survey confirms two factors that risk holding back the market in Asia – namely being a relatively new discipline there are few seasoned professionals to call on, and that not enough young people see the supply chain industry as an attractive career.

Entry-level talent acquisition may help to overcome this obstacle and enable companies to develop local leaders. Kim Winter, CEO of the Logistics Executive Group, states that: 'In developing markets such as the Asia region, management teams were previously dominated by expatriate leadership. However, over the past 3 years, companies have by necessity embarked on the road to localization of management talent, deploying leadership development strategies for high potential locals, thus gradually reducing the dependency on expats.'

While 73 per cent of respondents were currently hiring full-time they still have a constant requirement for the right qualified talent and skills to develop supply chain and logistics solutions their clients are looking for, including customer-facing roles. The challenges posed by this survey will however be equally or even more familiar to organizations in the more advanced economies who need to compete against what may be seen as more attractive and stimulating careers elsewhere. In response to the question 'Which functions have you found it most difficult to recruit for?' the survey results showed the following as the top five categories:

1 Logistics and transport.

2 Supply chain.

3 Distribution and warehousing.

4 Sales and business development.

5 Customer service.

The shortage of skills challenge is reflected in feedback from senior executives who reported their top business challenges for the year ahead as shown in Figure 9.1.

FIGURE 9.1 Senior executive top business challenges in the year ahead

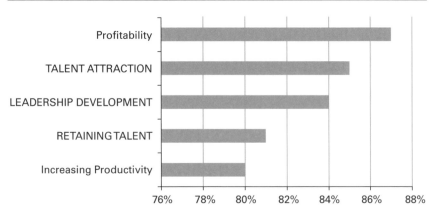

SOURCE Logistics Executive Employment Survey, 2013–14

This on-going skills shortage is affecting companies' business growth abilities for over 65 per cent of businesses, whilst almost 7 per cent say that the skills shortage is having a 'significant or critical impact' on their business.

How to attract and retain talent

Human capital assets are increasingly a major source of competitive advantage and are key drivers of profitability for the organization.

This is particularly true in service-oriented sectors such as logistics and transportation, where, despite large investments in information technology and physical assets, it is ultimately the employees' actions that empower the effective and efficient execution of the company's or client's supply chain ecosystem.

The current imbalance in the talent market reflects inadequate supply to meet the increasing demand – and this is increasing business costs, both directly on the payroll and indirectly through higher turnover and additional recruitment.

In such fast-changing and competitive markets, logistics companies in particular need to ensure that they set out their organization profile from a marketing perspective in order to attract and retain the talent needed to cope with demand. Long before the interview, potential employees may have acquired some pre-conceived awareness of the company in question which may heavily influence their career choices.

With fierce competition to attract the best talent, it is essential for organizations to adopt a public relations approach to human resources activities. Within their respective industry sectors, individual businesses need to promote their company image and build their brand as an 'employer', over and above their market positioning as a supplier. In the current environment companies are not only competing for customers, they are also competing for employees.

Particularly important for companies that do not have global brands or strong industry positions is the need to increase their presence and profile on the radar of potential future employees, through various market oriented activities.

Tactics include active and public participation in community activities, engagement with the relevant industry associations and regular exposure in the trade publications, which will all help towards positioning your company as an *employer of choice*.

In addition, with the increasing awareness and concern throughout society about environmental issues, a company having, but not articulating, clear policies and strategies on corporate social responsibility (CSR) is escalating in importance as one of the factors for consideration by potential employees.

Developing linkages with the relevant education sectors and institutions will assist in providing options for entry-level talent acquisition.

This represents a substantial opportunity for employers to attract local talent into their organization at grassroots level, deploy graduates through job rotation and management development programs, thus generating a home-grown pool of talent with high levels of commitment and loyalty to the employer.

Don't poach – attract

All too often, it seems that the majority of organizations do not have enough patience, management bandwidth or the investment perspective to adopt this approach. They may continue to poach talent from their competitors, thus exacerbating the challenges and increasing the costs for everyone.

In a recent Keystone Group survey of C-level (high ranking) executives, more than half of respondents describe 'experience within the industry' as the best source of talent (Keystone Group, 2014). This means that organizations prefer to improve their human capital by recruiting experienced people away from their competitors.

However, it's not just about money. As John Nolan, senior vice president of HR for Unilever in Asia commented: 'You have to offer employees a reason to want to work for you. Employees need to feel they are not only pursuing a career, but that they have a chance at impacting the world and the community.'

In addition to the dollars and cents of the salary and benefits package, companies that offer ongoing training and development programmes leading to varied career opportunities are likely to be successful in attracting good quality talent.

Successful selection supports retention

Careful and thorough recruitment and selection processes will increase the likelihood of successful employment and increase retention. Selecting the right candidate for the right role requires experience and expertise, combined with clear communications. One of the most common reasons for managers leaving within one year is when the job role fails to meet their expectations. Candidates may also use the job as a hopping platform to better offers. Thorough discovery during the recruitment process, engaging expert external resources as required, will play a large role in mitigating these risks.

Retention

Having successfully attracted the right talent and selected them to join your organization, the challenge then becomes how to retain them for as long as possible and to see your organization as one capable of offering a worthwhile career. Active retention should form a key component of your company's overall talent management strategy starting right from day one.

Successful on-boarding is an essential start to inducting new hires, including rapidly integrating new staff into the organizational culture and the company's day-to-day business. Structured induction programs providing broad exposure throughout the organization and deep immersion into the new employee's specific functional areas, together with developing a crystal-clear understanding of roles, responsibilities, deliverables and measurements, are all key elements of best-in-class on-boarding programmes.

The first few months of the new recruit's experience within your organization may have a significant impact on their longevity in your company. Hence the early days of the new employee's tenure, whilst they are getting up to speed, not necessarily delivering results during something of an investment phase, will play a major role in increasing employee retention rates.

Back-to-basics best-in-class business practices for supervision and management can make a huge impact. Some of the key drivers of employee satisfaction, which in turn has a major influence on retention, are enshrined in basic management principles.

Generally speaking, satisfied employees:

- clearly understand the requirements and expectations from them;
- feel they have the tools, time and training to do their job properly;
- see opportunities within the company to learn and grow;
- feel rewarded, recognized and appreciated.

Hence, working on employee satisfaction is a key part of employee retention. Other strategies to increase employee retention include nurturing a work environment where employees feel a sense of belonging to their team, their department and the company, both inside and outside of work hours.

A Vietnamese consumer products company improved staff loyalty and retention through three specific strategies:

- A job rotation programme allowed employees to progress horizontally across different departments at the same pay scale, providing opportunities to broaden their experience and learn new skills.

- They provided individual and team performance-related cash bonuses for specific results with opportunities to increase take home pay, all funded by results above and beyond budgeted levels.

- Company sponsorship of sports activities and company sports teams helped engender company belonging, loyalty and community spirit, with opportunities for workers to enjoy team and social activities together outside work hours.

The gender gap and opportunity

The role of women has changed and continues to do so. In many professions such as medicine and law they now outnumber men in many countries and having a job or career is now the norm in most countries.

This huge pool of potential talent is one that the logistics industry cannot ignore. Although logistics has traditionally been male-dominated, women are now coming up the ranks in ever-increasing numbers, and in all areas. With modern technology designed to de-muscle operations there are very few roles that women cannot be expected to fulfil.

In businesses worldwide women occupy senior board positions including CEOs and other executive roles. One high profile example in the UK is Hilary Devey, Founder, CEO and Chairman of Pall-Ex, which is the UK's leading palletized freight distribution network. Hilary is recognized as an inspirational role model for both male and female entrepreneurs. Having started from nothing, she now leads a network which boasts a combined turnover approaching $150 million and serves numerous blue chip customers.

Encouraging female employment provides social benefits too by increasing the potential household income and generating the holy grail of any developing economy, more disposable income.

In the UK, Women in Logistics was established in 2008 as a non-profit organization to support the careers of women in the industry. It currently has over 2,000 members with the aims of increasing the number of women in the sector, improving life for those women already working in logistics, addressing the gender imbalance issue and providing networking, support, mentoring and encouragement for members.

In the US, the Women in Logistics organization provides support and guidance for those in the industry and encourages women to improve their careers by using for example their LinkedIn group.

Why staff move on

In such a dynamic and fast-changing world with new industry opportunities competing with the logistics sector for staff, it is ever-more important to understand what makes people leave. Figure 9.2 shows that there are a number of incentives, with money and career needs being the most powerful incentives.

This makes it all the more important to select the right staff for the right reasons, and to provide a career path that will both satisfy their aspirations and enable them to achieve a commensurate and competitive income.

FIGURE 9.2 As an employer, what are the major factors contributing to people leaving your organization?

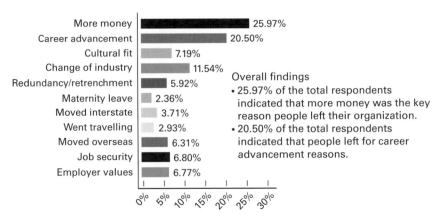

Overall findings
- 25.97% of the total respondents indicated that more money was the key reason people left their organization.
- 20.50% of the total respondents indicated that people left for career advancement reasons.

SOURCE 2012–13 Employment Market Survey by Logistics Executive Group

Make training and development pay at all levels

Much has been written recently about the need for improving the education and training of the logistics workforce. As important as this is, at least equal emphasis must be given to improving the quality of management if business is to succeed in achieving greater employee commitment and thereby its profitability.

The benefits of having the best-trained workers using the most advanced technology can be nullified by poor people management practices used by managers. In addition management skills need to be refreshed to meet changes in today's business conditions.

Logistics Executive Group's 2014 Employment Market report identified that companies fall short of satisfying the training and development needs of employees with just 32 per cent stating their organization offers on-site workshops and even fewer, 14 per cent, offering professional training. These figures contrast starkly with the 82 per cent who say they would be interested in such a development opportunity if it were offered. Clearly more needs to be done in the area of management training if we are to adequately equip our frontline supervisors with the right management tools and skills to lead in this critical area of a service-focused industry.

A best-in-class example of management development programmes is offered by 3PL company Fast Logistics in the Philippines. Their strategic direction includes investment in the leadership team through an Executive MBA programme which has proven to increase retention amongst their management team. Through working with the local university – one of the top academic institutions in the country – Fast Logistics have also helped to develop an increased focus on supply chain management centric topics in the curriculum.

President and COO Enrique 'Ike' C Castillo places great importance on how his people should seamlessly execute the delivery of services to the very reason of the company's existence – their customers. Ike, a Former President of SCMP – the Supply Chain Management Association of the Philippines – firmly believes that training and developing staff is essential in ensuring they develop the appropriate competencies that are core in making this service promise a reality.

He shares what he always tells his team: 'Fast Logistics is not in the business of logistics, looking for customers. We are in the business of customers needing value-adding Logistics solutions – and of equal significance, in the business of our people delivering them.'

There are two simple keys to success in today's environment of increasing competition and rapid change – an absolute passion for, and dedication to, excellence in customer service and the effective and enlightened management of our workforce. The latter encourages commitment, which in turn leads to achieving the desired standards in customer service.

Without employee commitment, there can be no improvement in any area of business activity. In the absence of good management, employees will simply treat their work, as a nine-to-five routine without any desire to accomplish any more than is necessary to remain employed. It does not take many uncommitted employees to prevent a business from prospering and thereby ceding a big advantage to its competitors.

To succeed in the face of increasing competition, a business needs improved productivity at all levels. This requires the enthusiastic commitment of all employees, which can only be achieved through better management practices. To be effective, the skills of good people management must be installed in an organization so they become part of its culture. In this way there will be consistency from the top down to the most junior employee. And it starts with establishing a commitment to ourselves.

The changing labour market

Globally the labour market is undergoing unprecedented, structural changes. These changes are fundamentally changing the way we work.

The new generation of flexible entrepreneurs is arriving. The growing number of skilled workers choosing self-employment and the relentless demand for their skills has given rise to the notion of the blended workforce – contractors, freelancers and consultants working alongside the permanent workforce in critical roles, and all evidence suggests it is here to stay.

Increasingly, organizations are learning how to manage diverse workforces, blended with employees who are permanent, semi-permanent, virtual and transient. Adding to this a novel situation whereby for the first time in history there are now four generations in the workplace, each with slight differing needs and desires.

If adapting to the shifting construction of our workforces wasn't enough, organizations now need to manage a generation gap of up to 50 years between the oldest and youngest workers. This mixed workforce means there is no room for a one-size-fits-all approach. Leaders and HR managers will need to create new solutions to workforce planning and talent management to overcome the cultural and practical barriers. There are a number of steps organizations can take to benefit from the skills and valuable flexibility this new breed of workforce can provide.

Take stock and assess the impact

Find out how many freelancers and independent contractors are already working for you today and where these employees sit in the organization. This will give you a good idea of how blended your workforce is. It may be more diverse than you think. Some questions you could ask include:

1 What impact does a contingent workforce have on your employee culture? What roles and functions do they perform today?

2 What additional roles and functions could a contingent workforce undertake in the future?

3 How can independent contractors and freelancers contribute positively to your culture?

For example, there could be a great opportunity for knowledge-sharing between contractors and permanent employees, while contractors may be more motivated to support organizational goals if they are included in team meetings and events.

Review and adapt

To seek differentiation and develop competitive advantage, companies can adopt a range of strategies and tactics:

- Inclusive. Review policies and procedures to ensure they are inclusive and relevant for contingent or diverse workers. Are we using the contingent workforce's unique position to assist in better understanding our organization? This valuable source of information, if we regularly gather feedback can guide us on what works and what needs to be improved. The key then is to channel this information back into the business and to update policies or create new ones where necessary.

- Work-life balance. The boundary between work and home life is disappearing as companies assume greater responsibility for the social welfare of their employees. Used to our advantage this can energize a workforce and create opportunities for talent which may not be able to commit to a work from office environment (such as professional mothers looking to return to work).

- Diversity. Make workforce diversity a meaningful, measurable goal in staffing your organization. It will be essential for attracting and retaining enough skilled employees in the decade ahead and to ensure you stay ahead in talent competition stakes.

Preparing for the millennial generation

The millennial generation (those born between 1978 and 2000) are now in employment in vast numbers. Their entry will reshape the world of work for years to come. Attracting the best of these millennial workers is critical to the future of your business. Their career aspirations, attitudes about work and knowledge of new technologies will define the culture of the 21st-century workplace.

Millennials matter because they are not only different from those that have gone before, they are also more numerous than any generation since the soon-to-retire Baby Boomer generation – millennials already form 25 per cent of the workforce in the US and account for over half of the population in India. By 2020, millennials will form 50 per cent of the global workforce.

However, although they will soon outnumber their Generation X predecessors, they remain in short supply, particularly in parts of the world where birth rates have been lower. They will also be more valuable – this generation will work to support a significantly larger older generation as life expectancy increases. CEOs tell us that attracting and keeping younger workers is one of their biggest talent challenges.

Summary

All of these facts lead us back to where we started. Having a tailored approach to workforce planning that considers the needs and motivations of employees at different stages of life and career development will ensure companies stay competitive and future-ready. It's an issue that organizations need to address quickly and immediately.

Paradoxically at a time when the world's population and work-force is continually increasing, the logistics sector, one of the biggest employment industries using a diverse range of skills and abilities, is at risk from lack of human capital. Without warehouse staff, drivers, crane operators, IT specialists, engineers and the like, if the move-ment of goods, the lifeblood of the modern global economy, stutters, the effect on every single country could be alarming. Every stake-holder in the supply chain infrastructure, whether private or public, must play its role in ensuring the industry is fully staffed with the skills that the mid-21st century industry needs.

CASE STUDY   Gender diversity in supply chain and logistics

'Gender diversity is well recognized as one of the great areas of opportunity for organizations across the supply chain. The fact that women are under-represented in our industry is unacceptable and ensuring a balance in all forms of diversity, cultural, skills/experience and gender is essential for a healthy business environment. It's been my pleasure to work with Mark worldwide over the last decade and in particular to support his work promoting the need for greater participation, engagement and recognition of women in the workplace globally.' Kimble Winter, Global CEO, Logistics Executive Group

Women in logistics and transport

With the vision to be 'the most sought after group for advocacy, professionalism and empowerment of women in supply chain, logistics and transport' the WiLAT organization (Women in Logistics and Transport) is the first and largest female professional body in the global logistics and transport sector.

Initially convened in Lagos, Nigeria in June 2012, Women in Logistics and Transport (WiLAT) was founded by a group of female members of the Chartered Institute of Logistics and Transport.

The Chartered Institute of Logistics and Transport (CILT) is the leading professional body associated with logistics and transport. With over 33,000 members working in over 100 countries worldwide, CILT holds unparalleled professional international recognition. Established in 1919 and receiving its Royal Charter in 1926, the principal objective of the Institute is 'to promote and advance the art and science of logistics and transport' which CILT achieves through both its membership and its educational qualifications. The Institute encourages women working within the world of supply chain, logistics and transport.

The mission of WiLAT is to promote the status of women in logistics and transport, to bring together those who support talent and career development of women and to provide a support network and mentoring opportunities for women in the sector.

By June 2014 WiLAT had over 1,600 members in 14 countries and continues to grow, with WiLAT Founder and Global Convenor, Aisha Ali Ibrahim, commenting: 'We are enjoying great success in cultivating a spirit of togetherness to survive in a male-dominated industry.'

Conclusion

As the leading industry organization furthering the cause of gender diversity, WiLAT helps individuals with career development and:

- serves as a pool for competent women in the industry that can key into government gender policies in the industry;

- sources, grooms and sustains women in the male-dominated industry;

- serves as an anchor for the women, through work life and during retirement;

- gives room for flexibility in career growth and development through the CILT;

- offers community services amongst other programmes for women and children concerning transportation;

- enables a holistic approach to solving challenges in the industry, as networking enables knowledge of the individual challenges of the different modes and expectation from others;

- serves as a professional female voice for the industry.

'The nature of the industry requires dealing with people from all walks of life. It is not perceived as an elegant industry and hence has been dominated in the past by males. However, the industry has evolved with globalization and technology advancements. 4A executives – Adaptive, Agile, Aligned, Architecting – are required to cope with today's challenges and these are the innateness of women to handle.' Vicky Koo, Convenor and Co-Founder, WiLAT Hong Kong.

Omni-channel supply chains

10

The brave new world of omni-channel supply chains

The digital revolution has enabled consumers all over the world, many of them 'digital natives', to shop via the internet from virtually anywhere, using an ever-expanding range of hardware devices and technology platforms to gain instantaneous access to unprecedented amounts of information.

Retailers therefore have to adapt accordingly and offer omni-channel solutions. 'Today's customers desire the option to start their shopping process in one channel and finish, fulfil or even return through another,' explained Bob Heaney, Research Director and Principal Analyst for the Retail and Consumer Markets division of Aberdeen Group.

The multiple different 'channels' that consumers may use for their shopping include desktop computer, mobile device, telephone, catalogue or physically in a store.

For taking delivery of their purchase, omni-channel supply chains offer consumers a smorgasbord of channels to choose from – over and above taking the product with them from the store – including deliver to consumer – at home or at work or elsewhere, consumer collects from another location such as a different store, a warehouse or an intermediary location such as a convenience store.

Transcending purely information sharing through to transaction processing has enabled connected consumers to extend their browsing to become shopping – and thereby purchase goods online, electronically placing orders and processing payments across the internet, online and in real time; hence the explosion of e-commerce!

Omni-channel retail is all about providing a seamless shopping experience for the customer on the front end – irrespective of which channel is used for shopping and purchasing. When combined together with full integration across multiple channels on the back end – through the fulfilment, logistics, delivery and returns processes – this becomes the omni-channel supply chain.

The latest generation of powerful, connected and smart hand-held mobile devices is rapidly overtaking desktop and laptop computers as the digital platform of choice for 'netizens' to access the internet. Gone are the days when online buyers had to wait to get back to their computer at home or in the office to make a purchase, they now shop online whilst on the move. Mobile has become massive – consumers can buy just about anything at any time and from anywhere – today's digital consumers are always-on, globally-connected and mobile!

E-commerce has spawned new start-up business enterprises that have risen from nothing to billions of dollars in just a few years – across the USA, China and Europe – and has given a new lease of life to many established catalogue sales and mail-order companies and traditional high street retailers. It's difficult to imagine any other business, technology or social innovation that has wrought such a profound and widespread change in the lives of consumers across the globe in just a few years.

Right at the heart of this revolution is the omni-channel supply chain, featuring all the additional complexities of e-commerce logistics, including the challenges of last mile and returns management. New generation supply chains have had to rapidly evolve to serve and enable omni-channel retail – where the offline world of retail stores, known as 'bricks' – seamlessly merge with the world of online retail – increasingly called e-tail and known as 'clicks'.

The seamless integration featured in the omni-channel world is resulting in convergence of what previously were clearly segregated roles of the retailer, an e-commerce business and the logistics service providers.

In this chapter we look at the supply chain implications of the digital revolution fuelling this e-commerce frenzy and explore how companies are dealing with the distribution challenges and opportunities of servicing often fickle online consumers. We consider how today's omni-channel supply chains are reacting to each new development to ensure that every consumer receives exactly what they have ordered, in pristine condition and on time – and that suppliers can build successful, profitable businesses.

What drives the e-commerce revolution?

Consumers today – using hand-held mobile devices such as smart phones, iPhones and tablets, or even home and office devices such as laptops and PCs – can place an order online for delivery to their home, for just about anything they want, from anywhere in the world at any time of day or night.

People living in rural areas far away from cities, who rarely if ever are able to visit a supermarket or department store, now have access to the same global brands and retail outlets as the most savvy city dweller. Using their mobile or smart phone they have leapfrogged a chapter in the development of modern retail and consumerism – from comparative isolation to unprecedented market visibility and choice, bringing a whole new segment of consumers into the world's economy.

Across emerging markets, we have millions and millions of digital-native consumers that have never been to a supermarket or a department store, who – now equipped with smartphones and empowered by always-on and all-pervasive internet access – can shop online as if they were in Macy's in New York or Harrods in London!

How big is the e-commerce market?

The simple answer is it is huge and growing very fast. According to eMarketer (2014), the global B2C (Business to Consumer) e-commerce market grew 20 per cent year on year to exceed $1.5 trillion in 2014, with their geographic analysis showing Asia at 35 per cent share becoming the largest region for the first time, overtaking North America with 32 per cent, whilst Europe and other regions make up the remaining 33 per cent of just under $500 billion.

Mobile is growing exponentially, particularly in developed markets where almost three out of four internet users now access the web through a mobile device, whilst mobile penetration in emerging markets is reported to be already over 40 per cent.

On just one day – 11 November 2014 – the singles-day shopping festival in China, the largest online e-commerce platform Alibaba set a new world record with over $9 billion of sales for the day, far exceeding single-day online sales for Black Friday or Cyber Monday. Alibaba reported over 400 million unique visitors to its sites – more than a third of the adult population in China – whose transactions generated over 150 million parcels for shipping, with 43 per cent of orders being placed from mobile devices.

Forecasts and statistics for e-commerce come thick and fast and while not always in agreement, they all point to continued rapid growth. Although actual reported volumes vary by sources, it is generally accepted that the largest e-commerce markets rank as follows:

1 China

2 USA

3 UK

4 Japan

5 Germany

6 France

7 Australia

8 Canada

9 Russia

10 South Korea

Back in 2010, e-commerce sales in the USA were double those of China, but with the explosive growth amongst Chinese netizens, China overtook the USA in 2014 to become the world's largest e-commerce market. Beijing-based iResearch (2014) projected that online retail sales in China – already having reached over $1 billion dollars per day – would continue to show annual growth rates of 30 per cent plus.

Across Europe, Forrester Research (2015) forecast online retail sales to grow by 11 per cent a year through to 2017, with the fastest pace of growth, at 18 per cent per annum year, coming from southern European countries like Italy and Spain. For the USA, Forrester report that E-retailers' aggressive marketing, pricing and customer acquisition tactics will contribute to continuing online retail growth in the coming years. They predict compound annual growth of 9.5 per cent through to 2018, when online sales will account for 11 per cent of total retail sales.

What do people buy online?

According to the website Statistic Brain, in the USA, the most popular products purchased by e-commerce are:

1 Women's apparel.
2 Books.
3 Computer hardware and software.
4 Apparel.
5 Toys and video games.
6 Videos and DVDs.
7 Health and beauty goods.
8 Consumer electronics.
9 Music.
10 Jewellery.

Why do people buy online?

The same website also listed the top reasons why US consumers purchase online, with 87 per cent of online users having made at least one online purchase, and 59 per cent of them having made multiple purchases (Table 10.1).

TABLE 10.1 Top consumer reasons for shopping online

Top consumer reasons for shopping online	Percentage of respondents citing reason
1. Time saving	73
2. More variety	67
3. Easy to compare prices	59
4. No crowd	58
5. Lower prices	55
6. Spend less on fuel	40
7. Less taxes	30
8. Other	3

SOURCE Ecommerce and Online Sales Statistics, 2014 Statistic Brain Research Institute, publishing as Statistic Brain, October 9 2014

We can see that in developed markets like the USA, the primary reasons for purchasing online relate to saving time, saving money and – probably most important of all – convenience.

In the USA, there is not much you can buy online if anything that you could not drive to the mall and buy in person – hence one of the primary appeals of e-commerce is convenience. But what about the millions of consumers who live in societies where there are no malls and the majority of people don't have a car? In these scenarios, e-commerce opens up completely new opportunities – hitherto unseen new products, new brands, enormous selection, massive choice, all visible and available and delivered to your home, for free – and hence the accelerated growth of e-commerce in emerging markets.

How digital technology empowers consumers

Digital technology has delivered many advantages that help consumers make better informed and more astute purchases. Wherever you may be, with mobile device and internet connection it is easy and fast to make online comparisons about price, performance and specification; consumers can see special offers from retailers keen to build business or just to clear old stock; customer reviews, social media and blogs provide comments and recommendations on what to buy and what to avoid, and placing orders is generally easy to do – any time of the day or night.

Traditionally shoppers expect to get informed advice from the sales assistants in the store. Today's consumer is often likely to have used the internet to carry out research and may well be better informed than the shop's employees. We are seeing a trend towards showrooming, where consumers visit the high street store or shopping mall in order to get some hands-on experience with product samples and talk to product experts, before actually buying online, maybe from within the showroom or from outside or back home. The term 'webrooming' refers to the opposite, where consumers conduct extensive research online and then visit the store to make their purchase.

Old and the new – from traditional retailers to new technology-enabled entrants

The internet and the web have delivered an additional benefit to the world of business by having minimal barriers to access, in that pretty much just about anyone can join in.

Millions of businesses from well-established international companies to the latest pure play internet retailers who operate 100 per cent online, have benefited from e-commerce business boosting revenues, stimulating trade and in some cases enabling whole new consumer sectors.

The rise of online shopping pioneer Amazon has been well-documented and with sales of over $75 billion the company continues to lead the field by a sizeable margin. However the sheer number of other e-commerce companies in the US, Europe and China are powering continued growth as new and innovative business model variants are launched to take a share of the market. E-commerce companies such as Amazon, eBay, Alibaba and many others took advantage of opportunities to build greenfield operations as purely online businesses, unencumbered by traditional retail outlets and distribution models. Their custom-built business models were game-changers that enabled them to go head-to-head with traditional retailers and rapidly build huge global enterprises.

However, in this omni-channel world, should these new entrants be considered as e-commerce companies or retailers? Increasingly becoming tagged as e-tailers, they are definitely competing with traditional high street, bricks and mortar retail – to the extent that many retailers have now established e-commerce businesses.

This convergence is extended even further with many of the e-commerce companies establishing their own fulfilment operations and delivery mechanisms – services traditionally outsourced to the logistics service providers. Operational supply chain activities such as warehousing, storage, inventory management, picking, packing, despatching, transportation, deliveries and collections are surely the domain of the third-party logistics companies? Not necessarily so in today's omni-channel world.

Amazon's counterpart in China – Alibaba – was first set up in 1999 as a business-to-business portal linking Chinese manufacturers with overseas buyers. Since then it has expanded into the consumer market, offering a full range of products and services for online purchases through their C2C platform Taobao, similar to eBay.com and their B2C channel TMall. Alibaba group's websites account for well over half of the online orders and sales within the total China e-commerce market. Having gone public in late 2014, in what has been described as the biggest IPO ever, Alibaba is now the Chinese e-commerce giant that makes headlines around the world. Offering China's largest e-commerce shopping websites, customers routinely shop online at Alibaba for shoes, clothes and other household necessities. But it's far more than that. There is a huge, diverse and sometimes exotic range of products for sale, including cow brains, live leeches, underwater restaurant construction materials and even robotic dinosaurs – all just a click away! China's insatiable enthusiasm for online shopping reflects the power and extent of the mobile phone penetration and massive internet population combined with relatively under-developed retail sectors.

In the developed markets, the more far-sighted of the established retail giants saw the potential threat from e-commerce and online businesses and companies such as Walmart, Tesco, Best Buy, JC Penney,

Argos and numerous others have developed online e-commerce websites to work alongside their traditional bricks and mortar models, thereby offering their customers the choice of purchasing online as well as offline – combining bricks and clicks into omni-channel.

One of the biggest challenges in discussing omni-channel and e-commerce is that both the volume and technologies driving the growth of this revolution are changing so quickly. Indeed it's almost impossible to make any comment about e-commerce without the risk of it becoming rapidly out of date. Nevertheless, it is such an integral and critical part of today's global supply chain ecosystems that all business managers need to be aware of this fundamental change and how it affects their companies and their supply chains.

Supply chain impact of omni-channel?

Providing a holistic, cohesive and seamless approach to the customer experience, omni-channel brings together the entire spectrum of consumer shopping channels available, including computers, laptops, mobile internet devices, smart phones, tablets, TV, direct mail, catalogues and bricks-and-mortar retail outlets. In turn the omni-channel model impacts every aspect of the supply chain ecosystem – products, inventory, warehouses, fulfilment, picking, packing, shipping, transport, distribution and the all-important information flows.

Across the supply chain ecosystem the most critical areas of impact from omni-channel retail and e-commerce are warehouse operations, last-mile delivery, product returns, customers becoming sellers as well as buyers and cross-border transactions.

Warehousing operations

Processing e-commerce order transactions involves picking and packing of orders within a warehouse-type operation, operated either by the retailer or outsourced to a logistics service provider. Typically referred to as a fulfilment centre (FC), this differs from a traditional retail distribution centre (DC) by differences in the nature of the orders and the activities undertaken; system and process considerations become quite complex, with some of the primary considerations summarized as follows:

Inventory visibility and order management – e-commerce brings new challenges to traditional order management systems with more inventory channels and demand patterns to manage and control as part of a holistic process. A robust order management system should balance factors such as order fill rate, service levels, delivery times and freight costs to make decisions about how to allocate inventory and serve the customer.

Is your warehouse management system (WMS) able to cope with the new environment? Companies often introduce new technologies to handle retail and e-commerce. However, if you want to put in place a cross-channel batch pick and sort system for retail, can the WMS and/ or ERP system recognize zones and break up orders appropriately? Can the same systems interface with pick-to-light and pick-to-voice solutions? If the WMS can't handle the requirements companies may be forced to consider adding another layer such as warehouse control or order management software.

Pick and waving logic – having multiple channels means finding the right balance when it comes to picking and waving logic. A retail-only DC may pick by category so that store shipments arrive for efficient re-stocking on a store friendly manner; while an e-commerce DC may be organized around SKU velocity to improve efficiency and speed of order processing. You may have developed efficient processes for picking cartons and pallets, but how will you pick one or two lines for an e-commerce order?

From the physical infrastructure perspective, retailers have to consider options for the operational facilities where they will inventory the products and process the orders. Whether they are purchased in-store or online, the actual products themselves are invariably the same, and so traditional retailers are therefore exploring the various options available for holding inventory from which to pick e-commerce orders:

- Fulfilment centre – establishes warehouse infrastructure dedicated to, and designed for, e-commerce orders; can organize processes and systems specifically for the e-commerce business to maximize operational efficiencies; default model for the internet only businesses.

- Distribution centre – picks e-commerce orders from the existing inventory within the existing distribution centre operations; facilitates use of common inventory, but challenging to process single unit orders in operational environment designed for bulk handling and distribution of pallets loaded with full cartons often despatched as full truckloads to a single destination.

- Combination DC/FC – re-configures and re-designs warehouse facilities and operations to hold common product inventory, whilst operational functionality is segregated for the two different channels of offline and online business; results in inventory optimization and shared allocation of resources.

- Pick from store – some retailers are experimenting with fulfilling e-commerce orders from the inventory in their retail stores, providing opportunity to reduce delivery costs by routing the order to the store closest to the customer's specified delivery location; minimizes transportation costs; better enables click-and-collect, where the online customer collects their order from the store.

Last-mile delivery

The last mile refers to the last leg of the supply chain, whereby the goods are finally delivered to the consumer. In the omni-channel supply chain, e-commerce transactions result in very large volumes of very small orders – small physically in size and in the number of units or pieces – that have to be delivered direct to consumers, typically at their residential address.

One of the key convenience features of online shopping – home delivery, frequently free-of-charge – actually results in the last mile often being the least efficient link in the supply chain, representing over one third of the total cost of the delivery. Last-mile delivery is fraught with challenges, including congestion in urban areas and distance in rural areas; invalid or non-unique domestic address locations; consumer not at home and therefore unable to take delivery; buyer remorse – consumer at home but refuses to take delivery; difficulties in accessing the location, eg lifts not working or no parking area for delivery vehicles.

Economies of scale, finely tuned operational efficiencies and advanced systems and technology– and profitability – are the keys to success in last mile delivery, as demonstrated by the leading global integrators (UPS, FedEx, DHL and TNT) for whom this is the daily bread and butter, but who are unlikely to be the cheapest solution in the e-commerce environment of 'free shipping'.

Ironically, in many markets home delivery is providing a new lease of life for post office organizations, whose traditional business models based on physical paper mail had become disintermediated by the widespread adoption of digital documents delivered via the internet, web and email. In many cases, well established post office networks of physical premises coupled with door-to-door delivery capabilities are being leveraged for efficient and effective last-mile business models serving omni-channel supply chain ecosystems.

Amongst all the challenges of last-mile delivery, an important factor to remember is that in the e-commerce world, the home delivery is most likely the only person-to-person interaction in the transaction between the supplier and the customer. There are therefore several additional considerations over and above pure operational efficiencies and economics – for example a myriad of customer service considerations, plus the reputation of the brand and the company. In reality, the person undertaking the final delivery of the goods to the consumer on their doorstep is the in-person representative of not just the delivery company they work for, but in effect is representing all the companies involved in the e-commerce supply chain ecosystem.

The click-and-collect model avoids many of the last-mile delivery problems – having ordered online, the consumer collects their product from the store themselves. This has implications for store layout, but is considered to provide incremental revenue opportunity in that many customers, whilst collecting their orders, will also go into the store to make additional purchases.

Extending the click-and-collect model beyond the store, omni-channel supply chain options now involve the seller delivering multiple orders to a single intermediary location, which acts as a collection point from where the customer collects their orders – examples include post offices (limited opening hours), networks of convenience stores such as 7-Eleven (limited storage space), and other easily accessible, open long hours, multiple outlet networks such as petrol stations. Of course this model works equally well for the pure play online retailers who do not have any physical retail footprint – e-commerce customers can collect their orders from hundreds of designated pick-up points.

This integrated intermediary model is now being further extended to technology enabled but unattended locations using smart lockers or locker boxes. Major Chinese B2C e-commerce player JD.com introduced smart lockers into the Chinese mainland in 2012. Once the consumer has ordered and paid, they receive a text message with a unique collection code that allows them to collect their merchandise from a number of designated pick-up points. Amazon soon followed suit by introducing its own smart locker network in the US in 2013 – located in convenience stores and drug stores and subsequently launched in Beijing in the middle of 2014. UPS also has plans to launch its own smart locker service in the US market.

As a convenient self-collection option appreciated by consumers, smart lockers are becoming another configuration parameter within the omni-channel supply chain ecosystem, an attractive option that reduces the number of delivery personnel required, lowers distribution costs and is estimated to improve overall delivery efficiency by 50 per cent.

All of these 'customer collect' options overcome many of the challenges of last-mile delivery, not least the economics! Consider the efficiencies of the integrated intermediary model of delivering 100 different customer orders to one single location – whether it be a petrol station, seven-eleven or installation of smart lockers, versus delivering each and every single order individually to one hundred different consumer addresses – all within a few square miles.

Product returns

Almost every retailer offers return policies that allow consumers to return merchandise – often on the basis of no questions asked – either for exchange or refund, subject to certain conditions. Amongst the intoxication of the e-commerce frenzy, 'free returns' seems to have become the norm and has become massively prevalent in the apparel category, where online shoppers order multiple style-colour-size options which they can try on at their leisure in the home – and subsequently return the unwanted items.

This wonderful customer service promise has ramifications for the supply chain ecosystem that are substantial and expensive!

Consider the additional transportation time and logistics costs to collect the unwanted items and return them to depot – over and above what was a free delivery in the first place. Upon receipt at depot – using a separate process to receiving incoming deliveries of brand new products from suppliers – consider what then has to happen to the returned items of clothing or footwear, before they can be classed as being re-available as new stock for sale – inspection, cleaning, ironing, folding, steaming, wrapping, packing and re-packaging.

Consider also the consequences for the financial transaction processing – do you charge for all items initially ordered and then process a refund when the unwanted items are returned – implications for revenue reporting and recognition, or are the products delivered to the customer on the basis that they will be charged only for the items they select to keep – reduces the burden of processing refunds, but introduces additional element of risk.

Other complications include offering additional options for the consumer to return the goods – instead of your courier delivery company collecting from the home (another opportunity for consumer not at home) maybe the customer can return the goods to your retail store, or send them back in the mail (what happens if they never arrive?) or take them to a designated drop-off point.

Of course, in addition to unwanted and over-ordered items, there are the normal returns scenarios that involve goods that upon receipt by the consumer are found to be damaged or faulty, in which case of course the seller is duty-bound to provide and fund the collection and exchange or refund transaction, which in many cases will involve the seller recouping their own costs by returning product to their supplier for credit or claiming for damage in transit.

Whatever the reasons and policies, in balancing the benefits of customer service, company reputation and brand equity, we must recognize that returns management procedures and reverse logistics activities involve additional levels of complexity in what are already very complex supply chain ecosystems.

Consumers become sellers as well as buyers

The power of digital networks increases consumer connectedness across the world – over one billion people are connected through Facebook. In many ways, this digital connectedness has also reduced complexity to further empower consumers through internet enabled digital platforms such as social media, crowd sourcing and group buying.

As described by Yochai Benkler, Professor at Harvard Law Business School and author of *The Wealth of Networks* (2007), 'The world is becoming too fast, too complex and too networked for any company to have all the answers inside'.

Digital technology has also enabled customers to sell as well as buy – online platforms such as eBay and Craigslist connect buyers and sellers around the world. Indeed, the C2C world – consumer to consumer – has been revolutionized by these e-commerce platforms, with devastating effect on some traditional businesses. It is not just the supply chain ecosystems that are being fundamentally impacted by the digitally enabled omni-channel world, in some sectors it disintermediates the entire business model and distribution channel – consider the effect on products and sectors such as books, music, movies, advertising, recruitment, real estate and travel.

Cross-border transactions

Of course the internet knows no borders, so the shopping, purchase and payment transactions can all be processed online in the digital, borderless, connected world. However, for order fulfilment and delivery, the global supply chain ecosystems operate in the physical world. Whether FMCG, consumer electronics or garment industries, the consumer products that were easily ordered online have to physically travel across continents and through countries on their journey – by a combination of air, sea, rail and road – to be delivered to the consumer, all the time optimizing the balance of speed, cost and quality.

These supply chain ecosystems that power e-commerce transactions involve several location-related entities and activities that could well be in different geographical locations, across different countries or continents – for example, where the internet retailer (website) is located, where the inventory is located and the order shipped from, where the buyer (online consumer) is located, from where the invoice is raised, to where the payment will be made and to where the product will be shipped.

E-commerce has empowered buyers to easily purchase products from sellers located in different countries and McKinsey has predicted that by 2020, 15 per cent of all online sales will be cross-border transactions. Such international online transactions can introduce additional complexities for consumers, businesses and authorities – in the areas of shipping costs, customs procedures, duties and taxes.

It's not just the purchasing that consumers can easily transact across borders; through the connected world they can search and consume product information globally – including user reviews from unknown but seemingly trusted fellow consumers – and equally importantly pricing details. Prior to executing their cross-border online purchase transaction, they can readily compare product prices across multiple locations, resulting in cross-jurisdictional pricing transparency that may not always be in the best interests, or indeed desirable, for the seller or brand owner.

Cross-border e-commerce trade provides a range of challenges for the authorities in terms of customs clearance, logistics, taxes and foreign exchange. This has led a number of commercial enterprises to develop international delivery options to overcome these obstacles. For example the US Postal Service has partnered with Hong Kong Post, China Post and Singapore Post to launch ePacket, a service aimed at eBay sellers in these territories in Asia who ship to buyers in the USA.

The Borderfree company of New York provides a full range of cross-border e-commerce services, including site localization, multi-currency pricing and payment processing, landed-cost calculation, customs clearance and brokerage, global logistics services and international fraud management. The company's clients include some of the leading retailers and brands such as Aéropostale, J Crew, Land's End, Macy's, Neiman Marcus, Under Armour and Williams-Sonoma.

Summary – what's next for omni-channel?

It would be a brave forecaster who dared to predict where e-commerce and omni-channel will take us in the next few years. The American and Chinese internet and retail giants will no doubt be battling for supremacy with new services and new technologies to take a competitive lead, if only for a few months at a time.

No doubt more consumers in more countries will become digitally connected and embrace e-commerce, with online sales increasing as a proportion of total retail – and mobile continuing to increase its share as the preferred shopping conduit.

Potential risks for the bricks and mortar retailers are recent warnings that the overall retail footprint needs reconfiguring to better suit the latest consumer behaviour trends – some are calling for fewer large megastores and many more smaller, local outlets; some UK retailers forecast that up to 20 per cent of their stores may close.

These shifts in the retail landscape combined with digital consumers' shopping preferences will continue to have profound implications for distribution operations and logistics networks. The boundaries are becoming blurred – the previously clearly segregated roles undertaken by retailers, internet companies and logistics service providers are converging, with many exciting opportunities and challenges ahead for omni-channel supply chains.

CASE STUDY   The Amazon phenomenon – internet business or logistics company?

No overview of e-commerce would be complete without a look at Amazon, a company that dominates the industry and continues to innovate and expand, evolving a unique and changing business model.

Back in 1994, founder Jeff Bezos opened an online store from a 400sq ft garage in Seattle. The concept was classically simple, yet brand new – to trade solely online, offering the convenience of home shopping for the consumer, with minimal costs for the seller. Today there is scarcely a consumer product that Amazon cannot offer either directly, or from one of its merchant partners. Amazon have also taken huge strides in e-fulfilment – as of 2014, they operated

145 warehouses around the world totalling almost 40 million square feet. Annual revenue exceeds $75 billion and the company is now working with more than two million partners who use Amazon's platform and services to sell their products online.

As well as offering an almost limitless range of products, Amazon continues to develop innovative new service offerings for both consumer and now business partners. Amazon Prime offers customers free two-day shipping across the US for a flat annual fee, whilst Amazon Fresh is designed to offer same-day delivery in key markets. Amazon Supply provides a marketplace for thousands of industrial suppliers and is the company's most significant move into the B2B sectors for business and industry. For e-fulfilment and logistics, the company is planning its own fleet of trucks and drivers. And Amazon Prime Air plans to use drones to deliver merchandise in 30 minutes or less, subject to US government approval.

Amazon wasn't the first online store, but the company recognized the potential to transform the way we shop by building the next generation platform and infrastructure that gives customers unprecedented choice, scope and value. By building the online shopping platform, Amazon radically reinvented the traditional retail business model and the fundamental dynamics of how consumers go shopping.

Amazon's impact on 3PLs

From the logistics perspective, with such a wide and growing range of services the question now being raised is 'Is Amazon a 3PL?' (third-party logistics provider). It could be argued that this has already happened, considering Amazon's extensive network of distribution centres and its latest developments of moving into transportation. In a survey reported in the *CSCMP Supply Chain Quarterly* (2014), the question 'is Amazon a 3PL?' was posed to a panel of CEOs of several of the world's largest 3PLs.

Eighty per cent agreed that Amazon had had a significant impact on supply chain management, including the role its high-speed deliveries have played in raising customer service expectations. Their e-commerce fulfilment services were cited as a 'game-changer' which has led to a greater demand for e-fulfilment services. The company was also credited for bringing together a broad range of services under a single platform and is seen to be a major factor in traditional retailers developing their own omni-channel strategies.

Other comments were less favourable. One respondent said that Amazon had substantial market clout but 'wields it so violently that it is not a customer of choice or a desired client'; another said that it kills firms with low prices.

Nine of the 25 respondents said that Amazon is one of their customers, with the services provided including distribution, warehousing, transportation services, bulk goods fulfilment and import/export services.

They added that many retail start-ups rely on Amazon to provide warehousing, inventory management and fulfilment, services that would otherwise be handled by a third-party logistics service provider, so in that sense, Amazon was effectively acting as a 3PL. Its huge shipment volumes and the demands it places on parcel delivery firms such as UPS and FedEx often take priority during peak periods, sometimes to the detriment of other 3PLs.

Six of the respondents considered Amazon to be a 3PL, with whom they compete in various aspects of their business, while others even described it as a 4PL. As to the future, 17 respondents said they viewed Amazon as a major threat to other 3PLs, whereby Amazon would be providing a broad range of logistics services including warehousing, transportation and order fulfilment, leveraging its formidable resources and platforms.

Conclusion

The survey concludes that the answer to the question is that Amazon does already act as a 3PL in many situations and that its strategy to target the business-to-business sector may well attract more clients away from traditional 3PLs. Is this a deliberate ploy on its behalf? Amazon certainly has the infrastructure and a reputation for innovation and service, so any prudent 3PL should be well-advised to prepare for them to make a major push into the B2B sector. Jeff Bezos has often been quoted as saying he is not sure whether retailing will continue to be its core business; if not, then it may well be as a 3PL service provider.

Africa – is it the next Asia?

11

What future for Africa by 2050?

The question 'Will this be Africa's century?' was posed by the OECD's *Observer* magazine in 2000 (Kamal-Chaoui, 2000). Has Africa's time really come, or will it continue to be dogged by the problems of the past?

Covering an area larger than China, USA, India and Europe combined, Africa's combination of fast growing economies, plentiful and cheap labour supply, gradually improving infrastructure and trade facilitation initiatives are synonymous with the key growth indicators witnessed in emerging Asia back in the 1970s.

Amongst the continued media reports of political instability, disease, famine, civil war and corruption, it is easy to forget that the continent has 54 countries with vastly differing levels of stability, development and political structures. What most of them do have in common are considerable mineral and agricultural resources, young and fast-growing populations, improving educational standards – and the potential to achieve China-like levels of growth.

In September 2014, London's *Daily Telegraph* reported a 'growth miracle' taking place on the continent (Lynn, 2014). Several African countries including Mozambique, the Congo, Liberia, Ghana and Nigeria have joined the 7 per cent growth club – alongside a select group of large emerging markets that includes China, India, Philippines and Vietnam.

Renaissance Capital's chief economist pointed out that real incomes have doubled since 2000, and that 'Africa is going to go from a $2 trillion economy to a $29 trillion economy by 2050'.

However, the continent offers a diverse range of challenges, from its limited transport infrastructures to tough terrains, from widespread poverty to bureaucracy and corruption, and with individual countries at vastly different levels of development.

The Economist magazine (2013) – having labelled Africa as the 'hopeless continent' back in May 2000 – published a new special report on Emerging Africa in March 2013, this time entitled 'Africa Rising' – which identified and predicted great opportunities and prosperity for the continent, especially the sub-Saharan Africa (SSA) region – which is the primary focus of this chapter.

The North African countries in the Maghreb region and bordering the Mediterranean – including Algeria, Egypt, Libya, Morocco and Tunisia – are generally grouped together with the Middle Eastern economies under the MENA region umbrella – Middle East and North Africa.

Sub-Saharan Africa is expected to be the second fastest growing region in the world in the next five years – after developing Asia. With 2014 GDP growth of over 5 per cent demonstrating further increase over 4.7 per cent in 2013, the region is well above the developing country average of 3.9 per cent. In fact during the last decade, growth has surpassed worldwide averages, driving unprecedented increases in economic prosperity and instilling a sense of optimism across much of the continent.

Seven of the world's 10 fastest growing economies (KPMG, 2014) are in sub-Saharan Africa – Ethiopia, Tanzania, Mozambique, Ghana, Republic of the Congo, Zambia and Nigeria – and by 2050 the region will have a larger and younger workforce than China or India.

Some SSA countries – South Africa and Nigeria in particular – are well on their way to building modern, affluent societies with rapidly growing economies; while regrettably others still need to find a peaceful solution to conflict before they can take the first steps towards sustainable economic growth.

Abundant labour for low-cost country sourcing

In 2014 Africa's population exceeded 1 billion people – speaking over 2,100 different languages – with an overall literacy rate of

62 per cent, but with income levels only one tenth of the world average.

With this huge population offering an abundant source of labour, many international companies are exploring low cost country sourcing opportunities in sub-Saharan Africa, particularly for large scale, labour-intensive production operations.

The region has the potential to provide strong and serious competition as a source of volume manufactured goods, particularly at a time when factories in China are facing steep wage inflation and labour shortages in the established manufacturing zones along the eastern coastal cities.

One recent report identified that some Hong Kong manufacturers, seeking to improve margins and increasingly aware of Africa's appeal, are considering investing in production facilities in Sub-Saharan Africa to capitalize on the abundant and cheap workforce.

Vice-chairman of the All-China Federation of Industry & Commerce, Li Yifu, also former Chief Economist at the World Bank, called for manufacturers in mainland China to consider moving labour-intensive factories to Africa, saying that the young labour force of the continent's 1 billion population was similar to China's profile in the 1980s, but with current average shop floor wages in Africa of around $50 per month – around one tenth of the labour rates in China. The World Bank's Africa Development Forum also sees potential comparative advantage for Africa in low-wage, low-skilled labour sectors.

From the regulatory perspective, light product manufacturers in sub-Saharan Africa enjoy duty-free and quota-free access to US and EU markets under the African Growth and Opportunity Act (AGOA) and also via the Cotonou Agreement, which is the most comprehensive partnership agreement between the EU and 79 developing countries from Africa, the Caribbean and the Pacific (ACP).

Therefore, in addition to the rapidly developing consumer market opportunities, there will also be expanding production activities across Africa, driving exponential increases in flows of materials and goods, particularly imports and exports.

Thus trade and commerce will expand, in turn driving GDP growth and consequently, more demand for logistics and supply chain management expertise and services.

Employment considerations

With such unprecedented economic growth continuing, Africa stands at the brink of an employment explosion where companies large and small alike will need to search hard to find the right talent to capitalize on the economic boom.

However, Sharmi Surianarain, Director of Lifelong Engagement at African Leadership Academy in South Africa (2015), cautions that employers are generally reluctant to look for talent beyond the well-established universities or the most familiar tertiary institutions. While academic excellence will continue to remain an important baseline, employers need to be mindful that some of their best employees will likely be the quickest learners, the most entrepreneurial, the most emotionally intelligent, and the most resilient – and not necessarily the smartest in the academic sense.

Most organizations across Africa also suffer from an over-reliance on expatriate talent to fulfil mission-critical positions. While expats fill an important role in helping import much needed skills and experience, African employers need to more actively recruit from within the African diaspora to meet their expanding workforce needs. Positioning organizations for growth on the continent will require a pan-African perspective in addition to the basic skills – for example, growing a retail brand in West Africa will require understanding of both Francophone and Anglophone markets.

Urban middle class drives rapidly expanding consumer markets

According to Spire Research (2014), many cities across Africa are racing towards, or have already achieved, middle-income status, creating wealth and improved job prospects for their residents. Forty per cent of the continent's population now reside in cities – by comparison the 2013 figure for China was 55 per cent – and urbanization across Africa is forecast to increase to over 60 per cent by year 2050.

This urbanization in turn is driving increased demand for healthcare, education, construction, water and sanitation services, as well

FIGURE 11.1   Sub-Saharan Africa's most populous cities

SOURCE AT Kearney

as internet, communication and commercial hubs, all of which generate new business opportunities for international companies.

As the world's youngest continent, more than half the population is under the age of 20, compared with 28 per cent in China. The age group of 16- to 24-year olds is expanding rapidly, making this segment very attractive for consumer marketers.

Although there is massive diversity and disparity throughout and across the various countries, a new consumer class is rapidly emerging, with increasing spending power, digitally empowered global awareness and the desire for international products and brands. From $680 billion in 2008, Africa's consumer goods sector is expected to more than double to $1.4 trillion by 2020, opening up new markets with millions and millions of new consumers. Africa's middle-class spending patterns, lifestyle developments and wealth expansion growth trajectories are all extremely attractive for global companies.

Rapid technology adoption

Across sub-Saharan Africa, technology adoption trends are firmly shifting many economies into the mobile and internet age, as well as reshaping the retail landscape. Telecommunications companies are seeing exponential growth in numbers of mobile phone users, and internet penetration is now over 25 per cent.

From the consumer technology perspective, the continent has 17 million Facebook users, accounts for 7 per cent of the world's internet subscribers, has 600 million mobile phone users and is the world's fastest-growing mobile phone market.

In Nigeria alone, over 70 per cent of adults own a mobile phone and there are 45 million internet users.

Digitally empowered and internet enabled, African consumers are embracing e-commerce, fuelled by mobile payment services that enable cashless transactions, with the result that 51 per cent of Africa's 1 billion-plus population are now shopping online.

Increasing foreign investment

With the diversification of economic activity in Africa gathering pace, growing employment levels are creating a new consumer class. This has paved the way for increasing foreign direct investment (FDI) in consumer-focused services and manufacturing sectors. Sectors other than extractive industries are growing in importance, especially the rapidly expanding consumer markets. Annual FDI first reached $50 billion back in 2012 and is now at the average run rate of over $1 billion per week.

According to EY (formerly Ernst & Young) in their Africa Attractiveness Survey (2014), Africa's share of global FDI projects reached 5.7 per cent in 2013, its highest level in a decade.

In terms of FDI recipients, while South Africa maintained its position as the top FDI destination, emerging hotspots for investment were reported as Kenya, Ghana, Mozambique, Uganda, Tanzania and Zambia. The number of new FDI projects in sub-Saharan Africa (SSA) increased by 4.7 per cent and the average size of FDI projects increased to $70.1 million in 2013, from $60.1 million in 2012.

EY reported the prime factors behind the sub-Saharan African growth story being strong macroeconomic growth and outlook, improving business environment, rising consumer class, abundant natural resources, democratic dividend and infrastructure development.

Prominent investing nations include China, and to a lesser extent India, whilst the USA, Japan and the Netherlands are all investing in Africa's energy industry. EY reports that whilst the UK remains the lead investor into the continent, intra-African investment continues to steadily rise. Investors are also looking beyond the more established markets of South Africa, Nigeria and Kenya to expand their operations, as well as moving into more consumer-related sectors as Africa's middle class expands.

From the supply chain ecosystem perspective, these exciting market developments, together with the massive diversity across Africa, will present both opportunities and challenges for local and international logistics service providers.

Diverse and complex

Sub-Saharan Africa (SSA) consists of 48 countries featuring massive variety in size, development, stability and economic potential. This diversity across the region is best explored and explained using two independent and transparent global studies, namely the Index of Economic Freedom and the Ease of Doing Business Index. Each of these studies compiles rankings of multiple economies across several different dimensions, portraying the complexity and variety of scenarios across this exciting region.

Economic freedom

The Index of Economic Freedom published by the Heritage Foundation takes a broad and comprehensive view of country performance, measuring 10 separate aspects, grouped into four broad categories or pillars of economic freedom:

1 Rule of law (property rights, freedom from corruption).

2 Limited government (fiscal freedom, government spending).

3 Regulatory efficiency (business, labour and monetary freedoms).

4 Open markets (trade, investment and financial freedoms).

Some of the aspects evaluated are concerned with a country's interactions with the rest of the world. For example, the open markets measurements examine the extent of an economy's openness to global investment or international trade through imports and exports.

Each of the economic freedoms plays a vital role in developing and sustaining national and individual prosperity. They are all complementary in their impact and progress in one area is often likely to reinforce or even inspire progress in another.

Each economic freedom is independently scored on a scale of 0 to 100. A country's overall economic freedom score is a simple average of its scores on the 10 individual freedoms.

The rankings are categorized into five bands, ranging from repressed (score below 50), mostly unfree (50–59), moderately free (60–69), to mostly free (70–79) and free (above 80).

As can be seen from Table 11.1, Sub Saharan Africa countries span the full spectrum of economic freedom rankings, but the majority of economies are at the lower end of the economic freedom scale, once again reinforcing both the challenges and the opportunities.

Ease of doing business

The doing business project is run by the International Finance Corporation and the World Bank, and provides objective measures of viewing business regulations across 189 economies.

Together they publish the 'Ease of Doing Business' model which measures and tracks changes in the regulations applying to domestic small and medium-size companies operating in the largest business city of each economy.

The Doing Business indicators cover 10 specific areas relating to the business lifecycle: starting a business, dealing with construction permits, getting electricity, registering property, getting credit, protecting investors, paying taxes, trading across borders, enforcing contracts and resolving insolvency.

The ranking on the ease of doing business in each of the countries measured is based on the aggregate scores across these ten indicators.

TABLE 11.1 2014 Index of Economic Freedom – Sub Saharan Africa (SSA)

SSA Rank	Country	2014 Overall Score	Property Rights	Freedom from Corruption	Fiscal Freedom	Government Spending	Business Freedom	Labor Freedom	Monetary Freedom	Trade Freedom	Investment Freedom	Financial Freedom
1	Mauritius	**76.5**	65.0	53.4	92.2	81.8	74.4	78.0	76.7	88.6	85.0	70.0
2	Botswana	**72.0**	70.0	61.2	81.0	69.8	68.5	69.7	72.4	82.7	75.0	70.0
3	Cape Verde	**66.1**	70.0	54.9	77.4	68.6	63.8	48.0	79.1	69.6	70.0	60.0
4	Rwanda	**64.7**	30.0	46.9	80.3	78.2	69.6	84.1	74.8	77.7	65.0	40.0
5	Ghana	**64.2**	50.0	40.4	85.4	83.3	62.6	60.2	65.8	64.8	70.0	60.0
6	South Africa	**62.5**	50.0	41.6	68.7	69.1	74.5	54.4	75.3	76.1	55.0	60.0
7	Madagascar	**61.7**	40.0	27.3	90.8	92.3	62.8	43.9	77.6	77.8	55.0	50.0
8	Swaziland	**61.2**	40.0	31.6	74.7	70.9	64.2	71.7	72.3	81.5	65.0	40.0
9	Zambia	**60.4**	30.0	31.3	71.8	82.9	74.9	50.1	68.0	84.6	60.0	50.0
10	Uganda	**59.9**	30.0	23.8	79.1	87.3	45.1	87.4	71.0	75.4	60.0	40.0
11	The Gambia	**59.5**	30.0	31.7	79.0	79.8	57.4	65.8	71.3	65.0	65.0	50.0
12	Namibia	**59.4**	30.0	44.2	66.9	58.8	64.4	81.9	75.0	82.9	50.0	40.0

(Continued)

TABLE 11.1 (*Continued*)

SSA Rank	Country	2014 Overall Score	Property Rights	Freedom from Corruption	Fiscal Freedom	Government Spending	Business Freedom	Labor Freedom	Monetary Freedom	Trade Freedom	Investment Freedom	Financial Freedom
13	Burkina Faso	**58.9**	30.0	31.3	83.0	82.3	60.7	55.0	78.8	67.8	60.0	40.0
14	Gabon	**57.8**	40.0	29.1	74.5	81.7	58.9	63.0	75.1	61.0	55.0	40.0
15	Tanzania	**57.8**	30.0	28.8	79.7	78.3	47.0	61.1	66.0	76.8	60.0	50.0
16	Cote d'Ivoire	**57.7**	30.0	22.1	79.1	79.8	55.1	59.0	80.6	71.4	50.0	50.0
17	Benin	**57.1**	30.0	29.5	68.3	86.1	51.0	50.5	75.4	60.0	70.0	50.0
18	Kenya	**57.1**	30.0	21.0	78.0	74.6	55.8	64.0	74.9	72.8	50.0	50.0
19	Seychelles	**56.2**	50.0	48.5	76.8	61.8	67.6	68.5	75.1	33.4	50.0	30.0
20	Djibouti	**55.9**	30.0	30.9	80.6	62.8	42.7	65.1	77.2	54.8	65.0	50.0
21	Mali	**55.5**	20.0	27.7	69.8	81.7	48.0	63.2	76.7	73.2	55.0	40.0
22	Malawi	**55.4**	45.0	31.9	78.0	63.0	38.9	60.3	64.1	72.7	50.0	50.0
23	Senegal	**55.4**	40.0	29.5	65.1	75.4	47.5	41.5	81.8	73.2	60.0	40.0
24	Niger	**55.1**	30.0	26.0	76.8	88.4	35.2	45.4	88.3	65.6	55.0	40.0

25	Mozambique	**55.0**	30.0	26.2	75.7	64.6	65.2	36.7	80.8	75.5	45.0	50.0
26	Nigeria	**54.3**	30.0	22.7	85.0	74.5	48.0	66.4	73.1	63.8	40.0	40.0
27	Guinea	**53.5**	20.0	19.2	69.3	86.2	51.8	73.4	64.1	61.2	50.0	40.0
28	Mauritania	**53.2**	25.0	23.9	81.7	75.8	38.0	53.1	75.5	69.0	50.0	40.0
29	Cameroon	**52.6**	30.0	21.9	71.7	86.0	45.0	56.1	69.4	61.2	35.0	50.0
30	Liberia	**52.4**	30.0	33.8	83.6	70.5	62.3	47.0	72.9	64.1	40.0	20.0
31	Burundi	**51.4**	20.0	15.9	73.5	51.9	59.8	63.1	68.2	71.8	60.0	30.0
32	Comoros	**51.4**	30.0	22.1	64.5	85.3	49.4	50.1	74.5	72.7	35.0	30.0
33	Guinea-Bissau	**51.3**	20.0	20.2	89.0	86.6	40.5	61.4	74.4	61.4	30.0	30.0
34	Sierra Leone	**50.5**	15.0	24.6	80.7	85.7	55.3	28.7	70.2	70.2	55.0	20.0
35	Ethiopia	**50.0**	30.0	27.0	77.5	89.9	57.8	54.7	59.0	64.2	20.0	20.0
36	Togo	**49.9**	30.0	23.8	69.7	82.4	43.3	42.8	79.3	62.8	35.0	30.0
37	Lesotho	**49.5**	40.0	37.1	67.4	-	54.0	62.4	75.5	68.6	50.0	40.0
38	Sao Tome and Principe	**48.8**	20.0	32.5	86.9	27.9	52.6	44.7	68.3	75.3	50.0	30.0

(Continued)

TABLE 11.1 (*Continued*)

SSA Rank	Country	2014 Overall Score	Property Rights	Freedom from Corruption	Fiscal Freedom	Government Spending	Business Freedom	Labor Freedom	Monetary Freedom	Trade Freedom	Investment Freedom	Financial Freedom
39	Angola	**47.7**	15.0	17.7	87.7	55.3	47.5	40.1	63.6	70.1	40.0	40.0
40	Central African Republic	**46.7**	10.0	20.6	65.1	92.6	33.9	40.4	72.5	51.8	50.0	30.0
41	Chad	**44.5**	20.0	15.9	46.2	80.0	24.9	43.3	69.8	55.2	50.0	40.0
42	Equatorial Guinea	**44.4**	10.0	16.6	75.5	62.6	43.4	41.5	75.4	53.8	35.0	30.0
43	Republic of Congo	**43.7**	10.0	20.6	67.5	79.6	35.1	47.0	72.0	55.6	20.0	30.0
44	Democratic Republic of Congo	**40.6**	10.0	17.6	69.4	74.6	30.0	38.5	63.0	63.0	20.0	20.0
45	Eritrea	**38.5**	10.0	22.9	57.0	66.1	18.6	63.6	57.6	69.1	-	20.0
46	Zimbabwe	**35.5**	10.0	19.3	63.3	64.0	34.5	22.2	73.0	54.2	5.0	10.0

SOURCE The Heritage Foundation
http://www.heritage.org/index/explore?view=by-region-country-year

FIGURE 11.2 Ease of doing business indicators

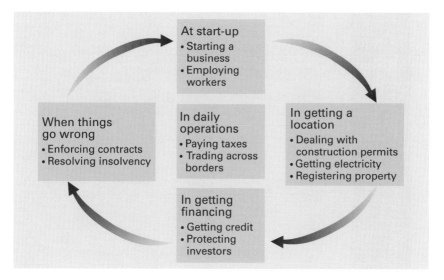

SOURCE World Bank's Ease of Doing Business Model

The 2015 figures show that within sub-Saharan Africa, the leading economy for Doing Business is Mauritius – ranked number 28th globally, ahead of South Africa at number 43 and Rwanda in 46th place. The last six countries in the sub-Saharan African rankings – being the Democratic Republic of Congo, Chad, South Sudan, Central African Republic, Libya and Eritrea – are also in the 10 lowest ranked economies around the world. This wide range of rankings for African countries once again reinforces the massive diversity in levels of economic development and business sophistication across the whole continent.

Logistics developments and the supply chain challenge

In such a vast continent with so many natural obstacles, moving goods efficiently and safely through well-developed supply chain ecosystems is an essential building brick in developing modern economic

TABLE 11.2 Sub-Saharan Africa Global Ease of Doing Business Rankings 2015

Ease of Doing Business 2015		Global	Sub Saharan Africa Economies from 189 countries ranked worldwide									
SSA	Economy	EDB	SAB	DCP	GE	RP	GC	PMI	PT	TAB	EC	RI
1	Mauritius	28	3	26	1	14	3	2	1	1	2	2
2	South Africa	43	7	4	27	13	5	1	2	5	4	1
3	Rwanda	46	15	5	4	1	1	18	3	33	9	13
4	Ghana	70	12	23	6	2	3	3	13	11	16	35
5	Botswana	74	26	17	11	5	7	14	6	26	8	3
6	Seychelles	85	18	7	16	9	40	3	4	2	18	4
7	Namibia	88	28	1	5	41	7	8	10	17	7	7
8	Swaziland	110	25	8	22	23	7	16	7	13	41	6
9	Zambia	111	8	21	14	31	2	7	9	41	17	10
10	Cabo Verde	122	9	25	18	6	10	43	11	6	1	39
11	Mozambique	127	13	16	29	15	18	11	19	14	38	16
12	Lesotho	128	14	36	13	10	32	14	17	22	20	22
13	Tanzania	131	17	41	9	20	32	30	26	18	3	15

14	Ethiopia	132	33	2	8	16	38	38	18	35	6	5
15	Kenya	136	24	19	23	25	15	20	14	25	25	28
16	Gambia, The	138	30	11	21	18	36	39	40	3	5	14
17	Sierra Leone	140	11	28	34	33	32	5	21	15	19	29
18	Gabon	144	22	14	15	45	10	31	29	16	33	24
19	Mali	146	34	20	17	24	18	31	25	32	21	17
20	Côte d'Ivoire	147	6	46	28	21	18	31	37	27	12	8
21	Togo	149	21	42	19	46	18	20	32	9	24	9
22	Uganda	150	32	37	44	22	18	16	16	30	13	11
23	Benin	151	16	9	35	36	15	28	38	12	39	18
24	Burundi	152	1	30	42	4	40	11	20	36	35	30
25	São Tomé and Príncipe	153	2	6	3	29	46	47	31	8	45	36
26	Cameroon	158	20	39	2	40	15	18	41	29	36	23
27	Comoros	159	37	3	7	17	18	20	33	21	44	39
28	Sudan	160	23	35	20	3	38	45	22	31	37	34

(Continued)

TABLE 11.2 (*Continued*)

SSA	Economy	EDB	SAB	DCP	GE	RP	GC	PMI	PT	TAB	EC	RI
		Global										
							Sub Saharan Africa Economies from 189 countries ranked worldwide					
29	Senegal	161	10	33	43	38	18	20	43	4	27	12
30	Madagascar	163	5	45	47	32	44	8	5	7	28	26
31	Malawi	164	29	12	41	8	32	27	15	37	32	37
32	Equatorial Guinea	165	46	18	10	27	10	20	35	20	10	39
33	Burkina Faso	167	27	13	38	28	18	20	28	39	31	18
34	Niger	168	41	27	30	12	18	31	30	42	22	25
35	Guinea	169	39	34	25	19	18	39	44	19	23	21
36	Nigeria	170	19	43	46	47	5	5	39	28	26	27
37	Zimbabwe	171	43	44	24	11	10	8	23	43	34	31
38	Liberia	174	4	31	31	43	36	46	8	23	42	38
39	Mauritania	176	31	15	32	7	40	41	47	24	14	39

Ease of Doing Business 2015

SSA	Country	EDB	SAB	DCP	GE	RP	GC	PMI	PT	TAB	EC	RI
40	Congo, Rep.	178	35	22	33	39	10	31	42	44	30	20
41	Guinea-Bissau	179	40	38	40	34	18	20	27	10	40	39
42	Angola	181	38	10	26	35	44	11	24	34	47	39
43	Congo, Dem. Rep.	184	36	24	37	26	18	31	34	40	43	39
44	Chad	185	45	29	36	37	18	31	46	45	29	32
45	South Sudan	186	42	40	39	44	40	44	12	47	15	39
46	Central African Republic	187	47	32	45	30	18	28	45	46	46	32
47	Eritrea	189	44	47	12	42	46	41	36	38	11	39

Key: SSA-SubSaharan Africa Ranking; EDB-Ease of Doing Business Global Ranking; SAB-Starting a Business, DCP-Dealing with Construction Permits, GE-Getting Electricity, RP-Registering Property, GC-Getting Credit, PMI-Protecting Minority Investors, PT-Paying Taxes, TAB-Trading Across Borders, EC-Enforcing Contracts, RI-Resolving Insolvency

SOURCE World Bank's Ease of Doing Business Model

structures, to enhance trade both with other African nations and the wider world.

Africa's transportation infrastructure lags well behind that of the rest of the world, with significant differences across and between the regions. A PwC (2014) survey (PricewaterhouseCoopers) found that while none of the African countries came close to the USA or China, the overall transport network in South Africa scored better than Indonesia and almost the same as India, whilst Kenya ranked higher than Vietnam.

In addition to the information technology systems and the physical assets of warehouses and trucks, the logistics and freight activities that enable supply chains to function are highly labour-intensive sectors. Developing modern supply chains across Africa will therefore provide employment for many millions of people using a wide range of skills, which in turn will provide a boost to the continent's states and help to raise a significant proportion out of poverty, providing much needed economic and social growth and stability.

The terrain across Africa also varies widely, from desert to mountains and rain forest. Such geographical diversity has a big impact on critical transport infrastructure often making it more challenging and costly to build road and rail networks, as well as much-needed bridges and tunnels. But even without extreme geographic and climatic variations, there is an enormous range in the levels of infrastructure maturity and development.

The Sub-Saharan Logistics report from Transport Intelligence (2012) cautions that challenges to doing business remain high, quoting 'weak transport infrastructure, lack of quality service providers, a disparate population, security issues and corruption', all of which make doing business in the region 'highly problematic'.

Domestic logistics weaknesses increase supply chain costs

Poor infrastructure across the continent is hindering the provision and development of domestic logistics services, which with related inefficiencies, are driving up logistics costs throughout Africa.

According to the World Bank, it takes just 12 days to export a container from Egypt, at a cost of $625. From Angola, the process takes four times as long – over a month and a half – and is nearly triple the cost – and it gets even trickier when you need to cross internal borders within Africa. By contrast, at the world's leading ports in Hong Kong and Singapore it takes just five days to export a container at a cost of $575 and $456 respectively.

Charles Brewer, managing director of DHL Express, sub-Saharan Africa, commented: 'Studies have suggested that the logistics sector in Africa costs anything between six and nine times more than in Europe, Asia-Pacific and the Americas'.

Such additional costs make goods less affordable to the population and are discouraging multinationals from establishing subsidiaries in the region. Brewer also added: 'The bureaucracies spelt out by customs procedures are derailing economic growth in many parts of Africa'.

The rate of domestic logistics development varies greatly across the continent. Marketing research firm Analytiqa (2013) confirms increased spending on logistics services by manufacturers and retailers, both in-house and outsourced services, with the total logistics market being worth $157 billion in 2016.

Rates of logistics outsourcing to specialist contract logistics providers are among the lowest in the world, but the outsourced logistics sector market is rapidly evolving and is projected to grow by some 38 per cent, with countries such as South Africa and Nigeria setting the pace.

Third-party logistics providers (3PLs) are set to take advantage of these new opportunities in the region, but they need to develop in-depth understanding of these new markets and accept the operational challenges that will inevitably arise.

International maritime gateways

Beyond the challenges and opportunities of domestic logistics, increasing imports and exports are vital to trigger growth and a number of countries are making bold efforts to put in place modern and efficient international maritime gateways.

Whilst Durban port in South Africa occupies the top spot for SSA, in North Africa the Suez Canal is by far the most important shipping route linking the Far East to the Mediterranean and Europe, with the transhipment centre at Port Said in Egypt having emerged as a leading state-of-the-art facility since beginning operations in 2004.

However, to put African port developments and ambitions into perspective, Port Said and Durban are the only African ports to feature in the world's top 50 container ports of 2013 – at number 43 and 50 respectively, together handling less than 6 million TEUs. Compare that with Shanghai and Singapore managing over 30 million TEUs each and in Europe the giants of Rotterdam, Hamburg and Antwerp between them processing 30 million TEUs.

East and West Africa have a number of competing ports, but they suffer from challenges with capacity, congestion and efficiency. Although there are several ports in the sub-Saharan region, it still lacks a clear hub. However, there are a number of strong contenders vying to win a bigger share of increasing sea freight volumes.

The port of Abidjan on the Ivory Coast looked to be a possible leadership contender but a local political crisis in 2011 set back their plans. The Lagos port complex offers direct access to the massive potential of the huge Nigerian market but is struggling to meet the growing demand. The situation could improve after 2016 when the new deep-sea port at Lekki is due to come on-stream. The operators forecast the demand for containers reaching Nigeria is expected to grow at an annual rate of 12.9 per cent up to 2025, such solid growth responsible for a projected 2016 capacity shortfall at container terminal facilities in Lagos of 800,000 TEUs.

In Ghana, Tema port operates in a stable political environment but has limited capacity and long waiting times. On the East coast Mombasa in Kenya and Dar es Salaam in Tanzania compete to be the preferred maritime gateway for East Africa. However congestion in Mombasa has led some shippers to move to Dar es Salaam, which is now putting further pressure on the port, specifically in the areas of capacity and administrative capabilities.

Comparing African ports to container ports on other continents, the OECD Port Cities programme report that African ports are generally less efficient, more congested and less connected, all of which are barriers to economic growth.

Olaf Merk (2014), OECD programme director, identifies a lack of good quality port capacity, saying the quality of most ports is substandard, with generally poor hinterland connectivity. Governance and regulatory frameworks add to the overall scenario of a container port sector in need of substantial improvement – there is generally a lack of competition, lack of professional management and an excess of cumbersome regulation and administrative procedures. But the upside of all these challenges is enormous opportunities!

Accessing the vast interior

Beyond the container ports, which are the key points of entry and exit for imports and exports, there are massive inland markets with plenty of potential. However, with many of the economies in sub-Saharan Africa being landlocked, the poor quality of inland transportation connections is restricting their economic development.

Enabling efficient access to this vast hinterland – adopting the geographical definition of the hinterland being the inland regions remote from urban areas – is one of the most important factors for Africa's future development. Continuing expansion of transportation infrastructure, much of it funded by foreign direct investment and through public private partnership (PPP) models, is essential in order to open up the full potential of the region.

Therefore, as the African economies continue to expand, governments will need to invest further in national transportation infrastructure and collaborate with the private sector to upgrade and enhance logistics capabilities, both for domestic distribution and to enable effective links with neighbouring countries for freight forwarding of imports and exports.

The map in Figure 11.3 shows that there is an established network of trans-African highways providing road access across the continent. However, the quality of this road infrastructure varies widely, with some sections – in particular the east-west Beira-Lobito land bridge corridor – considered to be barely functional as effective highways.

FIGURE 11.3 Trans-African corridors, gateways and infrastructure projects

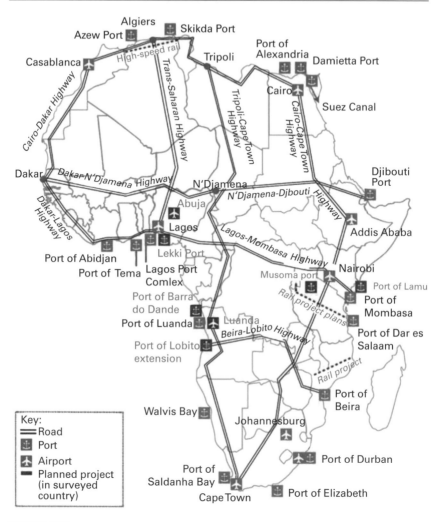

SOURCE PwC

Developing multi-modal hinterland connectivity is essential to opening up the potential of this vast continent, with many encouraging infrastructure developments already underway.

For example, expansion plans are being developed for the well-used Lagos-Abidjan-Dakar highway through West Africa. The five countries of Benin, Cote d'Ivoire, Ghana, Nigeria and Togo are involved in the Lagos-Abidjan Highway Corridor Project, which involves constructing a 1,028km road linking the region's major capital cities and ports.

On the east coast, new inland rail links are being constructed from Dar es Salaam which is the major regional maritime hub serving several landlocked countries including Malawi, Zambia, the DRC, Burundi, Rwanda and Uganda. The project will provide modern, rail-based transportation services in the East African Central Corridor, specifically a 1,672km rail network connecting Dar es Salaam to the key commercial centres of Kigali in Rwanda and Musongati in Burundi, which is expected to be complete in 2017.

Air freight hub and spoke networks developing

Air cargo plays a significant role in modern supply chain ecosystems, most notably where speed is vital over long distances. However, moving air cargo across sub-Saharan Africa is generally much more challenging than road, rail or waterborne freight, largely due to security issues. Africa has a number of international airports with the busiest being OR Tambo International airport in Johannesburg, followed by Cape Town and Cairo.

Several hub-and-spoke air cargo networks have been developed in the east and south of the continent. Hubs at Nairobi in Kenya, Addis Ababa in the east and Johannesburg in the south, are increasing connectivity in their respective regions.

West Africa lacks a strong hub and spoke structure, although two new airports are already planned at Angola's capital Luanda and in Abuja, Nigeria. Luanda airport is expected to have capacity for 13 million passengers and a cargo terminal with an annual capacity of 35,000 tonnes when it is projected to be opened in 2017. The large and growing size of the West African market together with rising consumer demand, indicate that more spokes will need to be developed to radiate from these future hubs.

So while air freight will only ever handle a small percentage of total cargo volume, having a well-structured network of air routes to complement ground and sea-based transport is a sign of a modern, developing transport and logistics infrastructure that will empower supply chain ecosystems.

Nigeria – Africa's largest and most populous economy

As Africa's most populous country and largest economy, Nigeria is seen as the up and coming powerhouse that will be the leader of Africa Rising. This is reflected and confirmed by Nigeria having by far the most newly registered companies on an annual basis – some 70,000, which is more than twice the number of second-placed South Africa with 30,000, followed by Kenya which has 22,000.

Despite many challenges including high levels of corruption, Islamic extremism in the north and health challenges, Nigeria has become the largest economy in Africa and 26th largest in the world. In 2013 its GDP was $510 billion, 14 per cent of which was from resources. In recent years retail and wholesale trade have become the biggest drivers of GDP growth whilst the IMF reported real economic growth since 2010 of 6.4 per cent.

A 2014 report from the McKinsey Global Institute (MGI) (Leke *et al*, 2014) provided encouraging reading for businesses looking to invest in Nigeria. In their 'Nigeria Renewal' report, MGI states that the country has the potential to achieve average annual growth of 7.1 per cent for the next 15 years which would make Nigeria a top-20 global economy in 2030 with GDP of more than $1.6 trillion. Most of the growth is expected to come from trade and infrastructure, which will lead to strong and steady improvement in the country's supply chain capabilities.

During 2012–14, Nigeria implemented a number of maritime reform measures aimed at enhancing the operational efficiency in the country's various ports, including implementing 24-hour operations at the Lagos port terminals, through which more than 60 per cent of the country's container traffic passes.

Nigeria is of course a major oil producer and exporter, but with a population of 170 million it has a huge domestic market for goods and services. While poverty is still a fact of life for some 75 per cent of Nigerians, MGI report there are already almost 40 million Nigerians in consuming-class households – defined as households with income of more than $7,500 per year in purchasing parity terms.

Furthermore, by 2030, MGI predict that some 160 million – of a projected total population of 273 million – will live in households with sufficient income for discretionary spending. Representing a market larger than the current populations of France and Germany combined, this will triple the sale of consumer goods and confirms the massive potential of this exciting but challenging economy.

Summary

The fact is that Africa's macroeconomic prospects remain favourable, with growth rates above the global average projections. However, as we have seen, growth performance and potential varies widely across the different countries and regions and such disparities are unlikely to disappear in the near future.

To further quote the *Daily Telegraph*'s September 2014 comment: 'Over the next two decades Africa will join the developed world… by encouraging industrialization, respecting property rights and allowing free markets to lift countries out of poverty'.

As much and perhaps more than any other emergent region, Africa has significant obstacles, whether in politics, instability, poverty, poor infrastructure, skill levels and bureaucracy. Yet as we have seen there are many green shoots and in the next decade or so, Africa may well become the emerging economic power it has so long hoped to be.

A long-term view is essential, because many of the issues facing Africa will not be solved in months or years; they will take decades. Companies should explore the numerous business opportunities across the continent being cognizant of the potential pitfalls – and prepared for setbacks. For those ready to commit to a long-term strategy, the rewards could however be immense.

For companies seeking to take their share of what may be a very large cake, it is essential to go in with eyes fully open, be ferociously practical and realistic about expectations, be prepared for setbacks and take a long-term perspective. For those with foresight, stamina and commitment it could well be a lucrative long-term investment.

CASE STUDY Walvis Bay Corridor set to make Namibia a leading logistics hub

The Walvis Bay Corridor Group (WBCG) is a service and facilitation centre which manages imports and exports for southern Africa via the Port of Walvis Bay in Namibia. Since being first established in 2000, WBCG has developed its port services portfolio to handle containerized cargoes and bulk commodities, whilst building an efficient transport network into Namibia's hinterland and further afield into neighbouring African countries. WBCG have also implemented a variety of incentives for local manufacturing and exports, helping to create much needed employment.

Walvis Bay port lies in the centre of the country on the Atlantic coast and with its natural deepwater harbour and stable weather conditions, is well placed to accelerate the growth of the region as a gateway to Southern Africa – including almost 200 million consumers in the Southern African Development Community. It has an efficient transport network linking it to the hinterland and neighbouring African countries in the form of all-weather highways, district roads and air links via Windhoek to numerous international airports across the region. Railway services connect to the rest of Namibia and Southern Africa to transport bulk commodities, containers, general cargo, refrigerated goods and fuel.

Two key road corridor systems – the Trans-Caprivi going north and the Trans-Kalahari going south – form a fast-flowing ground transportation network connecting Walvis Bay to major centres in South Africa, Botswana, Mozambique, Zimbabwe, Zambia, Angola, Democratic Republic of the Congo and other East African countries.

The logistics infrastructure and facilities at Walvis Bay offer an efficient and economical option for cargo trans-shipment between African, European and American trade markets which can help exporters and importers save at least eight to 10 days when shipping to and from these markets.

Telecommunication services are well developed in comparison to most other African states. High-quality digital telephony, data, internet, satellite, cellular and radio communication services are in place to enable companies to contact clients and business partners anywhere in the world at any time.

The Walvis Bay municipality has implemented programs promoting the development of local trade and manufacturing industries, including training for small and medium enterprise (SMEs) start-ups. The objectives included diversifying the dependency of the local economy from fishing, whilst assisting small traders to develop their businesses into fully-fledged enterprises, with the potential of exporting their products.

Most manufacturing activities are currently located in the export-processing zone (EPZ), an innovative approach that allows SMEs to take advantage of both home and export markets whilst also attracting larger, international businesses. SMEs in the EPZ are involved in manufacturing a diverse range of products including plastic products, automotive parts, fishing accessories, bathroom fittings and diamond cutting and polishing.

For international companies, the attraction to set up operations in the EPZ is that they can enjoy a tax-free investment environment with various benefits and advantages. These incentives are of unlimited duration and apply equally to Namibian and foreign firms, ensuring a level playing field.

International companies are allowed to repatriate their capital and profits, while enjoying freedom from exchange controls and the holding of foreign currency accounts at local banks, all in a politically stable environment with a reliable work-force and low production costs.

The only requirement is that foreign investors must employ Namibian labour. Companies who choose to upgrade the skills of their local employees are entitled to reimbursement of 75 per cent of all direct expenditure incurred on approved on-the-job training courses. A legally binding no-strike clause for companies with EPZ status ensures predictability of labour supply and availability.

The Walvis Bay region is also home to a wealth of natural resources, the commercialization of which benefits from having a well-developed and well-connected port, logistics and transport infrastructure.

The 3,500-hectare Walvis Bay salt field is one of the largest solar evaporation facilities in Africa. It processes 24 million tons of sea water each year to produce more than 700,000 tons of high quality salt, that is shipped to markets in southern and West Africa. The refinery recently installed the first robotic systems in the country which will drastically cut down on production time. Walvis Bay Salt Refiners is also a commercial producer of high-quality oysters supplied to customers throughout southern Africa.

The well-established fishing industry plays a vital role in the region's economy and over the past 50 years it has developed into a leading force in the world's fish supply market. The industry employs around 8,000 people, generates 10 per cent of the country's GDP and has more than 2km of landing quays, with extensive cold storage, processing and canning facilities. High-value fish and related products are processed for export to niche markets in Europe, Australia, the United States and Hong Kong, China.

Managed by the Namibian Ports Authority (Namport) the port operations at Walvis Bay processed over 750,000 tonnes of cargo in 2013, which – while modest on an international scale – represented a seven fold increase over the corresponding volume in 2005.

Improvements along the Trans-Kalahari hinterland corridor linking Namibia to Botswana and South Africa have improved the duration of cross border clearance procedures to just one and a half hours, reducing transit time between countries to a very competitive maximum of 48 hours.

Further investments and plans are in place including port expansion projects for 2016 involving a new container terminal and bulk port, and further development of railway links to all neighbouring markets by 2020.

Conclusion

The 10-year strategic objective is to leverage the established port and logistics infrastructure, together with the cross border connectivity, and develop Walvis Bay and Namibia into the leading gateway logistics and distribution hub for southern Africa by 2025.

The Chief Executive Officer of Walvis Bay Corridor Group, Johny M Smith who in October 2014 was named 'Africa's Logistics CEO of the Year' at an awards ceremony hosted by CEO Communications in Johannesburg, confirmed the vision: 'Namibia has taken a strategic decision to develop the country as a Logistics Hub for the Southern African Region and beyond, by focusing on being a transhipment and transit point for trade between Africa and the rest of the world.'

Supply chain innovation

Future considerations for global supply chain ecosystems

When considering the future, it is useful to contemplate the wisdom of management guru Peter Drucker who said 'the best way to predict the future is to create it' (Drucker, 2012).

In our complex, connected and highly competitive world, business today is much like the shark – if you don't keep moving, you die. The global supply chain ecosystems configured to service specific companies, business models and product portfolios, must continually develop and evolve to react and respond to changes arising from multiple external forces and macro factors.

Supply chain innovation comes in a variety of forms – technical, conceptual and commercially creative – but any changes proposed must meet various stringent criteria. Will such innovations help lower costs? Will they improve productivity and efficiency? Will they help to retain existing customers and/or win new ones? Will they improve customer service? Will they help lower the carbon footprint? And absolutely essential, will they improve the bottom line?

The need to embrace innovative technologies, systems and processes can arise from companies looking for opportunities to improve their business models, to tackle identified internal shortcomings or to respond to external, macroeconomic advances.

Infrastructure initiatives – typically led by government, but with both public and private sector participants involved in the funding, construction and operation – are critical drivers of economic development, whilst enabling regional and international trade, and reducing the cost and time of cargo flows.

Management attitudes towards innovation in the supply chain, not unlike other business sectors, can be contradictory. On one hand they are keen to adopt new technology, concepts and strategies to give them a competitive edge. On the other hand they are reluctant to be the first to commit and invest in the latest equipment or strategies, unless someone else has already acted as a test bed to validate that what is being proposed is practical and successful. But the prizes for second place are always less than for the winner so the spoils of success more than likely will go to those with the courage and the ability to accurately judge the potential of new proposals that may well put them ahead of the competition.

In this chapter we consider a number of examples of innovation impacting supply chain ecosystems, specifically focusing on technological developments, inland port developments and game-changing infrastructure initiatives.

Technology developments impacting supply chains

Supply chain ecosystems have to continually adopt and adapt the latest technological developments; as such they are voracious consumers of advances and applications in engineering, energy use, information technology, robotics, transport equipment – and in the near future, potentially even aviation.

3D printing

What once seemed science fiction is now a science fact. 3D printing – or stereo lithography to use the technical term – enables anyone to make a three-dimensional object in a variety of materials including metals, plastics, ceramics and glass.

The 3D printing process – also known as additive manufacturing – turns a whole object into thousands of tiny little slices, then produces it from the bottom-up, slice by slice. Those tiny layers stick together to form a solid object. Each layer can be very complex, meaning 3D printers can create moving parts like hinges and wheels as part of the same object. You could print a whole bike – handlebars, saddle, frame, wheels, brakes, pedals and chain – ready assembled, without using any tools.

If something is broken and the parts are not readily available, 3D printing means it is possible to simply produce the parts required. Even if the item needed is out of production and parts are no longer available from the manufacturer, with the digital specifications it is now feasible to 3D print the replacements.

For new product deliveries, instead of the supplier shipping the product to the user, they could transmit the digital files to allow local production on a 3D printer. Companies and even consumers can even design and produce a prototype, or an improved version of the product that they already have.

In fact, the projected rise of consumer adoption of 3D printers is not unlike the advent of the personal computer in the early 1980s. Manufacturers may be forced to reconsider their business models with applications such as small volume production runs, bespoke one-off items and on-demand spare parts being highly applicable to adopt the convenience and speed of 3D printing.

Leading hi-tech analysts Juniper Research (Smith, 2014) predict that sales of consumer 3D printers will exceed 1 million units by 2018, rising from an estimated 44,000 in 2014. While shipments are still at relatively low levels, Juniper expects them to increase significantly during the coming five-year period. Growth drivers include an ever widening scope of functionality and applicability, plus the entry – and growth – of the more established printing vendors, such as HP (Hewlett Packard) which together with increase in unit volumes will result in a more attractive pricing proposition for consumers.

What are the implications for supply chain ecosystems? The broader consequences for supply chain and logistics are yet to be fully understood and appreciated, but certain sectors are sure to be massively impacted, in particular service parts logistics.

Consider the spare parts scenario, where the service engineer is at the site of a machinery breakdown – mechanical handling equipment in a warehouse or a quayside crane, production machinery in a factory, motor vehicle broken down on the highway, malfunctioning hardware at a telecommunications' base station, computer data centre or centralized banking system. Having the correct spare parts available onsite is essential to being able to conduct a successful repair and restore the system/machinery to normal operational service. Such systems will involve an extensive portfolio of different spare parts – some worth thousands of dollars each – which would not be practically feasible or economically viable for the engineer to carry with them to every breakdown.

Equipping the field service engineer with the appropriate 3D printer, that in our connected world can download the digital specifications to produce any combination of spare parts, eliminates any possibility of 'waiting for parts' and enables repair scenarios to always have correct parts available, drastically decreasing downtime, while massively reducing the complexity (and cost) of services parts logistics.

Looking into the future, as the technology develops further and costs continue to decline, we will see 3D printing services become readily available to consumers on a service centre basis. For example, 3D printer installations in post offices, convenience stores or UPS, DHL or FedEx service centres, to where consumers would take – or send – the digital specification of the products they wish to have produced. Consider this an extension of the digital printing service bureau already available on every high street, providing printing, copying, binding and digital photo services.

We could then imagine potential scenarios where e-commerce purchases involve delivery of not the goods themselves, but the specifications of the products ordered – for the consumer to have them locally produced at their 3D printing service centre – such that e-commerce fulfilment becomes digital transmission of blue prints.

Maybe not totally mainstream, but for certain types of consumer products this could well be the supply chain ecosystem of the future, with substantial implications for the express delivery sector, whilst raising all sorts of questions around intellectual property ownership and copyright protection.

Warehouse robotics

During the past 30 years we have seen warehousing operations incorporate more and more automation as the systems become progressively more productive and hence far more widely used, largely by feeding off the enormous advances in equipment control systems and warehouse control software.

From the first fully automated high-bay pallet stores using stacker cranes and pallet conveyors, automated systems have advanced well beyond the storage and retrieval of unit loads. Modern systems are used for a variety of applications including unloading and loading pallets, unmanned narrow-aisle cranes in semi-and fully-automated warehouses; sortation, conveying, picking and packing systems enabling smaller unit loads such as totes, cartons, hanging garments and boxes to be processed automatically.

Automated systems work around the clock, don't get tired, are never late and carry out each operation in exactly the same manner. They can operate faster and more effectively than manually operated systems and free up labour resources for tasks where the human touch provides a more productive and flexible solution with the ability to improvise and make decisions as required. Fully automated warehouses can operate without lighting – saving costs, and automated chilled or frozen storage facilities can function without the need to make provision for staff working in very low temperatures. Automated guided vehicles can travel throughout the warehouse to bring inventory to workstations, saving picking times and allowing the human operatives to do what they do best in a more productive manner. They do break down occasionally, but so do people.

Full automation is not always the ultimate solution, but for a great many leaders in supply chain operations, automation has become an essential tool in the never-ending quest to reduce costs, increase productivity and improve service.

Robotics is the latest generation of technological innovation in warehousing operations, embracing both hardware developments and the all-important software. Steady and sometimes spectacular advances in information technology and software controls have made a huge contribution to the growth in robotic systems. Their ability to handle vast amounts of data about every aspect of goods movements, to instruct and manage storage, handling, fulfilment and other systems and equipment, and to provide management with real-time, accurate information have proved invaluable to supply chain management and logistics operations.

Without doubt one of the highest-profile events in supply chain innovation was when Amazon acquired US robotics company Kiva Systems for $775 million in 2012, a huge investment, even for the market leader.

Deployed in their huge fulfilment centres the robots carry goods to the person at the packing station. Following a complex grid and guided by sensors and wireless technology, the Kiva robots move around the warehouse floors picking up storage racks full of merchandise and transfer them to the final picking locations for customer orders. Warehouse operatives no longer need to walk up and down aisles to pick goods but now stay by their own workstation, making them far more efficient. Amazon claims that the robots will enable them to increase productivity by up to four times as many orders per hour.

Amazon's CEO Jeff Bezos told investors at a shareholder meeting at the end of 2014 that he expects to significantly increase the number of robots used to fulfil customer orders and that the company expected to have 10,000 robots in operation by the end of the year. There are currently about 1,000 robot workers deployed in Amazon fulfilment centres, and even with the significant increase in robots, the company stated that it would not change the number of actual people employed.

Prior to the acquisition by Amazon, Kiva had built a solid customer base including major US retailers such as Staples, Walgreens, The Gap, Office Depot and Crate & Barrel. These companies may have to consider whether the change of ownership may lead to possible shortages of Kiva robots, but also whether they want to do business with a direct competitor.

In the UK, online high-end fashion retailer Net-A-Porter is using a fully automated high-bay warehouse system and robot pickers to handle order fulfilment in its London distribution centre. They handle all e-commerce operations with the automated crane system storing products in totes, then picking them and placing them onto a conveyor system that takes the items to the upper floor for packing and dispatch, with every item being tracked via barcode. The system currently deals only with flat goods – items that don't require hanging. But that is set to change, with a semi-automated system to deal with goods on hangers about to start construction.

Drone deliveries

Once again pioneered by Amazon, who at the end of 2013 announced it was testing drones to deliver goods to customers under the brand name Prime Air, as part of its drive to improve service and productivity. Called Octocopters, the drones could deliver packages weighing up to 2.3 kg to customers within 30 minutes of an order being placed. Based on current volumes, this would represent some 86 per cent of all Amazon's orders – if the shift to the Prime Air service were to take place, for which at this stage there is no clear indication. Currently being pioneered in the USA market, Amazon acknowledged that it could take up to five years for the service to start on a commercial basis, because it would need approval from the US Federal Aviation Administration to use unmanned drones for civilian purposes.

In mid-2014, Amazon made a formal written request for approval from the Federal Aviation Administration to commence tests and was actively recruiting engineers and other staff for the Prime Air Team.

While the company is positive and enthusiastic about the project, there are a number of concerns and objections to overcome before drones delivering parcels become a familiar sight in the sky. If successful there could be dozens, hundreds or even thousands of drones in the air, which could well present a serious risk to commercial aircraft as well as small private planes, presenting air traffic controllers with an additional hazard to monitor.

What happens if the drone crashes, causing a traffic accident, a fire or fatality? Who is responsible and how can the risk be minimized? How can Amazon be sure that the merchandise reaches the correct recipient and does not land in a neighbour's back yard? Perhaps most pertinently, what premium will customers be prepared to pay to receive their shipment perhaps just half a day earlier?

Opposition to the widespread use of drones is, however, growing from the expected sources that fear the risk to civil and military aircraft and the potential they pose for terrorists to strike, as well as some less obvious quarters. According to *Computer Weekly* in October 2014, a University of Birmingham Policy Commission report (2014) concluded that the use of drones in the UK raises significant safety, security, and privacy concerns. The report was based on research led by David Omand, former head of UK intelligence agency GCHQ.

In the UK, police forces in Merseyside, Staffordshire, Essex, Wiltshire and the West Midlands have bought drones for surveillance, but the report said there should be strict guidelines governing their use. The report raises security concerns that drones could be used by terror groups, criminals and paparazzi.

With a different perspective *Wild Life News* (2014) commented that while drones could play a positive role in protecting wildlife by helping research and tracking poachers, they could also be used to hunt protected species and disturb wildlife habitats. In the US, the National Park Service in 2014 banned the use of drones in all its parks and soon after prosecuted users who had flown drones in Yellowstone and Grand Teton National Parks.

There's no doubt that the concept has caught the imagination of supply chain practitioners and e-commerce businesses alike. But with so many operational, security and safety hurdles to be overcome, as well as the fact that regulatory issues governing the use of air space are the preserve of individual governments, the big question, at the risk of a pun, will the project 'fly'?

Inland container port developments expand the ecosystem

By definition and practice, the further supply chain processes and activities reach into local, national and even international networks, the more integrated and effective they are likely to be, even though it may stretch management, communications and involve ever more stakeholders.

Many of the more successful container ports around the world no longer see their role simply as one of shipping and unloading cargo, but as an integral part of a wider and more inclusive service as critical supply chain nodes connecting the supply chain ecosystems.

Adjacent warehousing facilities, rail freight yards, container parks and multi-modal transport connections are just some of the modules that increasingly make up the modern container port and freight station complex, often involving additional operations outside the main seaport – known as dry ports.

As increasing cargo volumes have put further pressure on the capacity of container ports, congestion is now becoming a bottleneck at even the most well-organized and managed ports. Consequently, extending facilities by implementing dry port operations helps establish additional container handling operations and is becoming an increasingly attractive solution. The nature, extent and location of such dry port facilities will vary, but will reflect the type of trade being handled, the geography and transport infrastructure both in the sea port zone, also regionally and nationally.

In many cases the dry port facility is in close proximity to the container port and therefore functions as a node to enhance the sea port's capacity, productivity and throughput by moving containers to an additional facility, located close by, for handling, inspection and processing. In this case the dry port is effectively increasing the sea port's hinterland – being the inland region lying behind a port.

The second dry port scenario is that of a multimodal logistics interchange – alternatively known as an inland container depot (ICD). Particularly applicable for inland locations far away from the sea port – and specifically used in land locked countries – this platform provides a logistics facilities for handling of containerized freight together with a transportation hub – featuring road, rail and inland waterway connections – for further distribution of the cargoes, typically to destinations further inland.

Dry ports generally provide a single, integrated, logistics facility for containerized and other forms of freight and offer a range of services including:

- Storage, distribution and container management.
- Road, rail and in some cases, inland waterway links.
- Container cargo trans-shipment facilities.
- Customs clearance and documentation services.

The latest developments of implementing dry ports are a reflection of the advantages of having in one location all the facilities and services the modern supply chain ecosystem needs to function at its most efficient, beyond the immediate water-borne freight port.

In the Baltic states, recent developments include a dry port facility located adjacent to the existing sea port at Klaipeda in Lithuania, which is in turn connected through several inland container depot operations (IDC dry ports) all the way through to the Caspian Sea port at Aktou in Kazakhstan. Together with the all-important ground connections through containerized rail and road transportation linkages, such dry port developments expand the capabilities of the supply chain ecosystem, helping to increase trade and boost national and regional economies.

There are also plans for a dry port development at Karaganda – deep inland within Kazakhstan – giving this emerging economy a more efficient supply chain route to transport containerized freight from its vast interior to-and-from the main international sea freight routes.

Such new logistics infrastructure provides the sea-land multi-modal connectivity that enables containers of cargo from Kazakhstan, Uzbekistan, Iran, Azerbaijan and the Russian Federation to flow more efficiently throughout the region – readily transit and exchange within land locked countries – and connect to dry ports for access to the main ocean shipping lanes. Plans are in place to integrate aspects of the rail and maritime administrations in the participating countries by creating a single document for cargo movements from the sea port to a dry port. The main task is to organize the despatch of container trains using a single document, with all countries using it to create a fast and efficient transportation corridor.

Game-changing infrastructure developments could transform trade flows

As the global economic powers and their challengers compete in our connected world to take a bigger share of world trade, plans are being developed, some already underway, for a number of innovative and spectacular – not to say highly expensive and sometimes controversial – infrastructure engineering feats that could 'change the game'.

Should these game-changing infrastructure projects come to fruition, they may well shift the economic balance of power further east, as well as stimulating economic growth and expanding international trade by providing new transportation linkages and options for cargo flows – that improve global connectivity, shorten distances, reduce cost and save time.

Will the Nicaragua Canal change US shipping routes?

The Panama Canal opened in 1914 and transformed world sea trade by allowing shipping to avoid the long and arduous journey around Cape Horn, massively reducing the journey time between the Atlantic and the Pacific Oceans. With the advent in recent years of ever-larger container ships, the Panama Canal can no longer cope with a significant proportion of deep-sea freight as its 33.5 metre-wide locks are no match for the 50+ metre width of many current container vessels.

Lying north-west of Panama, Nicaragua had first considered a canal linking the two oceans as far back as 1826 and the US almost started work on one in 1899. Now a Chinese company HKND appears ready to revive the dream to construct the 278km waterway which will be longer, deeper and wider than the Panama Canal and will be able to accommodate the latest generation of giant container vessels, and even larger ships up to 23,000 TEUs.

HKND originally estimated it could complete the canal in five years at a cost of $40 billion, although later reports put the cost at $50 billion. However, some observers have pointed out that it has already taken more than 10 years to expand the Panama Canal, widening the channel and building additional locks on its 50-mile route at a projected cost of $5.25 billion.

Despite controversy over funding, security, its potential environmental impact and commercial viability, Nicaraguan officials are insistent their construction will proceed and have formally appointed – with great fanfare – HK Nicaragua Canal Development Investment Co (HKND), a Hong Kong-based construction management and infrastructure development company, to handle the project.

They were awarded a 50-year concession for the canal and an extension right of another 50 years.

The initial ground-breaking ceremony took place in late December 2014, amidst ongoing speculation about sources of funding and the canal's commercial viability.

Over and above the actual canal, the project is planned to include two ports, an airport, a resort and an economic zone for electricity and other companies and a 600-metre bridge that will cross over the canal.

This new infrastructure connecting the Pacific and the Atlantic oceans will introduce additional options for supply chain ecosystems currently using the Panama Canal and is likely to have significant impact on US container ports, particularly on the west coast.

Meanwhile, many east coast US ports already have plans underway to expand their physical infrastructure and capabilities in anticipation of handling the larger vessels that will be able to cross the Panama Canal from 2016, when its newly built locks will be 1,400ft long, 180ft wide and 60ft deep – and will be able to accommodate ships up to 1,200ft long.

The Nicaragua canal will provide a much larger channel and a slightly shorter alternative to the Panama Canal for goods being transported from Asia to the US east coast, which may well divert some trade away from the Panama Canal.

With over 70 per cent of all cargo imported through the west coast US ports being destined for distribution centres and consumer populations east of Chicago, many importers will consider reconfiguring their supply chains to take advantage of the expanded Panama Canal soon being able to handle ships up to 12,500 TEUs, and the subsequent Nicaragua canal accommodating even bigger ships. However the ecosystem comprises many different participants, with profound interdependencies, not least of which is the east coast ports' ability to physically accommodate and efficiently process such large container vessels.

Reducing transit times across South-east Asia

The ASEAN nation of Myanmar is planning a new deep-sea port, special economic zone and industrial park in Dawei, which will include highway, railway and pipeline connections through to South-east

Asia's largest industrial zone and Thailand's primary commercial hub embracing greater Bangkok and its major container port of Laem Chabang, which handles over six million containers per year.

This planned $8.5 billion project on Myanmar's south western coast will help cargo originating from western China, northern Vietnam and Thailand's industrial estates to transit overland and bypass the long sea journey through the Malacca straits, providing a shortcut for east-west trade, transiting through to Dawei with direct access to the Indian ocean, avoiding the long coastal route around China and cutting the journey by more than 2,000km.

The massive Dawei development project, still subject to questions over political will and financing, will comprise much more than the deep sea container port, including everything from a steel mill and oil refinery, to automotive assembly and petrochemical facilities, as well as a range of light industries such as food processing and garment manufacturing.

If and when the Dawei port and related infrastructure gets up and running, it could prove particularly relevant for the supply chains of manufactured goods whose production locations have migrated to Vietnam and inland China. It could also play a leading role in the supply chain ecosystems connecting the ever increasing volumes of south-south trade – cargoes being transported from the Far East to the Indian sub-continent and from China and ASEAN nations through to the rapidly developing economies of Africa.

The North-west Passage

For over 500 years, Arctic explorers sought a passage in the far north of Canada between the North Atlantic and Pacific Oceans to connect Europe and Asia. However, during the summer of 2007, Arctic pack ice, which had previously prevented ships from making the journey, began to melt as a claimed result of global warming.

Warmer conditions opened up an ice-free gap between the North American mainland and the Arctic sea, extending to the Bering Strait between Alaska and Russia, creating a connection almost free of all sea ice from the North Atlantic to the North Pacific – but available for just four months of the year. Located 800km north of the Arctic

Circle and less than 1,930km from the North Pole, the Northern Passage still poses significant challenges to shipping, including the claim that parts of the eastern end of the passage are barely 15m deep.

Political considerations have yet to be resolved with the Canadian government considering the North-western Passages part of Canadian Internal Waters while the United States and various European countries maintain they are an international strait and transit passage, and should allow free and unencumbered passage.

Given the vagaries of climate change, navigational obstacles and potential disagreements over sovereignty, opening and developing the North-west Passage as a new shipping route may be seen as an innovative supply chain development, but one that is not likely to become a major feature of international trade anytime soon.

China to the USA – by rail?

Possibly the most daring and game-changing infrastructure development is the proposed high speed railway line linking north-east China with the US. The proposed line will travel up through Siberia, pass through a tunnel under the Bering Strait, then run across Alaska and down through Canada into the US.

The link between Russia and Alaska would require a 200km undersea tunnel – four times the length of the Channel Tunnel connecting France and the UK – and the entire railway line would run for some 13,000km, carrying trains running at speeds of up to 350km per hour.

While China claims it has the technology and can finance the project alone, it is not yet clear that the other countries involved – Russia, Canada and the US – have been consulted or are in favour. However, China's ambitions go further and its press has listed several other ambitious high-speed rail projects under planning or development.

The first high-speed rail line would originate in London and run through Paris, Berlin, Warsaw, Kiev and Moscow, where it would split into two routes, one of which would run to China through Kazakhstan and the other through eastern Siberia. The second high-speed rail mega development would begin in the far-western Chinese city of Urumqi and then run through Kazakhstan, Uzbekistan,

Turkmenistan, Iran and Turkey to Germany. And a third project would begin in the south-western Chinese city of Kunming and end in Singapore.

Summary

In today's ferociously competitive world, companies and their supply chain practitioners must see continuous improvement as a core corporate value. This means innovation in their supply chain ecosystems, both within their organizations and outside, which in turn means that those responsible for directing the business need to keep up to date on developments and innovations within the industry and the wider world.

That does not imply that every new development is right for every company. It's vital to understand what such advances or new strategies mean and whether they are a sound and commercially viable fit for the business.

Technological innovation will undoubtedly bring operational efficiencies and cost savings. It is certain however that goods movements, whether they involve a one-mile-long container train travelling directly from central Asia to the heart of the US, or new and more cost-efficient ways to deliver a single product to an online shopper, will continue to change the industry landscape. There will undoubtedly be further exciting innovations in global supply chain ecosystems in the years ahead.

CASE STUDY   Innovative port solution for ocean freight
supply chains

Port congestion challenges inhibiting supply chain ecosystems

Already under pressure from steadily increasing container traffic, more and more container ports are suffering from congestion. The causes are many and varied and there is no simple answer as demand for container shipping will continue to increase and the advent of even larger capacity vessels will make the situation more critical.

Research into the causes of port congestion by Schwitzer *et al* (2014) identified numerous non-vessel related factors such as poor port management, labour relations, scheduling, loading and unloading procedures, handling equipment, truck driver shortages, traffic systems, customs delays and pollution issues as inhibitors to smooth transit of cargoes through the port community system.

Many variables can impede the throughput efficiency of cargo transiting through a container port, many of which are outside the direct control of the port operator. Just one example is on-time vessel arrival. In 2014 in the Asia-Europe trade lane, average reliability across all carriers declined from a high of 83 per cent on-time port calls in mid-2012 to just 51 per cent on-time. If ships arrive 'out of window', then terminal operators may not have the space or facilities ready to receive them, resulting in further delays.

In order to manage increasing trade flows and handle ever bigger ships, container ports also need to continuously develop and expand their operations and facilities. Ongoing investments are needed in infrastructure, handling equipment, information technology and human resources. These investments are never cheap, and not every port has the finances – or the land – available for expansion. Many port cities are struggling to expand fast enough to keep up with demand – particularly in the developing markets – which results in choke points such as berthing queues, container yard overload and land-side traffic congestion, all impacting the efficiency of supply chain, through delays and additional costs.

Chronic congestion at Indonesia's main import export gateway

An innovative port solution for ocean freight supply chains has been successfully implemented in Indonesia – the largest economy in South-east Asia and growing at 5 per cent plus, a G20 member with population over 260 million and a one trillion dollar economy.

In recent years Indonesia's booming economy has stretched the capabilities of its largest seaport Tanjung Priok in Jakarta. Since 2010, container throughput has increased by 40 per cent to 6.1 million TEUs in 2013, but Tanjung Priok port could not keep up with the increasing volume, resulting in serious congestion problems – both within the port itself and also in the road network servicing the seaport, connecting shipments to inner city Jakarta and surrounding hinterlands.

Innovative dry port solution eases congestion and empowers supply chain efficiencies

This is where Cikarang dry port provides an innovative supply chain solution.

Cikarang dry port is an inland dry port model that is providing an efficient and effective solution to chronic congestion and delays at the major import export gateway of Tanjung Priok.

Located on Java island, just 50 km from Jakarta, Cikarang dry port serves as an extension of the major Tanjung Priok gateway sea port – operating a hub and spoke model connected by highway and railway networks – and providing integrated port and logistics facilities with on-site customs and quarantine inspection services, operating 24/7.

Strategically located in the heart of the largest manufacturing zone of Indonesia along the Bekasi-Cikampek industrial corridor on the east side of greater Jakarta, Cikarang dry port is surrounded by some 12 industrial estates containing over 3,000 manufacturing companies, the majority of them being importers and exporters.

Cikarang dry port occupies 200 hectares of land, including an extensive logistics park, and enjoys multi-modal hinterland connectivity through its direct access to highway and railway networks.

Offering a one-stop-shop for cargo handling and transport solutions servicing international trade as well as domestic distribution, the dry port provides integrated port and logistics services for all supply chain ecosystem participants, such as shippers, consignees, carriers, customs agency, quarantine agency, container freight station operators, bonded transportation, third-party logistics providers, empty container depot operators, as well as banks and other supporting services.

'CDP have consistently delivered on its promises of efficient, reliable and cost effective shipments which are very important for our customers. There is no doubt that CDP will be a key gateway into the fast growing Indonesian marketplace.' David Chew – Commercial Director, APL Logistics Indonesia.

Cikarang dry port is the first and only integrated customs services zone in Indonesia, a new Indonesia Customs Agency model that makes it possible to conduct customs clearance activities in the dry port instead of the seaport. Using electronic seals and customs-bonded transfer, containers bypass the congestion at Tanjung Priok, are trucked to the dry port where all documentation formalities for customs clearance, quarantine clearance, and port clearance are completed.

Specifying the international port code IDJBK designation as port-of-origin or port-of-destination, cargo owners can choose any one of 18 shipping lines offering direct services to and from Cikarang dry port using a multimodal transport bill of lading.

'Indonesia needs new thinking to break the paradigm of high logistics costs. Cikarang dry port offers multimodal options and brings opportunities for

FIGURE 12.1 Location of Cikarang Dry Port serving Tanjung Priok

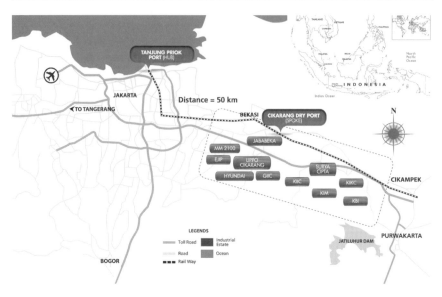

FIGURE 12.2 Bird's eye view of 200-hectare Cikarang Dry Port

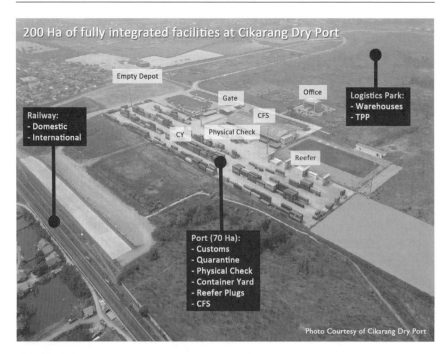

collaboration between importers, exporters and transport providers where all parties are winners. Maersk Line is proud to be in support of CDP since the opening. We see the growth as evidence of the success.' Jakob Friis Sørensen – President Director, Maersk Line Indonesia.

As at 2014, more than 300 manufacturing companies are using Cikarang dry port for their export and import shipment activities, increasing container throughput volume more than tenfold since opening in 2010.

Future plans include continuing innovation in further developing the 130-hectare logistics park, offering 'Integrated Port and Logistics Facilities', with the first container freight station (CFS) already operational in late 2014. Logistics park facilities will work as a buffer between the port and industry, opening further possibilities for enhanced logistics services such as just in-time operations, bonded area distribution centres, and export or import bound general warehouse service.

'As integrated port & logistics facilities, CDP team are smart to seize the developing opportunity in the context of Tanjung Priok congestion and fast growing Indonesia economy; they showed their hard work attitude, persistent and dauntless spirit, professional and thoughtful service ability, that will motivate them to new higher levels and acquire new achievements.' Jamie Liu – Managing Director, SITC Indonesia.

The success of this dry port supply chain innovation was reflected by Cikarang dry port being honoured with the Supply Chain Asia 2014 Award of 'Asia Logistics Centre/Park of the Year'.

Conclusion

With all forecasts indicating continuing growth of the Indonesian economy, which of course will result in further increases in trade and container flows, this innovative Cikarang dry port solution is enabling and empowering efficiencies in the flow of goods that save money and time for stakeholders throughout their supply chain ecosystems.

REFERENCES

Aberdeen Group CSCO (2014) Top three supply chain execution priorities, *Aberdeen Group* [online] www.aberdeen.com/research/8757/ai-supply-chain-priorities/content.aspx [accessed 2 March 2015]

Accenture (2014) Don't Play it Safe When it Comes to Supply Chain Risk Management: Accenture global operations megatrends study, *Accenture* [online] www.accenture.com/SiteCollectionDocuments/PDF/Accenture-Global-Megatrends-Operations-Supply-Chain-Risk-Management.pdf [accessed 4 April 2015]

African Leadership Academy (2015) Sharmi Surianarain: India, *African Leadership Academy* [online] www.africanleadershipacademy.org/building-foundation/academy/leadership-team/sharmi-surianarain [accessed 28 February 2015]

Allianz Risk Barometer (2014) Allianz Business Risk Baromter on Business Risks, *Allianz* [online] www.agcs.allianz.com/assets/PDFs/Reports/Allianz-Risk-Barometer-2014_EN.pdf [accessed 31 March 2015]

Analytiqa (2013) Africa Logistics: Keep cool for growth, *Analytiqa* [online] www.joc.com/sites/default/files/u52092/Arica.pdf [accessed 2 January 2015]

APICS (American Production and Inventory Control Society) Dictionary (2013), *American Production and Inventory Control Society* [online] www.feg.unesp.br/dpd/scm/claudemir/part3/Apics%20Dictionary.pdf [accessed 17 February 2015]

ASEAN (Association of South-east Asian Nations), *Association of South-east Asian Nations* [online] www.asean.org/communities/asean-economic-community [accessed 1 January 2015]

Baker & McKenzie (2014) Semi-Annual Supply Chain Briefing, 10 July 2014, Baker & McKenzie, 23/F One Pacific Place, 88 Queensway, Hong Kong. Attended by the author.

Benkler, Y (2007) *The Wealth of Networks: How social production transforms markets and freedom*, Yale University Press, New Haven, CT

Bowman, R (2014) While WTO Dithers, Traders Should Act: The path to harmonized and streamlined global trade is steep and strewn with boulders, *SupplyChainBrain.com* [online] www.supplychainbrain.com/content/index.php?id=5032&cHash=081010&tx_ttnews[tt_news]=29167 [accessed 4 March 2015]

Bradsher, K (2013) Hauling New Treasure Along the Silk Road, *New York Times* [online] www.nytimes.com/2013/07/21/business/global/hauling-new-treasure-along-the-silk-road.html?pagewanted=all&_r=2& [accessed 18 February 2015]

Brewer, C (2014) Great Things Awaiting Africa, *eyefortransport (EFT)* [online] http://goo.gl/UEU7Zy [accessed 14 April 2015]

Capgemini (2014) Third-Party Logistics Study: The state of logistics outsourcing, *Capgemini* [online] www.capgemini.com/resources/2014-third-party-logistics-study-the-state-of-logistics-outsourcing [accessed 31 March 2015]

china.org.cn (2013) China to Introduce Carbon Tax, *china.org.cn* [online] www.china.org.cn/china/2013-02/19/content_28003242.htm [accessed 31 December 2014]

Christopher, M and Peck, H (2004) Building the Resilient Supply Chain, *International Journal of Logistics Management* , 15 (2), pp 1–13

Clean Cargo Working Group (CCWG) [online] www.bsr.org/en/collaboration/groups/clean-cargo-working-group [accessed 31 December 2014]

Combined Logistics Networks [online] http://combinedlogisticsnetworks.com [accessed 31 December 2014]

Computer Weekly (2014) Drones a threat to privacy, says former GCHQ chief David Omand, *ComputerWeekly.com* [online] www.computerweekly.com/news/2240233131/Drones-a-threat-to-privacy-says-GCHQ-chief-David-Omand [accessed 31 December 2014]

CSCMP Supply Chain Quarterly (2014) Is Amazon a 3PL? *CSCMP Supply Chain Quarterly* [online] www.supplychainquarterly.com/topics/Logistics/20141027-is-amazon-a-3pl/ [accessed 31 March 2015]

Damardono, H (2014) Pendulum Nusantara: Revamping ports, expanding trade, *Indonesia Infrastructure Initiative* [online] www.indii.co.id/news_daily_detail.php?id=5893 [accessed 3 January 2015]

Dobbs, R, Remes, J and Smit, S (2011) Urban economic clout moves east, *McKinsey Quarterly* (March) [online] www.mckinsey.com/insights/economic_studies/urban_economic_clout_moves_east [accessed 31 December 2014]

DP World (2014) Major Milestone for DP World London Gateway Common User Facility, *DP World London Gateway* [online] www.londongateway.com/media-page/press-releases/major-milestone-dp-world-london-gateway-common-user-facility/ [accessed 31 December 2014]

Drucker, P (2012) *Quote Investigator* [online] http://quoteinvestigator.com/2012/09/27/invent-the-future [accessed 7 May 2015]

Economist Intelligence Unit/KPMG International (2014) Competitive Advantage: Enhancing supply chain networks for efficiency and innovation, *Economist Intelligence Unit/KPMG International* [online]

www.kpmg.com/Global/en/IssuesAndInsights/ArticlesPublications/
global-manufacturing-outlook/Documents/competitive-advantage.pdf
[accessed 22 April 2015]

Emmett, S and Sood, V (2010) *Green Supply Chains: An action manifesto*,
John Wiley & Sons, New York

European Commission (2013) Eurobarometer Survey: How green are
European SMEs? *European Commission* [online] http://europa.eu/rapid/
press-release_MEMO-13-1152_en.htm [accessed 31 December 2014]

European Commission (2014) Trade, Agreements, *European Commission*
[online] http://ec.europa.eu/trade/policy/countries-and-regions/
agreements/ [accessed 20 March 2015]

EY (2014) Africa Attractiveness survey 2014: Executing growth,
EY (formerly Ernst & Young) [online] www.ey.com/Publication/
vwLUAssets/EY%E2%80%99s_2014_Africa_attractiveness_survey_:_
Executing_growth/$FILE/EY-Africa-attractiveness-2014-infographic.pdf
[accessed 7 May 2015]

Fast Logistics [online] www.fastlogistics.com.ph/ [accessed 31 January
2015]

Fiorletta, A (2014) Revising the Supply Chain for an Omni-Channel Era,
retailTouchPoints [online] http://retailtouchpoints.com/features/special-
reports/revising-the-supply-chain-for-an-omnichannel-era [accessed 2
March 2015]

Forrester Research (2015) Forrester Research Online Retail Forecast, 2013
to 2018 (US), *Forrester* [online] www.forrester.com/Forrester+Research
+Online+Retail+Forecast+2013+To+2018+US/fulltext/-/E-RES115941
[accessed 8 May 2015]

gCaptain (2012) By the Numbers: how much does Somali piracy cost?,
gCaptain [online] http://gcaptain.com/somali-piracy-cost-report/
[accessed 31 December 2014]

Global Cool Foundation (2010) It's Official – Consumers Really do
Take the Green Option, *Global Cool Foundation* [online] http://
globalcoolfoundation.org/2010/12/ocado-green-delivery-shows-
consumers-will-take-the-green-option/ [accessed 1 May 2015]

Green Council of Hong Kong (2010) Report of the Research Study on
the Current Status and Direction for Green Purchasing in Hong Kong,
Green Council [online] www.greencouncil.org/doc/GPSurvey2009_
report_FINAL.pdf [accessed 8 February 2015]

Green Marine (2014) About us, *Green Marine* [online] www.green-marine.
org/about-us/ [accessed 31 December 2014]

Heaney, B (2013) Supply Chain Visibility: A critical strategy to optimize
cost and service, survey, *Aberdeen Group* [online] www.gs1.org/docs/
visibility/Supply_Chain_Visibility_Aberdeen_Report.pdf [accessed 31
January 2015]

Honda (2012) Honda Issues 2011 North American Environmental Report, *Honda* [online] www.honda.com/newsandviews/article.aspx?id=6469-en [accessed 3 December 2014]

Honda (2013) 2013 North American Environmental Report highlights, *Honda* [online] http://corporate.honda.com/environment/2013-report/ [accessed 3 December 2014]

Hong Kong Economic and Trade Office, San Francisco (2015) Transport and Industrial Maritime – Cleaner Air in Hong Kong Ports, *Hong Kong Economic and Trade Office, San Francisco* [online] www.hketosf.gov.hk/sf/whatsnew/fair_winds_charter.htm [accessed 15 April 2015]

Hudson, S (2004) The SCOR Model For Supply Chain Strategic Decisions, *Poole College of Management/SCRC* [online] http://scm.ncsu.edu/scm-articles/article/the-scor-model-for-supply-chain-strategic-decisions [accessed 31 December 2014]

International Organization for Standardization (2014) We're ISO, *International Organization for Standardization* [online].iso.org [accessed 2 March 2015]

Jennings, R (2014) Quoted in: Shoring Up a Supply Chain Against the Unexpected, Mary Shacklett, *World Trade WT100* [online] www.worldtradewt100.com/articles/90427-shoring-up-a-supply-chain-against-the-unexpected?v=preview [accessed 31 December 2014]

Journal of Commerce (2014) Maritime Piracy, *joc.com* [online] www.joc.com/maritime-news/maritime-piracy [accessed 1 April 2015]

Journal of Commerce (2013) Top 50 Container Ports 2013, *joc.com* [online] www.joc.com/special-topics/top-50-container-ports [accessed 1 April 2015]

Kamal-Chaoui, L (2000) Will This be Africa's Century? *OECD Observer* [online] www.oecdobserver.org/news/archivestory.php/aid/229/Will_this_be_Africa_92s_century_.html [accessed 31 December 2014]

Karrenbauer, J (2014) Quoted in: Shoring Up a Supply Chain Against the Unexpected, Mary Shacklett, *World Trade WT100* [online] www.worldtradewt100.com/articles/90427-shoring-up-a-supply-chain-against-the-unexpected?v=preview [accessed 31 December 2014]

Kemp, T (2014) Crime on the High Seas: The World's Most Pirated Waters, *CNBC* [online] www.cnbc.com/id/101969104# [accessed 18 February 2015]

Keystone Group (2014) Middle Market Trends: Offshore manufacturing and sourcing, *The Keystone Group* [online] www.thekeystonegroup.com/documents/Middle_Market_Trends_Offshore__Mfg_and_Sourcing_vF.pdf [accessed 31 December 2014]

Kiron D, Kruschwitz N, Rubel H, Reeves M and Fuisz-Kehrbach S (2013) Sustainability's Next Frontier, *MIT Sloan Management Review/The*

Boston Consulting Group [online] http://sloanreview.mit.edu/projects/ sustainabilitys-next-frontier/ [accessed 2 February 2014]

KPMG (2012) Supply Chain Agility: Managing change, *kpmg.com* [online] http://www.kpmg.com/US/en/IssuesAndInsights/ArticlesPublications/ Documents/supply-chain-agility.pdf [accessed 31 January 2015]

KPMG (2014) Africa's Top 10 Fastest Growing Economies, *KPMG Africa* [online] www.blog.kpmgafrica.com/africas-top-10-fastest-growing-economies/ [accessed 31 January 2015]

Leke, A, Fiorini, R, Dobbs, R, Thompson, F, Suleiman, A and Wright, D (2014) Nigeria's renewal: delivering inclusive growth, *McKinsey Global Institute* [online] www.mckinsey.com/insights/africa/nigerias_renewal_ delivering_inclusive_growth [accessed 3 April 2015]

Loadstar (2013) Large shippers urge logistics providers to report emissions data, *The Loadstar* [online] http://theloadstar.co.uk/large-shippers-urge-logistics-providers-to-report-emissions-data/ [accessed 7 May 2015]

Logistics Executive Group (2012) Supply Chain & Logistics: 2012–2013 Employment Market Survey Report, *Logistics Executive Group* [online] http://logisticsexecutive.com/cms/Logistics%20Executive%202012-2013%20EMS%20Report.pdf [accessed 24 January 2015]

Logistics Executive Group (2014) Supply Chain & Logistics: 2013–2014 Employment Market Survey Report, *Logistics Executive Group* [online] www.logisticsexecutive.com/cms/2014%20EMS%20Report%20 210314.pdf [accessed 24 January 2015]

Logistics Management (2014) Managing global trade: Rising importance but lagging execution, SCM World, *logisticsmgmt.com* [online] www. logisticsmgmt.com/article/managing_global_trade [accessed 31 March 2014]

Lynn, M (2014) Africa's Rapid Growth is Down to Industry and Free Markets, *Telegraph* [online] www.telegraph.co.uk/finance/ economics/11100698/Africas-rapid-growth-is-down-to-industry-and-free-markets.html [accessed 3 February 2015]

Manners-Bell, J (2014) *Supply Chain Risk: Understanding emerging threats to global supply chains*, Kogan Page, London

Manners-Bell, J (2015) A Year of Innovation Ahead in the Supply Chain and Logistics Industry, *Ti* [online] http://www.transportintelligence.com/ briefs/a-year-of-innovation-ahead-in-the-supply-chain-and-logistics-industry/3052/ [accessed 10 January 2015]

Merk, O (2014) African Ports: Challenges and opportunities, *Port Finance International* [online] http://portfinanceinternational.com/features/ item/1278-african-ports-challenges-and-opportunities [accessed 31 January 2015]

MindTools (2014) Plan-Do-Check-Act (PDCA): Implementing new ideas in a controlled way, also known as the PDCA Cycle, or Deming Cycle,

MindTools [online] www.mindtools.com/pages/article/newPPM_89.htm [accessed 4 April 2015]

National Environmental Education Foundation (2014) Knowledge to Live By, *National Environmental Education Foundation* [online] www.neefusa.org/about/index.htm [accessed 18 March 2015]

Office of Government Commerce (2008) Buy Green and Make a Difference: How to address environmental issues in public procurement, *UK Office of Government Commerce* [online] http://toolbox.climate-protection.eu/search/?cmd=view&uid=2f1e6bd7 [accessed 12 March 2015]

Overholt, W H (2014) It's Time to Update our Thinking on Trade, *East Asia Forum* [online] www.eastasiaforum.org/2014/08/03/its-time-to-update-our-thinking-on-trade/ [accessed 25 February 2015]

Pezzini, M (2014) An emerging middle class, OECD Yearbook 2012, *OECD Observer* [online] www.oecdobserver.org/news/fullstory.php/aid/3681/An_emerging_middle_class.html [accessed 9 February 2015]

Port of Long Beach (2011) Clean Trucks, *Port of Long Beach* [online] www.polb.com/environment/cleantrucks/default.asp [accessed 31 December 2014]

PwC (2014) The Africa Business Agenda 2014, *PwC* [online] www.pwc.com/ke/en/africa-business-agenda/index.jhtml [accessed 3 November 2014]

Robertson, C (2012) The Business Interview: Charles Robertson, Global Chief Economist, Renaissance Capital, video, *France 24* [online] www.france24.com/en/20121207-en-business-interview-charles-robertson-africa-the-fastest-billion/ [accessed 31 December 2014]

Schwitzer, M, Martens, K, Beckman, J and Yoo, Y S (2014) Port congestion, PowerPoint presentation, Iowa State University, n/d [online] www.bus.iastate.edu/cwalter/portcongestion.ppt%2025.ppt [accessed 2 February 2015]

SCM World (2011) The Chief Supply Chain Officer Report 2011: A research study by Dr Hau Lee, Chairman, SCM World, Kevin O'Marah, Faculty Member, *SCM World* [online] www.scmworld.com [accessed 28 March 2015]

Serafeim, G (2014) Turning a Profit While Doing Good: Aligning sustainability with corporate performance, *Brookings Institution* [online] www.brookings.edu/⊠/media/research/files/papers/2014/12/12-sustainability-corporate-performance-profit-serafeim/serafeim.pdf [accessed 2 February 2015]

Skills for Logistics (2013) Employer survey 2013, *skillsforlogistics.org* [online] www.skillsforlogistics.org/media/19858/skills-for-logistics_employer-survey-2013.pdf [accessed 30 April 2015] slideshare.net (2011) Green Brands, Global Insights 2011, *Cohn & Wolf/ Esty Environmental Partners/Landor/Penn Schoen Berland* [online] www.slideshare.net/WPPGreenBrandsSurvey/2011-green-brands-global-media-deck [accessed 8 March 2015]

Smith, S (2014) 3D Printers For Home-Use To Exceed 1 Million Unit Sales Globally By 2018, cites Juniper Research, *Yahoo! Finance/ Marketwired* [online] http://finance.yahoo.com/news/3d-printers-home-exceed-1-075800829.html [accessed 31 December 2014]

Sourcing Innovation (2014) Blog, *ToP KaTS Consulting* [online] http:// blog.sourcinginnovation.com/ [accessed 5 April 2015]

Spire Research (2014) Africa's Middle-Class Powers Ahead – Consumers leading the way to growth, *Spire Research and Consulting* [online] www.spireresearch.com/wp-content/uploads/2014/06/SpirE-Journal-Q4-2013_Africas-middle-class-powers-ahead.pdf [accessed 18 December 2014]

Supply Chain Insights LLC [online] http://supplychaininsights.com. Content from Lora Cecere supplied with permission.

Supply Chain Risk Leadership Council (SCRLC) (2014) Supply Chain Risk Leadership Council, *SCRLC* [online] www.scrlc.com/about.php [accessed 8 May 2015]

The Economist (2012) Daily Chart: The world's shifting centre of gravity, *The Economist* [online] http://www.economist.com/blogs/ graphicdetail/2012/06/daily-chart-19 [accessed 31 December 2014]

The Economist (2013) Emerging Africa: A hopeful continent, *The Economist* [online] www.economist.com/sites/default/files/20130203_ emerging_africa.pdf [accessed 4 April 2015]

The Economist/HSBC (2014) FTAs in South-east Asia: Towards the next generation, Insights, *The Economist/HSBC* [online] www. economistinsights.com/countries-trade-investment/analysis/ftas-south-east-asia [accessed 31 March 2015]

thegreensupplychain.com (2014) Research shows companies with high levels of sustainability gain major stock price advantage, *Green SCM* [online] www.thegreensupplychain.com/NEWS/14-12-09-1.php [accessed 23 December 2014]

The Telegraph (2011) How the 2010 Ash Cloud Caused Chaos: Facts and figures, *telegraph.co.uk* [online] www.telegraph.co.uk/finance/ newsbysector/transport/8531152/How-the-2010-ash-cloud-caused-chaos-facts-and-figures.html [accessed 2 December 2014]

Transport Intelligence (2011) Briefs detail: Kuehne + Nagel tops ranking of largest freight forwarders, *Ti* [online] www.transportintelligence. com/briefs-feeds/kuehne-nagel-tops-ranking-of-largest-freight-forwarders/2126/ [accessed 26 April 2014]

Transport Intelligence (2012) Sub-Saharan Africa Logistics 2012, *Ti* [online] www.transportintelligence.com/market-reports/report-sub-saharan-africa-logistics-2012/296/ [accessed 26 April 2014]

Transport Intelligence (2013) Global freight forwarding 2013, *Ti* [online] www.transportintelligence.com/market-reports/report-global-freight-forwarding-2013/311/ [accessed 26 April 2014]

Transport Intelligence (Ti) (2014) Ten reasons why M&A activity in the global logistics industry is about to take off, *Ti* [online] www.transportintelligence.com/briefs/ten-reasons-why-ma-activity-in-the-global-logistics-industry-is-about-to-take-off/3036/ [accessed 26 April 2014]

United Nations (UN) (2013) Composition of Macro Geographical (Continental) Regions, Geographical Sub-regions, and Selected Economic and Other Groupings, *unstats.un.org* [online] http://unstats.un.org/unsd/methods/m49/m49regin.htm#asia [accessed 22 March 2014]

University of Birmingham (2014) The Security Impact of Drones: Challenges and opportunities for the UK, *Birmingham Policy Commission/University of Birmingham* [online] www.birmingham.ac.uk/Documents/research/policycommission/remote-warfare/final-report-october-2014.pdf [accessed 7 May 2015]

VanGervin, A (2014) Quoted in: Shoring Up a Supply Chain Against the Unexpected, Mary Shacklett, *World Trade WT100*, 1 August 2014 [online] www.worldtradewt100.com/articles/90427-shoring-up-a-supply-chain-against-the-unexpected?v=preview [accessed 4 February 2015]

Vietnam Briefing (2014) Vietnam Consumer Confidence on the Rise, *Dezan Shira & Associates* [online] www.vietnam-briefing.com/news/vietnams-improving-economy-reflected-increased-consumer-confidence-fdi.html/ [accessed 31 December 2014]

W. Edward Deming Institute (2015) The Plan, Do, Study, Act (PDSA) Cycle, *W. Edwards Deming Institute* [online] https://deming.org/theman/theories/pdsacycle [accessed 18 February 2015]

Waller, A (2012) Supply Chain Strategy in the Boardroom, *Solving Efeso/Cranfield* [online] www.solvingefeso.com/upload/2012_06_18_SC_Strategy_in_the_Boardroom_the_reality.pdf [accessed 22 Janaury 2015]

WhatIs.com (2014) Drone, definition, *WhatIs.com* [online] http://whatis.techtarget.com/definition/drone [accessed 8 April 2015]

World Bank (2013) Data: GDP growth (annual %), *World Bank* [online] http://data.worldbank.org/indicator/NY.GDP.MKTP.KD.ZG [accessed 25 March 2014]

World Bank (2014) Logistics Performance Index (LPI), *World Bank* [online] http://lpi.worldbank.org/ [accessed 17 February 2015]

World Trade Organisation (2014) Annual Report, *World Trade Organisation* [online] www.wto.org/english/res_e/booksp_e/anrep_e/anrep14_e.pdf [accessed 8 May 2015]

Zamsky, D (2014) Quoted in: Shoring Up a Supply Chain Against the Unexpected, Mary Shacklett, *World Trade WT100*, 1 August 2014 [online] www.worldtradewt100.com/articles/90427-shoring-up-a-supply-chain-against-the-unexpected?v=preview [accessed 4 February 2015]

INDEX